CAMBRIDGE LIBRARY COLLECTION

Books of endurir

Travel and

The history of travel writing dates back
and the Crusaders, and its many theme
recreation. Explorers from Columbus t
visited by Western travellers, and were followed by merchants, missionaries,
and colonists, who wrote accounts of their experiences. The development of
steam power in the nineteenth century provided opportunities for increasing
numbers of 'ordinary' people to travel further, more economically, and more
safely, and resulted in great enthusiasm for travel writing among the reading
public. Works included in this series range from first-hand descriptions of
previously unrecorded places, to literary accounts of the strange habits of
foreigners, to examples of the burgeoning numbers of guidebooks produced
to satisfy the needs of a new kind of traveller - the tourist.

A Ride through Asia Minor and Armenia

Henry C. Barkley (c.1825–c.1895) was a civil engineer and author. His travel
books included *Between the Danube and the Black Sea* (1876), which covers
the five years in which he was working on the construction of a railway line
linking the Danube and the Black Sea, and *Bulgaria before the War* (1877),
written at the time of the Russo-Turkish war. (He also wrote a guide to rat-
catching for public-school boys, and *My Boyhood* (1877), a collection of tales
from his own childhood.) Published in 1891, this work recounts the author's
adventures on a journey that took him in 1878 from Bucharest, through
Istanbul, across Asia Minor and back to Trebizond (now Trabzon) on the
Black Sea coast, a distance of 1400 miles, completed in 96 days. He describes
with zest and humour the habits and customs of Christian and Muslim
communities that he encounters on the way.

Cambridge University Press has long been a pioneer in the reissuing of out-of-print titles from its own backlist, producing digital reprints of books that are still sought after by scholars and students but could not be reprinted economically using traditional technology. The Cambridge Library Collection extends this activity to a wider range of books which are still of importance to researchers and professionals, either for the source material they contain, or as landmarks in the history of their academic discipline.

Drawing from the world-renowned collections in the Cambridge University Library, and guided by the advice of experts in each subject area, Cambridge University Press is using state-of-the-art scanning machines in its own Printing House to capture the content of each book selected for inclusion. The files are processed to give a consistently clear, crisp image, and the books finished to the high quality standard for which the Press is recognised around the world. The latest print-on-demand technology ensures that the books will remain available indefinitely, and that orders for single or multiple copies can quickly be supplied.

The Cambridge Library Collection will bring back to life books of enduring scholarly value (including out-of-copyright works originally issued by other publishers) across a wide range of disciplines in the humanities and social sciences and in science and technology.

A Ride through Asia Minor and Armenia

Giving a Sketch of the Characters, Manners, and Customs of Both the Mussulman and Christian Inhabitants

HENRY C. BARKLEY

CAMBRIDGE
UNIVERSITY PRESS

CAMBRIDGE UNIVERSITY PRESS

Cambridge, New York, Melbourne, Madrid, Cape Town,
Singapore, São Paolo, Delhi, Tokyo, Mexico City

Published in the United States of America by Cambridge University Press, New York

www.cambridge.org
Information on this title: www.cambridge.org/9781108037570

© in this compilation Cambridge University Press 2011

This edition first published 1891
This digitally printed version 2011

ISBN 978-1-108-03757-0 Paperback

A RIDE THROUGH ASIA MINOR
AND ARMENIA.

A RIDE THROUGH

ASIA MINOR AND ARMENIA:

GIVING A SKETCH OF THE CHARACTERS,
MANNERS, AND CUSTOMS OF BOTH
THE MUSSULMAN AND CHRISTIAN INHABITANTS.

BY

HENRY C. BARKLEY,

AUTHOR OF

"BETWEEN THE DANUBE AND THE BLACK SEA,"
"BULGARIA BEFORE THE WAR," ETC.

LONDON:
JOHN MURRAY, ALBEMARLE STREET.
1891.

CONTENTS.

CHAPTER VI.

CHAPTER VII.

CHAPTER VIII.

CHAPTER IX.

CHAPTER X.

CHAPTER XI.

CHAPTER XXIX.

CHAPTER XXX.

A RIDE THROUGH ASIA MINOR
AND ARMENIA.

CHAPTER I.

Bucharest—Improvements—A chat with Turkish prisoners—Detained
in Bucharest—More Turkish prisoners—Giurgevo—Passports—
Wallachian bathers — Rustchuk — Bumptious Bulgars — Russian
management—Varna to Constantinople.

TOWARDS the end of August, 1878, I received a letter
from my brother G—— telling me that business was taking
him to the land of the Turk, and proposing that I should
accompany him on the journey. Before I had finished the
letter I had quite made up my mind to accept the tempting offer, and within half an hour I had written to say
I would go. I had several reasons for doing this. First,
I knew that G—— was an old and accomplished traveller,
both in lands of luxury and in lands of hardship, and that
with him as a companion rough roads would become
smooth, dry bread a cake, a camp bed a luxurious couch,
and hardships, pleasures. Then, for some years I had
longed to revisit Turkey, and this longing had increased
through the great interest I had taken in the war just
finished in that unfortunate land. I knew what I was

B

undertaking, for as an engineer, I spent thirteen years in Bulgaria, returning some eight years ago, and with a little knowledge of most of the inhabitants of the Levant, I had picked up a smattering of Turkish.

A few days in London, and our outfit was ready and packed, and a few days more of rapid travelling carried us to Bucharest; and though this is the capital of a country that is now independent, it had so recently emancipated itself from the suzerainty of the Sultan, that I shall commence jotting down what we saw there, as an introduction to our long journey farther eastward. Some years ago we had both of us lived much in this town, and knew it and its people well, and we were not prepared for the great strides in improvement both town and country had made. Instead of being slowly dragged into the town boxed up in a " diligence " over muddy roads, we dashed up to the barrier in an express train, and, after a few minutes spent in collecting our luggage, we drove in a comfortable little open carriage, through well-paved, well-lighted streets, to the Hotel Bróff, opposite the Opera House, where another pleasant surprise awaited us. Instead of the old, dirty-smelling hotel of former days, we found ourselves in a house as clean and comfortable as the good old hotels of Vienna, with an attentive host, civil waiters, respectable chamber-maids, and no smells ; and we afterwards discovered there was yet another hotel in the place, equally good, and much larger. Then, as to the town itself, twenty years ago I saw a horse bogged in a mud-hole in one of the chief streets. Fifteen years ago the main street

of the town was paved with round river-boulders set in
the mud, which soon became full of holes, the stones loose
and decidedly trappy. In summer the dust was in pro-
portion to the air we breathed as 8 to 10, and of so fine
a quality that it insinuated itself through and into everything, and it smelt as no other dust ever did in Europe.
In winter the dust became mud, inches deep in the best
parts of the town, and feet deep in others, but retaining
the smell of the defunct dust. Then all the streets were
lighted with petroleum lamps, or, rather, darkness was
slightly diluted by them and made yet more hideous.
Now we found that excellent pavement of square granite
stones had in all the main streets replaced the boulders,
and, moreover, that this pavement was kept clean and well
watered, to the destruction of dust and dirt. The fine rich
old odour was nearly on its last legs, and only to be found
in its former strength in side streets and retired corners.
The petroleum lamps had given place to gas, and there
was a general appearance of cleanliness and prosperity.

I must not forget to mention also that in many of the
streets tramcars were running; but they appeared thinly
loaded, and, owing to the steep gradients, I should say
they did not answer. The birgir—a little open carriage,
drawn by two quick, active little horses, and driven by a
sect of Russians called Skopti—is the proper and justly
popular conveyance, and will, I believe and hope, hold
its own for some years more.

The first morning after our arrival we went all over
the town, and noted with pleasure these good signs; but

even in this improved Bucharest we soon tired of walking about the streets, so, after an early lunch, I determined to take a turn in the Lipscani Gardens, and, if possible, have a chat with some of my old friends the Turks, who, I am sorry to say, still lingered on in Bucharest to the number of two thousand as prisoners of war.

On entering the garden I soon began to meet my friends, but having plenty of choice, I passed the first few I met—some because they had ruffian written on their faces, and others stupidity. At last I came to one who was sitting alone on a wooden bench, and, liking the look of his handsome sunburnt face, blue eyes, and stalwart graceful figure, I opened fire by saying, " Ah, neighbour, is your soul ravished with weariness ? " He seemed for a moment surprised at my speaking Turkish, but quickly answered, " Ah, much—much ravished. Sit down, Tchel- laby." I took the vacant seat beside him, and soon got into the flow of conversation by telling him, in answer to his questions, that I was an Englishman, on my way to Stamboul, and, as I hoped, to the interior of Asia Minor. In return, he told me that he was a native of Stamboul; that for years he had served in the army; that he first saw a shot fired on the Servian frontier; and, after that campaign was over, he had been sent to Widin, and from there marched on with the great Suleiman for Plevna. It is impossible to repeat all he told me, nor would it be interesting; but perhaps some who yet take an interest in the great defence may care to hear a few of the things he said.

"Did I fight much? Yes, day and night. Day and night for five months there was no rest; for, when we had done the fighting, there were the earthworks to make and repair. Suleiman was a great soldier—the only pasha soldier—he feared nothing. I myself stood beside him when a box-sort of thing smashed to pieces at his side; he never moved, but only said, 'Come, children, come, let us see,' and continued his walk with the bullets falling all around him. No, Tchellaby, he did not order where the batteries were to be placed. We had an English pasha, a bearded pasha, who did all that.

"You ask, Am I sure of this? Oh, quite sure; he used to come every day and say, 'Make a battery here; a trench there; make them so-and-so.' Yes; he worked hard all day, and most nights too, and was a great soldier. Do you ask how it was the Russians did not get him when they took Plevna? Why, just before they shut in our rear, the English pasha wished Suleiman to abandon the place, and break through or between the Russians, but Suleiman only said, 'No.' Then the Englishman said he would leave; he had done all he could, and he could do no more. Suleiman gave him an escort, and he rode away. He had no name, except 'The English Pasha.' He had a brother with him, or perhaps he was a friend, but he was an Englishman too. The war was a great sham. It was all the fault of the big pashas. Midhat Pasha has ruined our country. The Sultan may be good—who knows!

"What do you say, Tchellaby? Midhat going back directly to Constantinople, is he? Well, let him go; he

will soon have his throat cut there.   Mehemet Ali is
murdered in Bosnia!   It is better so; he was very rotten."
And then he continued, " Our soldiers are the best in the
world—they never fear; but what good are they when
their commanders are bad?   You know, Tchellaby, the
Russians crossed the river on a bridge of boats; but did
you know the boats they used were *gold* ones?   Every
soldier knows it.   Ask any one.   The Russians did not
want to fight.   Our pashas made them, because, before the
war, they thought it would make themselves big and rich,
and because they thought the English would come and
fight.   When the Russians took us prisoners they gave us
bread, when they had it, and were kind to us.   I and my
fellow-prisoners fell into the hands of the Wallachs and
were marched off.   There were two thousand of us altogether; and within a few days half were dead—frozen and
starved.   We did not die on the march; we died at night
as we sat.   They put us as close as we could squat into
stables, and said if we huddled together we should be
warm enough; and there one thousand died, sitting so,
crouched up.   Ah, it was very bad in the morning, to
look round, as I did, and see the man on my right, the
man on my left, and the man before me dead, frozen.
My flesh is sound, so I lived through those nights.   Then
there came an English doctor with a friend.   He came
amongst us, and when he saw the state we were in he
stood so, and kept hitting his thigh and nodding his head;
and then, telling us he would help us, he went off, and
soon returned, and gave us bread, honey, some spirits,

tobacco, and other things. He had the dead carried away, and then some of us were put into hot rooms, and those of us that were left had straw given us and a fire. There was an English woman, who nursed the sick, and worked very hard. God reward her! God reward the doctor and his friend; they saved us! It is very hard being kept here, but we get enough to eat. The bread is a little musty at times; but we are soldiers, and it does not matter. I am well off. My wounds were very slight, and I am quite well; but there are yet some here whose wounds are still open." He afterwards said, "Take me to Stamboul with you, Tchellaby. It is quite easy. Some dozen or so have escaped through Bulgar merchants coming here, giving them caps and other *à la Franca* clothes, and then taking them back to Turkey as their servants."

I said to him, "I like the Turkish soldier, and generally admire him, but you did a most disgraceful thing in killing all your prisoners and wounded at Plevna." "By Allah, Tchellaby, we soldiers did not do it, and Suleiman did not order it to be done. He hanged one soldier and shot another for killing some wounded. I saw them executed. No; if we had wished to do so, we dared not—it was against orders. It was done by the Bashi-Bazouks and Circassians. They came out at night after every fight and killed and robbed all they could find. By Allah, Tchellaby, they killed the Osmanli soldiers themselves for the sake of plunder."

I took this last part with a grain of salt, for what is a Bashi-Bazouk? Simply a lower-order Turk; and what

is a soldier but the same? Putting on a ragged old
uniform cannot alter the nature of the man, and I believe
the soldier that fought in the light often became a cut-
throat in the dark.

"Here, my interesting blue-eyed friend, is a bakshish for
you; but, please God, you may never cast those blue eyes
on any friend of mine as he writhes wounded on a battle-
field—ten to one if you do, his sufferings will be speedily
over!"

I wrote down this account within two hours of my conversation with the Turk. I have told it to the best of
my power, without alteration, and I may mention that all
I heard was told me *willingly*, not *extracted*.

I avoided putting leading questions or letting the man
see where my sympathies were until after he had said his
say, for I remembered of old how quick the Turks are
in divining your opinions, and in leading the conversation
round to suit them.

Much against our will we were detained three days in
Bucharest, for we had managed to arrive there just too
late to catch the through service to Constantinople. It
was no use proceeding to Rustchuk or Varna, as one
might have done, for the Russians swarmed all over the
country between those places, and the chance of our
finding beds would have been very small. Our inquiries
about other routes, such as *viâ* Kustendji or Galatz, met
with no success, and it was amusing to hear the cheerful
tones of those who informed us that we must stop on in
Bucharest, for they evidently thought that any detention

in that (to them) most charming town must be a subject
of congratulation to us! We killed time pretty well, for
to any one who has eyes, the numerous nationalities
congregated there must afford amusement, especially at
this time, when to the Wallach, the Hungarian, the Jew,
the Greek, the Bulgar, and the scores of no one knows
what, are added numerous heroes late from Turkey—that
is to say, the victorious Russian, and the defeated but
brave, patient, and manly looking Turk; the former
waiting to be called home, covered with honour and
glory, the latter to be released from imprisonment, and to
return, as best as he can, unrewarded, to his far-away
village in Asia Minor, there to vegetate till old age
exempts him from serving again, or until the Padishah
blunders again into another war, when he will without
a murmur come once more to his help.

The next day, being driven from my rooms at the hotel
opposite the theatre by the deafening clatter of hundreds
of carriages that continuously pass to and fro day and
night at a furious rate, I took my way to the Tchesmagu
Gardens, and lolling there in the shade and quiet, I once
more entered into conversation with various Turkish
prisoners. They were glad of a chat with a stranger, and
yet more glad of the cigarettes I gave them. They nearly
all tell the same tale; they are from the centre of Asia
Minor; they had been fighting throughout the entire war;
they had endured fearful hardships, and now they are
prisoners. They had had no news for months past, and
were not sure the war was over. They had no idea when

they would be released. Not one in a hundred had heard
a word of or from their friends at home since the war
began; but then, they are soldiers, and "What's to be
done?" As prisoners, they have nothing to complain of.
They are free to walk about the town when and where
they like; they have enough food, a barrack to sleep in,
and a reed mat to lie on; besides which, they get five paras
(one farthing) a day, with which to buy such luxuries as
'baccy. Please God, they might get away before the winter,
for they dreaded the cold; besides, their clothes were in
tatters, and they had no money to buy more. Then, as to
their late enemies—the Wallachs fought well, but the
Russians better; but then, the Russians were always drunk
when they attacked. Their officers gave them spirits,
which made them fear nothing. They rushed forward
towards the batteries and trenches, over the open space,
when the bullets were falling like rain; and when, if they
had been sober, they would have seen certain death before
them. They must have been drunk, or they could never
have done it. Osman Pasha was a "male." He was the
only soldier among the pashas in the Turkish army; all
the rest were bad and knew nothing.

Not one of these men (and I talked with over twenty)
asked me for money. All appeared marvellously cheerful, and as resigned as only those can be who believe in
"Kismet." I do not think any attempted to deceive me,
but I did not quite accept all they said. For instance,
I did not believe what they said of the Russian soldiers
being always drunk. They really judged them by them-

selves—they themselves being the best of soldiers behind
an earthwork, but incapable of an attack in the clear open,
where death seemed certain, or at all events incapable of
renewing an attack after repeated failures.

I asked these men about the English pasha, who my
friend of yesterday said had superintended the fortifying
of Plevna; but not one of them had seen him, though, as
one remarked, there might have been a dozen Englishmen
there without his knowing it, as for months he never left
his post in the trenches, and an English engineer would be
in a Turkish uniform, and occupied where new trenches and
defences were to be made, and not on old ones. Personally,
I feel inclined to think Osman Pasha had help from some
one, but I do not think it was from an Englishman.

We were heartily glad to take our departure from
Bucharest, which we did on September 13th, travelling by
rail to Giurgevo in a train filled with Russian officers.
We had been told at Bucharest that travellers were
allowed to pass *out* of Wallachia free, without regard to
custom-houses and passport-visés; so we, therefore, on
arriving at the station, put our luggage into one carriage,
and getting into another ourselves, started off at a rattling
pace for the bridge of boats which the Russians had made
across the Danube some three miles above Giurgevo and
opposite the town of Rustchuk. But we were in a land
of obstructions. First the road was not a road, but just a
track over dried mud and huge holes; over a series of
mounds like the graves of giants, amidst dust and smells,
under a broiling sun.

When we had arrived close to the bridge and were just congratulating ourselves that our drive was over, a nondescript sort of a creature, half soldier, half civilian, stepped into the road and demanded our passports. He first studied them most carefully himself, and then enlisted some half-dozen loungers to assist him. Not being able to understand them (which was but natural, as he held them upside down), he insisted on our returning to Giurgevo to have them inspected there by his chief. We mildly remonstrated, and offered bakshish, and did all we could to resist our fate; but no, we must return, not only on account of our passports, but to have our luggage examined at the custom-house. There was nothing for it, so back we went, over the dusty detestable road, to the custom-house on the quay, only to learn that the officer had gone to dinner, and would not be back for two hours!

I had often stood in years gone by on that same quay, undergoing the same annoyance, and I may safely say I have lost as much temper on that spot as would supply an army with that article; but I think I never felt worse than I did on this occasion. We resigned ourselves to our unhappy fate, and sat down for a two hours' sulk in the burning sun, when a man came up and, addressing us in Turkish, told us that, though it was forbidden to leave Wallachia by the bridge without passports and luggage being examined, yet we might have a boat and depart at once.

In less than five minutes we were slowly passing down the creek that leads to the Danube in a tub of a

boat pulled by two men, hardly believing in our luck at
being at last free of the beastly place.   But so we were;
and the only further discomfort we had to endure till we
reached the railway station on the Turkish side (which is
built on a quay on the river a mile below Rustchuk) was
the intense heat that nearly parched us.

Just below Giurgevo Quay, opposite the town, and in
full view of the houses, and within a hundred yards of
them, were some six or eight women disporting themselves
in the water and on the muddy banks, and the only
covering they had upon them was a little mud upon their
feet!   We passed within ten yards of them, but they paid
no heed to us, nor did they appear to mind a man and
some boys who stood on the bank and talked to them.
They splashed about in the water, struggled out on to the
shore, chattered and laughed like a set of monkeys, and
exhibited about as much modesty as those sagacious
animals would show.

At Rustchuk railway station we found Mr. Harrower,
an old acquaintance, who not only passed our luggage
through the custom-house, but took us to his pretty little
house above the station, gave us rooms and a hearty
welcome.   During the afternoon we drove into Rustchuk
and then took a walk over the town, accompanied by Mr.
Harrower, to examine, as far as we could, the damage done
by the bombardment, and from what I could see I cannot
think the Russians treated the town badly.   True, the
government offices which used to cluster round the konak,
or governor's house, with the house itself, were a heap of

ruins. A mosque near, on which, we were told, the Red
Cross was flying, had been hit a few times, but it stood
only some thirty yards to the right of the line of fire, and
close to the konak. In the line of fire before and behind
the government offices, houses were hit, and some quite
demolished, but in the main portion of the town little or
no harm had been done. I knew Rustchuk well some
eight years ago, and the only change I could see in it had
been made by the wear and tear of time. Nothing was
improved, nothing altered, and I felt, as I walked through
the old familiar streets, that the last eight years must have
been a dream. The town swarmed with Russian soldiers
and officers, all busy and business-like looking, and apparently getting on well with their late enemies the Turks
and with the other inhabitants.

In one street we found a large gang, half Bulgars and
half Turks, macadamizing the road, and, what is more,
doing it well. It was undertaken by the orders of the
Russian governor, and, if he were wise, he would largely
increase his working gang, for I saw many hundreds in
the streets that I am sure could only be kept out of
mischief by work. I spoke to many of the natives, both
Turks and Christians, and from what I could gather they
appeared to be reaping a rich harvest from the Russians,
and to greatly appreciate it.

Mr. Harrower told us that the newly freed Bulgars
were not pleasant to deal with. They are very bumptious,
and hardly know their position, and are decidedly not
ripe to govern themselves without foreign help. One

story I was told, which I believe to be perfectly true, will show that they have something yet to learn.   Directly the Russian governor had opened business, a deputation of Bulgars waited upon him and requested that he would prohibit foreigners settling in the town or selling anything, as they would themselves sell all they required! The governor gave them a lesson they well merited by sending them all off to prison, there to reconsider the petition.

We were told that the Turkish inhabitants were leaving as fast as they could, and that *all* would probably leave as soon as they could dispose of their property; and, from what I know of the Turks, I feel sure that within another five years hardly one of them will remain in the Free Bulgaria.

When first the Russians entered Rustchuk, they determined to work the Varna and Rustchuk Railway themselves, and had a lot of waggons sent over for that purpose, besides having locomotives ready for it in Wallachia.   I saw also in readiness for use, but for some reason not used, a very good steam-ferry, with rails laid down to it that apparently might at once transport a train across the river.

Finding the excellent manner in which Mr. Harrower worked the line, the Russians left it in his hands, contenting themselves by putting a Russian beside every single employé on the line, from the chief cashier to the watchman at the guard-houses.   No train was allowed to start from any station until the Russian duplicate station-master gave permission; and it took him so long to bring his mind into a proper state for giving it, that on the morrow, when we were passing over the line, we lost over four hours at the few stations, and were altogether twelve hours doing the hundred and forty miles. We did not, therefore, reach Varna till 7 p.m., and then we had no time to enter the town, as the Austrian boat, the *Nile*, was supposed to start at 8 p.m.

Even to us, who were interested in recognizing every inch of the country we passed through, and in seeing many old friends and workmen—among the latter, Tom Bilby, who has been an express driver on that line for twelve years, and Patrick Keefe, who has been there as long, acting as inspector,—even to us, the journey was wearying, and we heard many a sigh and groan from our companions. However, the weariness of the land journey was nothing when compared to the horrors of the sea passage. The steamer from end to end was crowded with Turks, Greeks, and Russians, besides the usual mongrel assortment. The sea chopped, and the steamer rolled, and I do not think there were twenty people who did not suffer more or less—I for one was doing the *more;* and our misery was protracted till 2 p.m. the next day (15th), when we reached Constantinople. But the voyage is a remembrance so distasteful to me, that I turn squeamish at the very thoughts of it, so shall say no more, but land myself at Miseri's old familiar hotel.

CHAPTER II.

Constantinople—A kiosk—A victim of the war—Hiring servants—
Constantinople to Moudanieh—On the road to Brusa—An abortive
railroad.

THE Crimean war, and the late troubles of Turkey, have
in turn excited so much interest, that faggots of able pens
have for years past been constantly employed on the
subject of Constantinople, and everybody knows exactly
what it and its surroundings are like, so I shall not
attempt any description of the scenery, but shall content
myself by saying that the eight years that have elapsed
since I last saw it have brought no improvements that I
could discover, except that a number of fairly good houses
have been raised on the spots where huge fires have
cleared the ground of the old native hovels. The streets
smell as badly as ever; the paving is as bad as of old;
and, while I was there this time, the streets were scarcely
lighted at all at night. There was not nearly so much
eagerness and bustle in the streets as of yore, and the
complaisant self-satisfied expression on the thousand faces
that used to pass Miseri's door after business hours were
over, had changed to a hungry, frightened look that plainly
told that things were going badly at Galata. Hardly any

C

ships lay at anchor in the Golden Horn, and the dense crowd that used to swarm to and fro over the bridge had shrunk to a quarter of the former number. The "young bloods" of Pera, clothed in superfine cloth, patent boots, flash jewellery, and kid gloves, had changed into a collection of shabby, melancholy youths; and even the street dogs did not appear so numerous nor so lively as of old.

As for us, we had a busy time, and were out and about all day. A tent, saddles, saddle-bags, pots, pans, and a host of small things had to be bought, and this from a people who would rather not sell at all than do so quickly.

I did find time one afternoon to drive with a friend to the Sweet Waters, where we found one old Turkish hag who begged of us, and two or three small children who did ditto. A small bakshish to the soldier at the gate opened for us the garden which surrounds the Sultan's kiosk or summer palace; but, small as the bakshish was, I do not think what we saw of the garden repaid us. It was something after the fashion of the public gardens in a small German town, but all had gone to rack and ruin—the walls broken down, the shrubs unkempt and ragged, and the paths covered with scorched grass and weeds.

The outside of the palace, a lath and plaster building, was fast crumbling to pieces, and the only thing we saw that was at all in decent order was a large marble-floored summer house, with a fountain that did not work in the middle of it.

The windows of this looked out on the river, which had

been here dammed back to fall over a series of artificial cascades, but these were broken and covered with stones, whilst the river had cut through the bank at the side, and flowed on without having to jump from cascade to cascade.

I can well imagine that at one time, when all was new and in order, it was very pleasant on a summer's evening for the Sultan to lounge in the cool summer house, listening to the gurgling water, sipping his coffee, smoking his pipe, and carrying on with the last new wife (that is, supposing a Sultan has sufficient "go" in him to do so, which I much doubt the last three or four to have had).

A second bakshish opened the palace itself for us, and we wandered all over it with a Turkish guide, even into the women's rooms. He told us that everything was exactly as it had been left when Sultan Azis last left it; and if he spoke the truth, I can only say the said Sultan was not overwhelmed with luxuries. The rooms were very large, but bare, comfortless, and most unhome-like. In each room there was a divan in the corner, and round the walls, a few gaudy armchairs of French manu-facture—the sort of things one sees in the best bedroom of a country inn; chairs that spoke for themselves, and said plainly, "I was made to be looked at, and I refuse to give you the least comfort in any position you may try." The walls and ceilings were painted in the worst possible style and taste, and here and there hung huge mirrors that gave one about as satisfactory a sight of one's self as a shop window does on a wet day.

The only really nice thing in the place was the bath, which was all of white marble, even to the ceiling, and if it had been heated I could have enjoyed a bath greatly. There was little difference in any of the rooms, except that the floor in the Sultan's sleeping-room was entirely covered with a splendid Turkish carpet, whereas all the other rooms were carpeted with grass matting. This latter looked cool, clean, and nice, and I should have preferred it to the carpet in so hot and insect-troubled a country. None of the sultans since Azis have even entered this palace, and I have no doubt but that in a few years it will be a heap of ruins.

As we drove back to Pera, we could see on the distant hills inland the thickly clustered white tents of the Russians; but we were told these were rapidly disappearing, as the Russians retired either to Adrianople or were shipped off to Odessa.

While in Constantinople I saw very little actual misery and poverty myself, though I was told there still were multitudes in the khans and mosques that were just kept alive by a miserable pittance from Government or by charity. One incident that happened to me told a pitiable story, and gave me a glimpse behind the scenes. I was walking alone in the bazaars one day, when a tall gaunt-looking Turk, fairly well dressed, made a rush at me, and before I knew what he was about, gave me a kiss on each cheek; and then, before I could recover from my disgust, began pouring forth a string of flowery speeches, denoting his pleasure at seeing me again.

Little by little I recovered myself, and then recognized one Salih Binbashi (Salih the colonel), whom I had known years ago when I lived at Varna. Then he was a rich man and a great swell, now he was starving and very humble.

He had taken his regiment to the Shipka Pass with Suleiman Pasha. There he had fought for some months, and had his head split open in a ghastly manner by a Russian soldier; this had left a scar across his head which had the appearance of the closed lips of a horse's mouth. While he was away fighting, his house in Stamboul had been burnt, and his two small children burnt in it. He had had no pay for months, and in a whisper he told me, " I have not touched food for twenty-four hours, and had only a scrap in the twenty four before that; and " (laying his hand on his stomach) " I am very hollow here, and all I possess in the world is the clothes I stand in. For the love of God, friend, give me five or ten piastres" (five piastres are a shilling). I gave him something, and then, thinking he looked like kissing again, I bolted, heartily pitying my old friend.

In Constantinople we hired a young Greek cook, Antonio by name, and, if I mistake not, fool by nature. But there was little choice; for, thanks to the numerous newspaper correspondents, Red Cross, and other travellers who had been of late at Constantinople, and who had been paying war prices for the most miserably inefficient servants, the cook and servant tribe in general had got such exalted ideas, that they looked upon the rate of £200 or £250 a year for their services as quite beneath their acceptance, and scoffed at the low wages we offered, which were yet double what they got before the war. Antonio had never been on a journey before, so accepted our place as a stepping-stone to something better.

Then we engaged, through the help of a Mr. Thompson, who carries on a large business in Angora goats' hair (mohair), a Turkish cavas named Ali Agha—a quiet likely looking man of about fifty-five or sixty years of age. He had only arrived from Angora two days before we were to start on our journey, so could give us the latest information as to the roads, etc. He had travelled all over Asia Minor, and was as much at home in Brusa, Angora, Sivas, and Diarbekir, as in his own village. Besides this, he had been twice to London, and once to the Cape of Good Hope, with goats for Mr. Thompson, who gave him a first-rate character.

It was on Saturday morning, September 20th, that we at last made a move from Miseri's hotel, accompanied by a young Frenchman who was visiting the Levant, and was on his way to Brusa for a few days.

After the usual quarrel with the porters and boatmen, because we would not pay them four times too much, we found ourselves on the densely crowded deck of the Brusa boat, having had to bribe the custom-house officer not to open our luggage in the boat at the steamer's side. As we were only going from one port to another in Turkey, and in a steamer that went nowhere else, we thought we should have been able to get away without this annoy-

ance; but there is an export duty of one per cent. on all
goods leaving Constantinople. However, of these duties
and other like troubles I will write further on.

The steamer should have started at 7.30 a.m., but we
were not astonished at being kept waiting till 9.15. We
were thoroughly disgusted to find, when we did start, that
she was a very slow boat. Fortunately the wind, such as
there was, was favourable, and the Sea of Marmora like
glass, or I verily believe we should have been there for
days. As it was, we reached Moudanieh two hours later
than we ought, but as we had the day before us, a pleasant companion, and a shady seat, we enjoyed the voyage.
As we rounded the Seraglio Point, we met a monster
steamer crowded with Russian soldiers on their way home.
They were cheering heartily, and were being watched by
some hundreds of Turkish soldiers in the forts. I wonder
which were the most pleased, the Russians to see the last
of the Turks, or the Turks of the Russians.

The morning was beautifully fine and bright, and the
sea was one sheet of the deepest blue, studded far and
near with the white sails of small boats, whilst in the
distance, snug under the Princes Isles, could be seen the
English ironclads. Moudanieh, with its white houses
with red tiles and numerous trees, strikes one as very
pretty and peaceful-looking as one looks at it from the
sea, but it will not bear a closer inspection. The wooden
pier stretches out from a flat coast without any sort of
protection, and it can only be in calm weather, when the
sea is like a duck-pond, that a steamer can come alongside,

and even then half her length projects beyond the end of
the pier, and necessitates the landing of men and goods
from the forepart.

Not being in any great hurry, we sent our cavas to
engage carriages for ourselves and baggage, and then sat
quietly till the nondescript mass of passengers had cleared
off. Then our troubles began again. First we had to pay
for landing on the pier, then our passports had to be
looked at, and, as our French friend passed by presenting
an old letter he had in his pocket, this must be of infinite
service to the police regulations. Then our luggage had
to be examined, or, rather, bakshish paid that it should
not be examined, and then we had to pay for leaving
the pier.

At last all was over, and we and our luggage in the
street, or, rather, in the filthy ditch that is here called a
street, and soon were all stowed away in the waggons or
carriages. The vehicle that I and my two companions
occupied was a full-sized landau, old and rickety, drawn
by two meagre, wretched-looking ponies, and driven by a
ruffianly looking young Mussulman-Greek, who never left
his wretched cattle alone for one minute, and kept bobbing
about on the coach-box like a pea on a drum.

For the first eight miles out of Moudanieh the road
passes up a narrow valley thickly planted with olive trees,
vineyards, and mulberry trees, from the luxuriant growth
of which it is evident that the soil (of decomposed volcanic
formation) is very rich.

For the first two or three miles these gardens were filled

with dirty, half-starved, wolfish-looking Circassian emigrants, who were waiting till the Government of Brusa should send waggons to cart them inland, and meanwhile existing on a pittance doled out to them by the said Government.

About nine miles from Moudanieh the road, which had been all the while ascending on a steep grade, gained the top of the ridge that separates the valley of Moudanieh from that of Brusa, and, on reaching this, a magnificent view of the valley, with Mount Olympus and other smaller mountains, lay before us, with the town of Brusa, apparently quite near us, nestled at the foot of Mount Olympus. Little time was allowed for admiring the rich scene before us, or for taking a last look at the Marmora in our rear; for our coachman, with a hideous yell, started off his horses down the steep hill and so on and on, with only a halt of five minutes at a roadside café, until, at the end of some ten miles, he brought us to a standstill at the door of the Hotel Bellevue, just at the entrance of Brusa.

But before we settle ourselves there, I must hark back again to the *road*. It had been constructed under European management, at the expense of the Government, some eight years ago, and had been for some years, I was told, "superb"; but since the days when it was first opened until now, not one hour's work nor one para has been expended on its maintenance, the result being that it is one mass of grips and holes that look impassable, and that no one but a Turk would ever think of attempting to cross with a carriage. With the constant traffic that goes on the holes must so increase that I feel sure the entire road must be impassable this winter. So much for the road; and now for another piece of Turkish enterprise.

About eight years ago the Turkish Government set to work and actually constructed a narrow-gauge railway from Moudanieh to Brusa. The earthworks were finished, the bridges made, and the rails laid. All was completed except the stations, which were to have been built after the line got to work. Five locomotives were bought and landed at Moudanieh, and one was run over a part of the line to see how it worked. Then these five locomotives were locked up in a shed at Moudanieh, and there the enterprise ended! It cost £7000 per mile, about double what it would have done if made by a good European company. The gradients were so steep and the curves so sharp that, practically, trains could not work; and, lastly, the engines bought did not properly fit the rails. It is now four years since the locomotives were imprisoned, and nothing further has been done. The sleepers are rotting and the locomotives rusting, whilst the patient soldier trudges along the twenty miles of weary road to fight for the Padishah, and when the war is over, if not killed by the enemy or muddled to death by his officers, probably trudges back again.

Thousands of tons of war material and war provisions have been hauled over these hills to Moudanieh, by half-starved, over-driven horses and bullocks, when a fraction of the cost would have put the line in working order in

a month. No; I am wrong about the *cost.* It would have
cost the Government something to put the line in order,
and it cost them nothing to order the peasants and their
carts on to the road. The line, as it exists, might have
been conceded to foreigners to finish—their payment being
so many years' working of the line; but then, perhaps it
might pay them, and why should foreigners make money
out of the Turk? No; let the line crumble away, let the
bridges fall in, and the locomotives rust. As it was in the
beginning, it is now, and it always will be; and God
save "the splendid Turk," for he will not save himself!

CHAPTER III.

Hotel at Brusa—Brusa—A street scene—Sight-seeing—Horse-dealing
—Silk factories—Armenian orphanage.

As we were driving across the wide plain of Brusa, I said
to my companions, " I will tell you what I should like
to-night—a nice clean hotel, good beds, and a wide
balcony where we might sit out and enjoy the cool of the
evening." My remark only elicited a smile at the pre-
posterous wish, but to our infinite astonishment it was
more than fulfilled. The Hotel Bellevue is a large, spacious,
airy house, very clean, and the beds were by far the best
I had slept on since I had left my own spring mattress;
and then there is not only one balcony to the house but
three, and in the deep cool shade of the one on to which
our bedrooms opened we spent some peaceful hours. After
this, we should not have been astonished to have found
a duplicate of St. Paul's Cathedral at Angora, a Crystal
Palace at Sivas, or a St. Pancras railway station at
Diarbekir.

It was almost dark when we arrived, and quite dark by
the time we had finished a fairly good dinner, so we saw
nothing of Brusa the first night; but we were up early the

next morning, and after a cup of chocolate cooked in our etna, we started off to take a preliminary run through the chief streets of the town and the bazaars, and call on the Director of the Ottoman Bank.

There is much to be desired in Brusa, and it would not be a Turkish town if there were not; but of all the towns I have ever seen where the Turk is master, this is the prettiest and nicest, and it might, with a little trouble, be made the jewel of Asia Minor. Standing as it does at the foot of Mount Olympus, but raised well above the plain, almost every house has a splendid view, while the rear is sheltered and shut in by the grand old mountain that rises immediately behind it. Down almost every street there runs a clear mountain stream, and drinking fountains are nowhere many yards apart. The chaussée runs well up into the middle of the town, and is there wide and airy, but the houses on either side are old fashioned and poor. Then innumerable streets and bazaars, huge khans and mosques, are scattered about, with here and there monster palm trees shading quiet corners, whilst on the higher slope above the town is a large Turkish burial-ground, dirty and untidy, but yet made picturesque by the splendid cypress trees that are thickly scattered over it.

So much we saw on this our first outing, before the bracing air from the mountains sharpened our hunger to such an extent that we hurried back to our hotel and there had a good breakfast. When I say a *good* breakfast, I mean good for *Turkey;* for nowhere else would thick muddy coffee, or rancid butter full of coarse hairs, or sour unleavened bread be tolerated.

After breakfast we took our cigarettes to the balcony in front of the house, and spent an hour or so watching the numerous passers-by. Thick and fast they came—a string of pack-horses loaded with wood they had fetched from a river by which it had been floated down from the mountains. Five Circassian emigrants followed, clothed in dirty rags and carrying the never-absent dagger. Then two Turkish women riding donkeys—they were perched up on old pack-saddles so high above their beasts, that they were able to cross their feet on the top of the donkeys' necks. A bullock-cart or two, followed by more pack-horses. A Greek woman on a donkey, with huge panniers on either side, one filled with grapes, the other containing a girl about ten years old, the load altogether being somewhat bigger than the donkey. The donkey stopped to take a nibble at a stalk of Indian corn, the woman dragged at the one rope rein, vainly endeavouring to get its head up, at the same time swearing at it frantically. Failing in her object, she takes off her slipper and whacks the donkey till it lifts its head, when she hits it on the right ear with the slipper, and round goes the little beast and starts off briskly in the direction from which it came. There is more whacking and swearing, in the latter of which the young one in the basket joins, but I feel sure her strong expressions were directed against her mother for being such a poor donkey-rider. Mother and daughter screech and yell, four Jewish women join in the row, a small

Greek boy rushes out with a pointed stick to prod the donkey, when suddenly it catches sight of a lady of its own species, and, being filled with love at first sight, it sets up a loud and hideous bray, ambles off up a side path with its tail set out straight behind, its ears stuck forward, and its mouth wide open, and we hear its roar and its riders' oaths dying away in the distance till they are finally lost in the screeching of the wheels of some bullock arabas, and the jingling of the bells of a string of camels that lope past at a stealthy walk. An *à la Franca* Turkish effendi, accompanied by an *à la Turca* Greek, trot past on ponies with French saddles, brass stirrups, and rusty bits. They turn out of the road for no one, and the Greek therefore runs his knee against a pack-load of logs, and swears deeply, while his Turkish friend evidently rejoices at the pain he suffers, and while chuckling at it he rides over a family of dogs that have taken possession of a hole in the middle of the road for a bed. The brutes sit and howl in an aggressively injured voice for ten minutes, just under the noses of three old Turks who are seated on low stools chatting under the shade of a monster cypress opposite our hotel, and the said Turks calmly suspend the even flow of their talk till it may please the dogs to stop theirs.

Having heard much of the beauty of the mosques here, we hired two diminutive donkeys in the afternoon and, with our cavas in attendance, started to inspect the one said to be the most beautiful, and after jolting and stumbling over the stones of the miserably paved Turkish quarter for a mile, reached the "Green Mosque," which stands on a small mound overlooking the town and plain. Externally, there is not much worth seeing, nor is there any architectural beauty about it. In 1855 it was greatly shaken by the earthquake, and to this day large rents and cracks gape open all over the walls. We had been told that the Turks of Brusa were very fanatical; but we saw no signs of this, for on reaching the yard of the mosque a small urchin produced the key and offered to do showman. Knowing it is bad form in Turkey to enter a mosque with shoes on, and not relishing the idea of having to unlace our boots, we pulled up at the door; but both the boy and a priest, who joined us shortly after, pressed us to enter, and when we refused, the priest insisted on our going up a winding staircase in the wall to a sort of big opera-box looking down into the building.

The mosque is cruciform, with a lofty domed roof over the centre part, painted green, and touched up with gold and bright colours. Here and there the walls were inlaid with porcelain, after the fashion of mosaics, which must have been very pretty when perfect, but the small pieces had nearly everywhere been partially knocked out, which gave an untidy, ruined appearance to the whole. In the middle of the mosque was a marble basin, some twenty feet in diameter, filled with running water. The floor was all covered with grass matting, and the only thing to relieve the bare monotony of it was a very high pulpit in the far right-hand corner, and on the left a

sort of low reading-desk. I cannot say there is much
grandeur or beauty about the edifice, and as we were
told this was the finest mosque in the town, we contented
ourselves with inspecting but one other, which was very
much in the same style.

No one who has not lived in the East can have any
notion what a time it takes to make a purchase of the
smallest description, but those who have had that experience will easily understand that the chief of our time
for four days was occupied in horse-dealing. We only
wanted three beasts, and we did not care to have any
fancy high-priced article, which was lucky, for all the
decent, well-bred horses of this part of the country had
been swallowed up in the war, and their places were
being filled by wretched, under-bred, over-starved Russian
troopers' and artillery horses that arrived by each steamer
that came in from Constantinople.

Every Monday there is a large market for all sorts
of local productions, and especially horses, and from
early morning we had seen crowds of natives—Turks,
Greeks, Armenians, Jews, Circassians, and Tartars—
flocking past the hotel, and from the number of horses
we saw, we thought we could have no difficulty in suiting
ourselves; but on pushing our way through the reeking
mass of humans into the horse-market, which is held
in a yard about twenty yards square, and the adjacent
lanes, our hopes were greatly dashed. There were horses
by the score, all alike in two respects—they were all
small and all bad. Most looked half-starved, and not

D

one of them would have fetched £10 in England. We soon had a ring of the poor beasts around us, with their attendant "jambas" ("lost souls," or copers—are not the names occasionally synonymous even in England ?), each vaunting the praises of his own particular animal. If I had been a millionaire, I would have bought them all and then shot them, to put them out of their misery ; but, as it was, for the space of two hours we were riding the best of the bad lot up and down a street, perched on Turkish saddles that almost cut us in halves, to see if we could find one with a hidden virtue. At last we selected three, one, a chestnut, the only well-bred horse in the market, and the other two wretched brutes. Giving the owners instructions to follow us to the hotel, we adjourned there, and after riding them for some time, we ended by buying the chestnut for about £9, and we found in him a good horse. Our next horse we bought from Mr. Gilbertson, the Acting-Consul of Brusa, and though it was a higher price than the other, yet it proved a cheap and useful little beast. His one great fault was his amorous propensities towards the softer sex, and proportionate hatred to the gentlemen of his species. The latter made it necessary to keep hobbles on him all the time he was in the stable, and to give the other horses a wide berth when on the road.

Our third purchase was by far the most useful looking animal of the three. "Fourteen, one" high, a big body, short legs, powerful hocks, and a good trippler. We saw him passing the door with a zaptieh on his back,

and after a short bargaining he became ours. Next
morning, as I was leaving the house, a small boy who
was sitting on the steps said to me, "You bought my
father's horse yesterday, how do you like him?" In
fun I said, "Oh, he is a good-for-nothing brute;" and
the boy answered, "Not quite that—he is rather rotten
and is lame. A short time ago he had something the
matter in his inside, but we gave him medicine, and he
is better; he eats a little now, so perhaps he will not be
ill again." This did not sound hopeful, as we were
starting on an eight days' ride to Angora, which would
probably be the first place where we could get another
horse.

On our third day in Brusa, we took a long walk
through the town, accompanied by a German, who is a
silk-broker there.

We paid a visit to the principal silk-spinning establishments here, the first belonging to an Armenian, the
second to a Frenchman. They both consisted of a long
room, with a row of some fifty women on either side, each
with a big pan of hot water before her, and a winder at
her back. In the water bob about the cocoons, and from
four at a time the women wind the silk, that is, they
attach to the twisting threads new cocoons as the old
ones are spun off, whilst the thread so made passes over
their heads to the winder behind. In the Armenian
Factory we found several Turkish women and girls hard
at work, and, what is more, they had no yashmaks on,
nor did they attempt to hide their faces from us in the

least. At the present time there is exported from Brusa and the immediate neighbourhood about 50 bales of silk. A bale weighs 2 cwt., and costs there £250. There is, therefore, some £12,500 earned by this industry alone, and if the export duties were only moderate, and a little encouragement given by Government, this might be greatly increased. But, as it is, it has been going down-hill for some years. The native worms have had the disease badly, and the seed (eggs) of the country only suffices to keep the factories at work for two months in the year. All the seed comes from Japan, Italy, or Bagdad, and the two former are of a very inferior quality.

The factories are worked by steam-power, and the man that drives the engine, and the owner of the factory, are the only males about the place. The women earn from two to three shillings a day, and look clean, well dressed, and well fed. Their hours of work are very long, however, being from sunrise to sunset, with two stoppages in the day, of an hour each, one for breakfast, and another for dinner.

Besides the silk-spinning, there are other industries in Brusa, such as tanning leather, and weaving cotton. The former trade is fast dying out, owing to the inhabitants having found out that foreign, and notably Russian leather, is both better and cheaper than the local manufactures.

All the cotton thread used here comes from England, and is taxed both on coming into Turkey and on going out. I visited one or two wretched sheds, where Turkish towels and embroidered handkerchiefs were being made, and nothing could have been rougher than the old-fashioned hand-looms; but the Turkish owners evidently looked on the miserable frames as something to be proud of.

We also visited, one day, another kind of manufactory, and, as far as money goes, I fear not a very thriving one. It was a manufactory of Protestants. The mistress of this establishment, Mrs. Baghdarian, is an English woman married to an Armenian. Some two years ago, she opened a house in the Turkish quarter for the reception of orphans and destitute children, and when we visited her house she had twenty-seven small girls under her care, and expected two more Bulgarians from Philippopolis in a few days. Her establishment is connected with the "Turkish Missionaries Aid Society," and, for further particulars, I was referred to the Rev. Henry Jones, 8, Adam Street, Strand. The house in which the orphanage is now established is a Turkish one—spacious, clean, and airy. The great salaamlik upstairs, is fitted up as a schoolroom, from which opens two dormitories, with beautifully clean, comfortable-looking beds. The children were all neat and tidy, and nicely dressed in cotton frocks; and, at the mistress's request, they sang to me some rather gushing hymns. Their singing, I should say, was rather above the average of village-school children in England, but, as none of them understand English, the words were somewhat lost upon them. I looked over their sewing, which seemed, to my poor male eyes, very well put together, and evidently the small creatures were uncommonly proud of their performances. They struck me as looking pale and unhealthy, and generally doltish ; but the mistress told me this was only on the exterior, and that they were seldom ill, and were as sharp as possible, and could learn anything.

The scheme, as far as I could gather, on which the orphanage works is a good one. The children are cared for and educated, and are brought up as Protestants ; then the most capable are sent to the Armenian villages in the interior, where they open schools, the Armenians gladly paying their salaries. Those that are not up to this, are sent into Armenian families as domestic servants.

As usual, *money* is the great thing needed. Mrs. Baghdarian says that living in a Turkish quarter (there are no other houses in Brusa large enough for her) she is a good deal annoyed by the Turks. For instance, the children are not allowed to play in the yard, or even sing much in the house, for fear of disturbing the faithful. She said she was hoping to raise £400, for which sum she could, with her husband's help (who, being a native Armenian, is up to the way of getting things done cheaply), build a good house in the Christian quarter, with many more rooms, so that she could take in double the number of children. She also hopes to be able to raise sufficient funds to enable her to open a hospital, under the management of a trained nurse from England.

There is also a school in Brusa for Greek girls, under the management of an American lady; but, as the school was closed for the holidays, we were unable to go over it. This school is in connection with the American missionaries.

CHAPTER IV.

The gallows-tree—A Circassian thief—Rice-growing—A start for
Angora—The first day's ride—A night in a khan—The vale of
Enni-Gul—Enni-Gul.

SITTING as we did evening after evening on the balcony
of our hotel, refreshed after the heat of the day by the
cool yet soft air, and listening to the hushed sounds of the
town that spread away to our right, Brusa appeared a
very pleasant, peaceful spot, just the sort of place for any
one tired of the turmoils of the busy cities of the West to
retire to, and there pass in ease and comfort the evening
of his days. No town could be more fitted for this, and
in all the town no pleasanter spot for a quiet life could be
found than the shaded balcony; but, just as we had come
to this conclusion, a friend sitting with us disturbs our
quiet by saying, "You see that splendid cypress on the
other side of the road, with one limb growing out at right
angles? I saw a man hanging from that not long ago.
He had killed a man in the vineyards near here, was
caught red-handed, tried, and condemned to death. Years
passed, and the sentence was not carried out till, one day,
Ignatief paid a visit to Brusa, and, being told of the
murder, he hinted to the governor that it was a shame to
keep a man so long with a rope dangling over his head.

The governor took the hint, and the next day, as I have told you, the man was swinging there."

As he finished his story, some twenty dogs dashed past below, in pursuit of a trespasser of their own species, pursuers and pursued all yelping and howling at the top of their voices. Was it the story, or was it the dogs that destroyed the feeling of peace and rest? "Ha! ha!" went on our friend, "I saw a good thing from this balcony the other day. An old Turk came riding down the road yonder, leading a pack-horse. Just as he got opposite here he passed a Circassian, who slipped up behind, cut the halter of the pack-horse, and in the twinkling of an eye was on the beast's back, and the next moment went dashing past the astonished Turk, who for a full minute kept looking first at the cut rope in his hand, and then after the fast-vanishing steed. At last he realized what had happened; but, instead of at once giving chase, he jumped off his horse, and began hobbling and shouting after the robber. There is a guard-house a mile up the road, and had he at once galloped after the man, he might have roused the guard, and they could have shot the thief as he passed."

Again, was it our friend's story that took away from us the last remnant of a feeling of rest and quiet enjoyment; or was it the two young Greeks who, hand-in-hand, lolled down the street howling out a hideous sound they fondly supposed to be a song?

To the ordinary tourist, or to any one visiting these regions who had only a slight knowledge of Turkey, and

had not previously learnt the masterly fashion in which
the governing Turk contrives to " kill the goose that lays
the golden egg," Brusa and its neighbourhood would
appear a most favourable spot for Europeans to settle in
and open out industries, such as farming, mining, and
manufacturing silk. It is near home, easily reached, has
a good market only a few hours distant at Constantinople.
Then the climate is most agreeable, the land in the plains
cheap, and capable of producing anything and everything
grown in Europe. Plentiful streams cross the plains in
all directions, and irrigation might easily be used. Labour
is cheap, and fairly good. Although the population all
suffer from occasional attacks of fever and ague, this rarely
kills, and may be set off against such epidemics as typhus
and scarlet fever, diphtheria, measles, etc., those scourges
we so often suffer from in Europe, and which rarely visit
Brusa and its environs.

Brusa is a favoured spot in all ways, and to the uniniti-
ated it appears strange that there are not more Europeans
engaged there in commerce, agriculture, etc. ; but it is not
so to those who know the Turk. Again and again men
from various parts of Europe have made a start there,
but invariably with the same result. A few years of
struggle, more or less money wasted, and failure. There
seems to be no exception ; and of the numberless men
who have commenced farming, mining, etc., in this district, we could not hear of one who had succeeded or even
retired taking with him the original capital he brought
with him into the country. The great cause for this is

the utter insecurity of property held by a European. Say he buys a farm, a mine, or a manufactory. In the purchase every formality has been observed, proper papers taken out, and title deeds secured. Years pass, and perhaps the undertaking begins to look prosperous; when in steps a Turk, or an Armenian with a Turk to back him, who claims the property. It belonged to his great-grandfather, and was illegally taken from him. He has no papers to show this; but he has a number of witnesses to prove it. Turkish law is set a-going; weary days and months are wasted over it; and at last it is almost invariably decided that the European is a trespasser. Ambassadors are appealed to, more time and money expended, and the decision is reversed; when the Turk begins all over again in another court, with more witnesses and more evidence, till at last the European, disgusted at his works having been stopped and at the hideous injustice he meets with, throws all up in despair and, if he is wise, abandons the country. The victorious claimant either sells his unjustly acquired property to some fresh flat or lets it all fall to ruin and decay.

But should the European, by the help of a powerful ambassador, succeed in gaining a verdict, and, after paying for his law and other expenses, continue his industry, he is worse off than if he had been driven from the country. The Government officials feel sure he is prospering, and as prosperity is a crime in their eyes, all are against him. He is obstructed in all ways. The stream that watered his land or turned his mill is diverted at its source. His crops rot on the ground while waiting for the tithe-collector. He is overtaxed, and illegally taxed, and in one way or another is always in hot water; till, little by little, his profits are *nil*, and to save being utterly ruined he realizes what he can of his original capital, and leaves a country that has used him so ill. And so it was, that in all our journeys through Asia Minor, we never saw a man who was succeeding in anything.

As I have said, to be successful is sure to create jealousy. and opposition. "Why should this Christian be making money in our land; why cannot we, the owners of the soil, make money as he is?" It is useless to point out that by his prosperity he is enriching the Government and country; that he employs labour, pays taxes, and creates wealth for the community. The governor and his officials do not individually pocket a piastre that they know of, and therefore they set to work either to prevent the Christian from succeeding or to get the industry into their own hands.

A year or two ago a few enterprising people started to work to grow rice on the flat plain some five miles below Brusa. They bought land, they diverted streams for irrigation, and made thrashing-floors, and were eminently successful, and the great extent of waste unprofitable land that now exists had the prospect of becoming one of the richest spots in Turkey. The success of the undertaking was its ruin. The jealousy of the Turks was aroused, and so they reported to Constantinople that the rice-fields produced fever, and an order was sent that no more rice should be grown. As I have said, the rice-fields were five miles from the town; between them and it extended a vast stagnant swamp sufficient to breed fever for the whole district, a swamp that might at a small cost be drained and brought under cultivation, and which, if the rice-fields had turned out well, would have been reclaimed and cropped, and so rendered harmless. But the fact is, the Turk can bear with the fever—"it is sent by God;" but he cannot bear the successful Christian—he is sent by quite another power!

When we left Brusa there was some hope of starting the rice-fields again. Bakshish was being used to soften the hearts of the megliss (council); but, as our informant remarked, "it will end in nothing, for they will require so much bakshish year after year, that the profits will be all swallowed up and the enterprise abandoned."

From inquiries we made, we learnt that as far as Angora there was a track sufficiently good to allow a carriage to pass over it, and as our cavas, Ali Agha, discovered a friend who had come from Angora with a two-horse araba, and would be glad to get a return freight, we settled to hire him for our luggage. And now, having finished all our preparations, we at last made a start on Saturday, September 28th; and though we knew that in leaving the hotel we were leaving for some time all comfort, and that fatigue and rough fare were before us, yet the feeling that our real Asia Minor journey had now begun in earnest was most agreeable and inspiriting.

As is usual in Turkey, the actual start took some time.

First G——'s horse got loose and raced up into the town ;
then the arabaji groaned like a camel as each piece of
luggage was loaded up ; then the wrong saddle got on the
wrong horse, and the horses—the runaway having been
recovered—set to work to kick. Then bakshish had to
be given to some and refused to others ; but the start
came at last, and away we went, G—— and I first,
Ali Agha next, then a zaptieh, then the araba, and the
rear closed by the other zaptieh. Jolt, jolt, went the
araba ; jog, jog, went we, up this street, down that, till
at last we were free of the town, and found ourselves on
the chaussée, which lasts for four miles. The Turks made
it, and a splendid specimen of their industry it is. They
have just rummaged to the surface all the loose stones,
and then their work was done, and the entire road consists
of a mass of boulders from the size of a cocoa-nut to that
of a bushel, and the track zigzags about to avoid the big
ones. Here and there has been made a culvert or bridge
over the numerous streams that pour down from Mount
Olympus, but most of these have fallen in, and one has
to plunge and struggle in the watercourses.

The first four or five miles of the road was over the
plains, but then we had to mount some steep hills that
divide the Brusa valley from that of Enni-Gul, and before
we had gone five hundred yards up the first pitch our
araba stuck fast. The road, which was just the width
of the araba, had been washed away into such deep ruts,
first on one side and then on the other, that the araba
must have gone over had it not been for the perpendicular

banks on either side on which it fell, and against which
it had to be dragged, and this made the work so heavy
that the horses jibbed, and eventually sat down like dogs
on their haunches.   There was nothing for it but to tie
up our riding horses, unload the araba, and then altogether
give it a shove, till the horses with a plunge took to drawing and rushed on for a few hundred yards, to stick fast
again, and this they did so often that it was an hour before
we got to the top, a distance of a mile.   Then all the
luggage had to be fetched up and reloaded, so that our
progress could not be said to be rapid.   To make matters
worse, a heavy thunderstorm came on, and we were soon,
in spite of our mackintoshes, a cake of mud and slush,
and went sliding and slipping about in an awful manner.

Just at sunset we arrived at the small village of Ak-Su,
and located ourselves for the night at the khan, and a
more beastly place cannot be found.   Below is a large
room with raised wooden divans, on which squat all day
and nearly all night the idle and aged of the village,
drinking coffee and smoking, whilst above are a lot of
rooms, some ten feet square and six high, round two sides
of which is a raised divan, covered with insect-infected
smelling rags and cushions, and the whole so disgustingly
dirty a pig would object to it.   We made the best of this
we could, by spreading a waterproof sheet on the divan,
with our big saddle-bags to rest against, and for supper
we eat some of the cold chicken we had brought with us
from Brusa, and helped it down with some tea made in
our etna.   We saw numberless bugs all over the wood-

work of the room, and to our disgust we found that a bug, after being buried in insect-powder for five minutes, jogged off as if refreshed by it.

On getting up next morning we found it was raining fast, but there was nothing for it but to pack up our traps, put on our mackintoshes, and make a start; but when half-way up the hill out of the village our araba stuck again, and after half an hour spent in trying to get the horses to give a pull, we had to send back to the village and hire a pair of buffaloes.

When these arrived, we unfastened the horses, and hanging the buffaloes on, they slowly but surely dragged the araba up the hill, Ali Agha standing first on one step and then on the other, to prevent it over-balancing. Little by little we crept on in drenching rain, till after two hours we were free of the hills, and the splendid vale of Enni-Gul was before us, some twenty miles in length, and including the sloping ground on either side, that might be easily cultivated and even irrigated, averaging about six miles in width.

Down the centre of this valley runs a branch of the river Sakaria wending its way to the Black Sea, and to this descend from the side hills innumerable little streams that might be used for irrigation, and while so used would convert this rich valley into a perfect garden. As it is, not one half of the ground has been cultivated, and the streams, instead of being a source of wealth, have been allowed to meander just where they pleased, washing away rich fields here, and causing stagnant swamps there.

The villages we passed were few and far between, and a general appearance of poverty pervaded them. Half way up the vale we arrived at the town of Enni-gul, built on the flat in a swampy and most unhealthy situation, and though in the Asia Minor of to-day it may be called a *town* it is only a collection of mud huts with unpaved mud grips winding their way among them and doing duty for streets.

It had rained all day and been cold and cheerless, so, bad as the khan in the market-place proved to be, we were thankful for its shelter, and felt quite comfortable when squatting on the flaps of our big saddle-bags in a dirty room about nine feet square, with the teapot steaming between us.

E

CHAPTER V.

Zaptiehs — A zaptieh chaoush — The Akka-Dagh — Brigands — A
dangerous gun—An uncomfortable night—An alarm of robbers.

IT is customary for the European journeying in Turkey
to take from town to town one or more zaptiehs—first as
a supposed protection against robbers, and secondly as
guides; but I have little faith in them as protectors. A
guide could be hired from village to village or from town
to town at half the cost of these men. Theoretically they
cost nothing, as to escort travellers is part of their duty,
for which they are paid by Government; but in reality
they each cost in the customary bakshish about five
shillings a day, and if this were not given, they would give
such a bad name to the traveller that his next zaptieh
would be insolent, careless, and lazy. The traveller would
get little to eat, bad lodgings, and only be able to do a
few miles journey each day instead of the usual twenty-
five to thirty miles. The real good of these men is to
impress the villagers with the notion that the person they
are escorting is some one of importance. Without them
he would be considered no one—not worth feeding or
lodging; and any village lout would feel justified in treat-
ing him with insolence. The more zaptiehs the greater

the respect shown, and therefore the better fares the
traveller in the way of lodging, food, and general civility.

Some zaptiehs are better than others, and will lend a
hand to push a carriage out of a mud-hole, load and
unload the pack-horses, and make themselves generally
useful as a servant. These are men who have a lively
faith in favours to come, and think wisely that the more
they oblige the higher their bakshish will be. Now and
then one gets a stupid lout or a bumptious beast; the
first, through stupidity, just rides on in front and shows
the way and does nothing more, and the latter is too big a
man to demean himself by helping a giaour even for
the sake of the extra pay he may get.

In starting on a journey the traveller should either get
a passport or, as we did, secure the Sultan's firman, which
is a document only carried by Europeans when they are
considered people of importance. On arriving in a town,
you either present your firman or send it to the governor
by one of your men, and in compliance with an order in
it, zaptiehs are told off for the next stage, and should be
in readiness on horseback when you want to start in the
morning. In reality they never are ready, and I can
safely say that at every town where we took fresh zaptiehs
we lost two hours waiting for these men after all was
prepared for the start. In fact, they are doubtful blessings
and undoubted nuisances, but cannot well be dispensed
with.

Travelling as we were, just after the great war, the
zaptieh force was in a most disorganized state, and bad as

it has always been, it was now little better than a band
of ruffians. Their pay had been reduced and reduced
until they only got £1 8s. a month, on which they had to
keep themselves and their horses, and to live they had
therefore, like all other Government officials, to rob and to
swindle. In dress and accoutrements no two were alike.
One day we had a man on a fairly good horse, dressed in
complete, though worn out, uniform, armed with a splendid
Winchester repeater. The next day we got a creature in
rags, without a shred of uniform, armed with a club and an
old flint pistol, and, wretched as he was, his horse and its
trappings were worse—the poor beast so thin and weak
it could hardly drag itself along; so we were either obliged
to creep along and do a short day's journey or else ride
away and leave it.

After eating what we were pleased out of habit to call
our supper at Enni-Gul, we had a visit from the head of the
police, and as he seemed an intelligent sort of a man, we
asked him to stay and have a chat, an invitation he
readily accepted, and for two hours he babbled on, giving
us all the news he could. As a sergeant he had served
in the Crimea under Omer Pasha (and was pleased to
approve of the Englishman as a soldier), then for years he
had been cavas at a Constantinople embassy, and now he
was a zaptieh. "It is the life of a dog, but what's to be
done? The country is ruined, ruined by our big men. In
years gone by we fought everybody, and were always
victorious—so we should be now if we were but content
with the good old arms that served our fathers, and did

not spoil our soldiers by putting them into à la Franca
uniforms, over drilling and giving them these useless, new-
fangled breachloaders. The country has been bad for
years, but the war has made it much worse. All the
youngest and strongest of our men have been called away
to fight. Ten go, and out of the ten, one returns—the
rest are rotting in Bulgaria. Then those who are left
starve. The women have done wonders. They have
ploughed and sown, reaped and thrashed, and many have
produced more this year without their husbands than the
husbands themselves would have done, but they have had
to work hard and taxes have been heavy. I cannot live
honestly. I get for myself and horse, all told, £1 8s. a
month, and I cannot keep myself upon it, so if I did not
rob, my horse and my family must starve. Oh, I rob, if
I did not do so I could not do the Padishah's work." This
was an honest confession. I believe the only honest
thing about the man ; but it showed to what straits the
people were driven.

Having been told by our police friend that on the next
day's journey we should have to cross the Akka-Dagh, a
more formidable hill than we had yet seen, and further
that the road over it was as bad as it could be, we
arranged with him to send on one of the two zaptiehs he
was to give us to a village at the foot of the hill, there to
hire and have in readiness a pair of buffaloes to drag our
araba to the summit. This he promised to do ; but on the
morrow, when we reached the village, we found the zaptieh
sitting under a wall, surrounded by half the men of the

place, and on being asked, "How about the buffaloes?"
he said he had not yet been able to make a bargain—so
much was asked, and he had offered so much. "But sit
down, and we will make a bargain." We would not sit
down, but promised what was asked, and then were told
the buffaloes were feeding on the hills, and must be
fetched in. "Never mind, Tchellaby; sleep here to-night,
and start in the morning." But, as we had only come two
hours, and there was a long day before us, we declined
this, and by the help of a little forcible language, induced
the villagers to send for the animals, and then, riding
forward ourselves to the foot of the mountain, we there
had the pleasure of waiting for two hours. At last the
buffaloes arrived, and were hung on to the araba, and went
creeping slowly over the steep rutty road at the rate of
about two miles an hour.

We rode on ahead from time to time, and then got off
our horses to let them rest while we chatted with the
zaptiehs; and, if half the stories they told us of outrages
committed on this mountain were true, it was by no
means the safest part of our road. Earlier in the year a
large band of deserters from the armies in Bulgaria had
lorded it over this road, stopping every one, rich and poor,
who passed along it, until it had such a bad reputation
that no one dared venture over it; so, business becoming
bad, they moved on to a fresh field. Since then, the Circassian emigrants had been extremely industrious in the
same line, and from the way our zaptiehs kept peering
about, and holding their Winchester repeaters in readiness,

they evidently expected a visit from these light-fingered gentlemen. Ali Agha, with an old English double-barrel, stuck close to the araba as a guard; but he did not look a very great warrior, nor do I think his double-barrel was half so likely to shoot a robber as a friend. When we were stuck fast in the mud near Ak-Su, Ali Agha went to the opening at the back of the araba to take out his gun, and giving it a tug, off it banged, the charge passing between the horses and within a few inches of the head of the arabaji. Ali Agha stood aghast for a few seconds, then exclaiming "Marshallah!" he pulled out the gun, and turning his head sideways, applied his right eye first down one barrel and then the other, as if he expected to discover the cause of the accident down there. The arabaji ducked his head low down behind his horses, expecting bullet No. 2 might come; but at last, finding it did not, he proceeded to examine his horses' tails, fully convinced the charge must have lodged in them.

We each of us had a detestable revolver strapped round our waists that caused us constant discomfort and some danger; but it was supposed to be the correct thing, and even if we never used them, the fact of their always being seen on us might deter a half-hearted robber from attacking us.

Besides robbers, these hills or mountains (they were two thousand feet above the sea) were celebrated for game, and though we saw none, yet from the favourable appearance of the land and forests, I have no doubt it abounds. Red deer, roe deer, wild boar, wolves, foxes, and jackals

are said to be numerous, and to these may be added hares,
pheasants, red-legged partridges, and at times woodcock.
Most of the forest consists of oak-scrub, from five to fifteen
feet high, all the larger trees having been cut down, burnt,
or otherwise destroyed, except in a few inaccessible spots,
and even there the oaks were not large or well grown.
On the summits of the hills a few stone pine appear, but
nowhere did we see any really valuable trees. It took us
about seven hours to cross the mountains, but we could
have done it easily in four hours had we not been so
much detained by the slow pace of the buffaloes.

After passing the Akka-Dagh, the country became more
open, trees disappeared, and rich corn land stretched away
in front and all around us, intersected here and there by
small brooks that might be used to irrigate thousands of
acres and make this a most fertile and productive spot.
As it is, not one-tenth of the land is under cultivation
and hardly any villages appeared in sight, and what there
were were poor looking and wretched.

Just before sunset we reached the large village or small
town of Bazardjik, and as the ground was wet from the
late rains, and the weather was still unsettled, we took up
our quarters in a small khan, and I must say were most
uncomfortable. Our room was up a flight of stairs, and
beneath it was the archway into the khan yard, and the
rough boards of the floor being some inch apart from each
other and no glass in the windows, we had a fine current
of air. Early in the evening, the cold drove us to our
little camp-beds, but having no mattresses on them, the

draught from below made sleep out of the question, and
the whole night was spent in first one and then the other
getting up to dress in great-coats, extra trousers, travelling
caps, etc.; and yet morning found us poor muddled-up
creatures, still shivering and feeling unfit for anything in
the shape of exertion, but quite determined to get something in the shape of warm coverlids at the first town we
arrived at.

After about two hours' ride out of Bazardjik, and just as
we were about to enter a narrow rocky gorge, some fifteen
horsemen appeared through the morning mist, riding
across the plain as if to cut us off at the entrance to the
gorge. The distance and the mist prevented our seeing
them very clearly; but after a halt of a few minutes to
observe their movements, our zaptiehs pronounced them to
be Circassians, and robbers. We had a feeling this was
a false alarm; but there was just sufficient chance of their
being the veritable article to make us feel anxious, and to
bring out the strong or weak points in the characters of
those with us.

First the Angora arabaji voted strongly and loudly for
flight back to the village, but this was scoffed at by all.
Then zaptieh No. 1 (generally full of swagger) proposed
retreating behind some rocks, and there waiting to be
attacked, showing thereby that he was of the same family
as those who had tumbled into Plevna, and, like them,
preferred fighting from a hole. The pros and cons for this
scheme were being hurriedly discussed, when Ali Agha
said, in a reassuring tone, "Don't fear; don't fear." At

this zaptieh No. 2 flew in a violent rage, and poured down a torrent of abuse on poor Ali Agha. "Fear! Who fears? I fear no one! I am an old soldier. You talk of fear as if we were women! You yourself are a coward! I dare fight a thousand! Follow me!" and off he dashed, very fast at first, but as he drew near the gorge where the horsemen had disappeared, he got slower and slower till he was joined by the other zaptieh and Ali Agha, both apparently full of valour and fight. Slowly the three disappeared from sight, while we halted with the araba till we should hear the result of their reconnaissance. In about ten minutes Ali Agha returned to say the supposed robbers were peaceable merchants, and that they were scouring the country to find some horses that had been stolen from them in the night by Circassians. We all now became brimful of valour, and went riding down the gorge feeling we had missed a chance of greatly distinguishing ourselves, but at the same time fervently hoping such a chance would not occur again.

CHAPTER VI.

Camels—Camel drivers—Out on the plains—Half-ruined villages—
Eski-Shehr (Doræloum)—Meerschaum—Drunkenness.

On our journey up this gorge we for the first time came
upon a flock of the real Angora goat, or, as it is there
called, " tiftik," the prettiest, jolliest, cleanest and most
profitable little beast in Asia Minor. Here, too, it was
we met the first caravan of camels we had seen on our
march.

The camel is an animal in every way fitted for the
Turk. He must have been specially created for Asiatics,
and for Turks in particular. There were about one hundred
and fifty of these creatures following in Indian file, the
first one being attached to a diminutive donkey, on which
sat a big man, whilst here and there other men on donkeys
acted as outriders to the procession. Each camel was
carrying two sacks of corn, and they were wending their
way at the rate of three miles an hour to the sea-coast at
Moudanieh or Ismidt, and as they only manage some
twelve or fifteen miles a day, a journey from the great
plains about Angora is a slow and costly affair.

It is only in a country like Asia Minor, where for
months at a time the roads are dry, that the camel can be
used with advantage, for when the roads are wet and

greasy the poor brutes slip and slide about, and are in a few hours completely knocked up. Again, they can only travel in comfort on sands or earthy roads, for stones and gravel soon injure their great fleshy feet and lame them. As it is, one often sees the poor creatures limping along, and looking (as I dare say they are) most sorry for themselves. The ordinary load for a camel on a long journey is thirty stone, but at a pinch they will carry more, and, besides, some camels carry half as much again as others with less fatigue. They vary in colour and size, some being almost black, and others a light fawn colour; all are equally slow in their movements, and during all our journey, though we passed thousands of these beasts, they were always walking at exactly the same pace, and we never saw a man attempt to drive them on faster or strike one.

Now and then a yearling camel, or one that has not had the odious pack put upon it, makes a feeble attempt at a gambol, but when it does so its ungainly legs get all astray, and the creature quickly settles down into its usual sober, quiet behaviour. At no time of their lives can they be considered cheerful beasts, but yet there is a pleasant, sagacious, wise look in their faces that forces one to respect them. There is no animal the Turk likes more, and I was often told wonderful stories of its sagacity. For instance, all camel-drivers believe that when passing through a country where robbers are supposed to be, if the numerous bells that are generally attached to the camels are taken off and muffled, the creatures know why it is done, and will step so lightly that they can pass within a few yards of a concealed enemy without being heard. Then their sense of hearing is supposed to be wonderfully acute. When camping out at night, if a stranger approaches, the camels, who are lying in a circle round the encampment, will hear him three miles off and become uneasy, waking up their sleeping masters by a series of grunts. I cannot answer for all this, but I can say that they are in other ways most sagacious and clever. At a word from the driver they will kneel down in a circle to be loaded and unloaded, and while the former process is taking place they evince a lively interest in the performance. They turn their heads back and inspect everything that is put upon them, and if they were being loaded with feathers would give a discontented grunt as each one was put on, which grunt becomes a roar as the last one is lifted up.

Thanks to the camel being so long in the leg, he can only be loaded whilst kneeling, and therefore the load is regulated by what he can rise with, and is never very excessive; and though the getting up is often a struggle, he knows so exactly what he can lift, that if he has too much he won't make an effort. When once on his legs he is all right, gives up grumbling, and walks quietly off. Unlike the horse or donkey, the camel never allows the one in front, to whose pack his halter is attached, to drag him, but always keeps his regular distance, the halter hanging slack.

When on the plains, where there are no trees, shrubs, or rocks to catch the load of the wanderer from the direct

path, the halters are often cast loose, and the camel then
browses on the herbage as he goes, ducking his long neck
to snatch a mouthful, but never stopping or altering his
one regular pace, and will make as good and as quick a
journey when browsing as when tied in a string.

Nothing in the shape of herbage seems to come amiss
to a camel, the driest thistle, or the big ball of the gum
tragacanth plant, which in shape and prickles are exactly
like a hedgehog, disappear down his throat one after the
other; but I believe, from what I have seen, that their
favourite food is the green leaves of the willows. Taking
a branch of this tree sideways between their teeth, they
swing their heads to and fro, and swish! off come the
leaves, which are caught in their great protruding lips,
the stick, except the tender end, being allowed to go free.
So roughly do they tear a branch through their mouths,
that one expects to see them cut and lacerated; but
apparently their lips are made of gutta-percha and nothing
hurts them.

When passing a string of them on the narrow roads,
they never do more than cast an eye on the stranger,
but should the unwary traveller hit or poke one with a
stick, the beast will swing out his ungainly heavy leg in
a surprisingly quick manner, and woe betide the man or
horse he fairly hits.

While on a journey, the long string of camels patiently
follow the leading donkey, but the Turks assert that they
feel humiliated at being towed about by such a little
beast, and will, if they get the chance when their masters

are not by, show this by biting the donkey, and at times
killing it; anyhow, the donkey is always tied apart at
night, well out of reach of the camel's long neck and
powerful jaws.

Most of the camel-drivers are Turcomans, and they do
all the porterage of the country with these creatures. In
the spring, as soon as the roads get a little dry, these men
hire the camels from the villagers, one here, and another
there, till they have collected one or two hundred, and
with these they contract during the summer to transport
goods for the merchants to and from the seaports. They
feed and care for the camels as if they were their own;
but should one die on the road during the summer, its
tail is cut off and returned to the owner in the autumn
instead of the living beast, and the owner puts up with
the loss.

Use works wonders, and, I dare say, it makes the Turcoman enjoy his life as a camel-driver; but, to my mind,
nothing could be more dreary than, day after day, week after
week, to go crawling over the dreary plains, scorched by
the heat by day, and chilled to the bones at night; never
entering a house, sleeping out in the open in all weathers,
and with food of the roughest description; constantly
bothered by loads shifting, backs getting sore, and camels
falling lame—the end to be a week or a month spent in
some stuffy khan yard or dirty suburb of a seaport town,
waiting for a return load, and then the long weary trudge
back. This kind of life continues till the snows of winter
force the man from the roads, when he restores the camels

to their owners, and himself retires to the bosom of his family, and spends the entire winter squatting on a rug in a chimney corner, rarely moving from it day or night— dirty, ragged, and vermin infested, his pipe his sole comfort and enjoyment, and a cup of black coffee now and then his one great indulgence.

A couple of hours' ride up the gorge, and we came to a spot where a main road branched away from ours south to Kutayah, and, at the same time, we rejoiced to find ourselves getting clear of the broken and somewhat mountainous ground we had been passing over since we left Brusa, and out on the great open upland. Had we but known what was before us—the apparently never-ending rolling sea of land, treeless, waterless, hideous in its vastness, desolate, burnt up, brown and barren—how different our feelings would have been, and, I believe, so would our journey, for we never could have faced it. I think we should have shirked it, and either gone south or north to get into the richer and better-watered lands on the coast of either the Black Sea or the Mediterranean, and to have worked our way to the East. As it was, we knew little about our route, and hour after hour, day after day, kept looking for something fresh, something green—a tree, a garden, a real mountain, *something* to break the dull monotony, but it never came; and so, hoping and expecting, we struggled on, getting more and more weary as each mile receded behind us. At rare intervals we passed through, or saw in the distance, a few huts clustered together that called themselves a village; but on an average

these were twelve miles apart, and, in nine cases out of
ten, they were scarcely more than the remains of villages,
and had apparently been getting smaller and the houses
fewer year by year. First we came to the village graveyard, covering, in an untidy fashion, acres of ground ;
then a lot of ruins, or just a few stones cropping up out
of the ground, that had once been the foundations of
buildings ; then a few broken walls, then huts and buildings, minus doors and roofs, and, lastly, the inhabited
houses themselves, which were only one degree removed
from the surrounding ruins.

Huge heaps of manure, the accumulation of generations,
stood in the midst; and as we passed the whole population,
old men and women, lads, children, and dogs, seized this
vantage-ground to squat upon and stare at us, and there
they might be seen squatting in the far distance, after
we had put miles and miles of road between them and us.

We had a long ride this day, thanks to the roads being
dry and the weather fine ; and, just as the sun was dipping behind the hills, we saw in front of us the town
of Eski-Shehr, built on the banks of a branch of the river
Sakaria, and surrounded at the distance of a few miles by
low, rounded, barren-looking hills. We pushed on quickly
to save daylight; but on getting into the narrow streets
of the town, we found that khan after khan we visited
was so crowded there was no room for us ; and had not
Ali Agha found up a Monsieur Joanaki Hordja, an
Armenian merchant, to whom we carried letters of introduction, we should have had to pitch our tent on one of

F

the numerous dirt-heaps, surrounded by filth and smells. As it was, we soon found ourselves settled in a large and comfortable house on the outskirts of the town, in a nice clean room, with Monsieur Joanaki Hordja and his brother-in-law, Mr. Godjamanoglu, giving us a most hearty welcome.

The ancient name for Eski-Shehr was Doralæum, and it was here that the Turcoman sultan, "Kilitch Arslau," after having been driven from his capital, Nicæa, in 1097, collected all his forces, and gave the first Crusaders battle, and where he was once again beaten, leaving the road to the Holy Land, *viâ* Koniyah Araklis, Marash, and the Taurus Mountains, open to his enemies. The Crusaders were commanded by Godfrey de Bouillon, and probably Peter the Hermit was also present at the battle.

We arrived at Eski-Shehr on October 1st, and stopped there until the 3rd; and from the moment we were out of bed till we returned there again, we had a constant stream of visitors—Turks, Greeks, and Armenians, all brimful of local information, and anxious to impart it; but, as I have learnt of old, that the information picked up in the East must be taken *cum grano salis*, I shall only repeat here what was freely salted, being confirmed by two or three witnesses.

First of all, Eski-Shehr is not a pleasant place to live in. It stands low on the banks of the river, and ague is always rife there—a fact one could see for one's self in the cadaverous, careworn faces one meets at each few yards along the street. On the day after our arrival our hostess

had a fit of ague come on when at dinner, and we only
saw her once again when her husband pointed her out,
through an open door, lying curled up on a regular
European bed, looking pale and miserable. Another
drawback to Christians living at Eski-Shehr is the fact
that, with few exceptions, the local government will not
allow them to buy land or build a house. The few wealthy
Christians of the place get over the difficulty by hiring
houses, and as they are all engaged in commerce, they can
dispense with land. For the Turk, if he can put up with
the fever, it is about the best spot in western Asia Minor.
Land is good, plentiful, and cheap, the distance to the
nearest seaport not too great to prevent exporting its
produce ; and the entire town is enriched by some meerschaum mines, that are worked in a hill about four hours
distant. We did not visit these mines; but from what
we were told we gathered that they were worked in a
most primitive manner. A man buys the right of sinking
a shaft, and what meerschaum he finds he sells in the
rough at a fixed price to the Government, and after it has
been trimmed up a little, and the inferior parts cut away,
the remainder is sold to traders, who despatch it to Austria
and Germany, where it is converted into pipes, etc. The
meerschaum beds are near the surface, on a sloping hill
that is full of springs ; and as a shaft is sunk, and never
a drift driven, the mines soon fill with water, and have to
be abandoned.

Yet, in spite of this bad system, the mines afford
sufficient labour to employ all those of the town who care

to work or who may stand in need of a little ready cash;
the result being that the inhabitants are the richest
we saw in Asia Minor, want for nothing, and are quite
content. As the Turkish Government wants a great deal,
and is never content, it seems strange that more is not
made of the mines; and I have no doubt that were they
let to a good European company, the revenues of Turkey
would be greatly increased, and the inhabitants of Eski-
Shehr made none the poorer, as their labour would still
be required, and their pay certain, which now it is not.

When first the meerschaum is brought to the surface
it is in blocks of about a foot square, very soft, and full of
moisture. Not the fourth part of these blocks is pure
meerschaum, and when the inferior parts are cut away
the remainder is of all shapes and sizes. We were told
by a merchant that over and over again people connected
with the trade had offered to buy the chippings, to grind
up and manufacture into masses, from which can be cut
pipes so like pure meerschaum, that only the "knowing
ones" can tell the difference. The Turks have always
refused to sell, assigning as a reason that, if they did so,
the market might get overstocked with pipes, and the
price of good meerschaum reduced.

When I first visited Turkey, over twenty years ago, it
was occasionally whispered about that such and such a
pasha, effendi, or bey, was given to strong drinks. The
old men shook their heads and said it was very bad, and
those who indulged kept their backslidings as much as
possible in the dark; and though from that time till

I quitted Turkey, thirteen years later, the vice had
steadily increased among the upper classes, it was not
indulged in openly, and had not spread to the lower orders.
Eight years have wrought a sad change; for not only is
drunkenness almost as common among the Turks as it is
with us, but they have apparently got over thinking it
a sin and disgrace, and it is both openly indulged in and
openly talked of. Few of the upper classes abstain, and
many make it a rule to go to bed drunk every night.

As far as possible a Turk does everything in the reverse
way to a European, and in getting drunk he makes no
exception. We sit over our wine after dinner; the Turk
before. This has its advantages: one being that you are
sooner drunk on an empty stomach, and it therefore
saves drink; besides, the arrival of dinner stops the
debauch. With our poor old-fashioned stomachs drinking before dinner would take away our appetite; but with
the Turk it has the opposite effect, and the more he
drinks the more hungry he gets. If, after eating, the
fumes of the precious drink are ousing out of his head,
he takes a fresh bumper, and then, in nine cases out of
ten, tumbles back where he sits, falls fast asleep, and is
then wrapped up by his servants and left all night to
sleep himself sober.

We found drunkenness everywhere in Asia Minor, but
nowhere carried to such an extent as at Eski-Shehr,
owing, I imagine, to all being able to earn enough at the
meerschaum mines to enable them to indulge freely. We
were told by an old man, a member of the megliss that in

the town alone eighty thousand okes of maastic were
drunk yearly, and this by a population of twelve thousand.
Now, we may suppose that children and some of the
women abstain, so that those who do drink get a heavy
share. I have said, some of the women, for both here and
at other places we were told that many of the women
drank as hard as the men.

The swell Turks delight in making up parties to the
kiosks in the neighbouring vineyards, taking their women-
kind with them. Several families will join in these
outings. All get drunk, men and women, for days
together. Husbands get confused and mistake their
neighbour's wives for their own; quarrels, fighting, and
murders often take place, and the generally phlegmatic
Turk becomes when drunk a raging madman. If this is
all true, and we had it so constantly repeated and confirmed in different towns that I cannot help believing it
is, the end of the Turk is nearer than I thought. With a
people as indolent and lazy as the Turk, a people as
incapable as children of commanding their passions,
drunkenness will find a ready victim, and will, if I
mistake not, make gigantic strides in a few years. I
had up to this time believed, and I am not now sure
I was not right, that the Koran forbade the Turk drinking
alcohol; but a pious Mussulman, much given to liquor,
informed us this was not so. It only says it is well to
abstain from fermented drinks. Others say the wine in
the days of Mohammed was bad and sour, and gave stomach-
ache. Had it been as good then as now, Mohammed

would have had a good word to say for it. My brother asked a Turk how it was that when both pigs' flesh and wine were forbidden to good Mussulmen they abstained from the one and indulged in the other. The answer was, " Oh, pig is filthy, and wine " (with a sigh) " is *so* nice."

We learnt another fact at this place, which is that a Turkish woman thinks she will lose her husband's affection if she becomes a mother, and therefore has recourse to drugs. Even those who do have children rarely have more than one or two, and then, owing to their ignorance of the most common treatment of infantile maladies, and to the absence of doctors, infant mortality is very great; and so, and so, the Turk is passing away !

CHAPTER VII.

Circassians from Bulgaria—Ancient bath—Soldiers from Russia—An
Eastern morning—A shot at bustards—A fine wheat country—
Flat-roofed houses—Camping out—Rough fare—Village visitors.

WHEN we were at Eski-Shehr, the town was swarming
with Circassian emigrants, who appeared in no hurry to
leave; and as the Government only allowed them a half oke
each man or woman (about 1⅗ lbs.), and each child ninety
drachms (⅞ lb.) of bread a day, it seemed strange to us
that they were so contented; but our host, on our mentioning this, soon gave us the key to the mystery. Pointing
to a large open shed opposite, he said, "Look in there; you
see the whole floor is strewn with sleeping men. Now, we
will look in again before we go to bed, and you will only
see women and children." As we happened to be passing
the shed at 11 p.m., on our way from a bath, we did
look in, and behold! what he said was true. Every man
was out marauding, and at daybreak one by one the band
would return, one with a chicken, another a bit of a cow,
the head of a horse, and so on, and these being put in the
common stewpot, would make a savoury mess, and greatly
help out the Government pittance. Our host concluded
by saying, "We are all robbed by them, we cannot
escape, they are so devilishly clever; but, thank God, there

will soon be an end, they are very rotten, and are dying fast!"

Having mentioned the bath, I must here give an account of this our first satisfactory wash since we left Brusa, for during our journey from there we had not been able to procure any sort of vessel to hold water for washing, and the largest we carried with us was a tea-cup. When fine and warm, we afterwards from time to time took a dip in some stream, or a good soaping at a roadside fountain, but in an ordinary way we had to put up with the fashion of the country, and make a bath of our hands, the water being poured into them from a bottle-shaped jug.

On asking our Armenian host for something to wash in, he said he had nothing, but that, if we liked, he would secure the bath for us in the evening, and we should have a real clean up. Agreeing to this, we started soon after supper, and accompanied by our host and his brother-in-law, ferreted our way out through narrow streets and by-lanes till at last we entered a solid stone dome-shaped building, in the centre of which was a marble basin four feet deep and ten or twelve feet in diameter; into this on one side ran a stream of natural hot water, and as quickly overflowed down a drain on the other. Round the edge of the basin ran a narrow path, and in the thickness of the walls were niches to undress in. Proper Turkish towels and body cloths had been brought with us, and soon we were un-dressed and ready. As soon as we appeared, our friends called out from their niches telling us to jump into the middle, but fortunately we thought it better to put in gently one foot at a time. We did so, and instantly pulled it out again with a scream, for the water appeared boiling hot. There was no cold water, so we kept dipping and dipping till we got used to the heat, and finally were able to get fairly in, where we stood in downright pain from the excessive heat. We were much laughed at by our Armenian friends, who, as soon as they were ready, came flop into the water, and then swam round and round as if it were only tepid. It was a very long while before we dare altogether dip under, and then we were struck by the apparently total absence of all support the water gave. Trusting to the water to let me down easily, I dropped on my knees and hurt them against the bottom as much as if I had done so on the stone pavement outside. By the time we had dipped all over the heat was insupportable, and we each returned to our niche, where for an hour we were in such a bath of perspiration we could not get on our clothes ; and though we did at last wriggle into them, all creased and rucked, we continued to perspire all night, and it ended in awaking in the morning with a bad head-ache. As for me, I felt all the better for my wash ; but my skin was all over the colour of a beefsteak.

We were told by the bathman that the bath was very, very old, before the days when the Turks took the country ; and from what we could see of the massive walls, we felt sure no Turk had made it. Probably this is one of the few remaining perfect specimens of the old Roman work in Asia Minor.

Between Brusa and Eski-Shehr, we constantly passed

groups of disbanded Turkish soldiers—poor miserable
creatures, all in rags, looking dejected and poverty stricken.
Many, though, had on good knee-boots, and these we found
had been prisoners, and had had the boots given them by
the Russians, of whom they all spoke well, saying they
had been well fed and cared for in Russia ; and by working at harvest and other odd jobs had been able to earn a
little money.   Just before leaving Ak-Su, we saw three
soldiers start in front of us ; two were on foot, and one
perched up on a pack-saddle, while the horse was led by
a comrade.   This poor fellow had had the fleshy part
of his thigh carried away by a piece of shell; his leg was
contracted, and he still suffered greatly with it.   Later on
in the day we overtook the same party, wearily trudging
on in the rain, and just as we came up to them, the man
led the horse into a deep little brook, and as the clumsy
beast slipped down the side, over it went, pitching its
rider over its head, half in and half out of the water.
Poor wretch ! he writhed with pain, but never said a word
as he dragged himself to land.

We left Eski-Shehr on the morning of October 3rd, soon
after daybreak, and for a wonder the two zaptiehs we had
asked for were at the door ready to start.   They were
very superior articles in the zaptieh line, being tidily
dressed in old, but not ragged, uniforms, armed with good
Winchesters and riding little thoroughbred Turkoman
ponies which, though small and light, appeared to do their
work well, and maintained their pluck and spirit to the
end of a long journey, in spite of the twelve-stone man,

one-stone saddle, and one stone of such extras as coats,
saddle-bags, etc., that they had to carry.

Hitherto, when starting on our journey, the mornings had
been either wet or cloudy, but on this day it was fine and
bright; and as we left the town we exclaimed, "How
truly Eastern!" and so it was, a morning that may be seen
for months together in the land of the Turk, but rarely
indeed in western Europe. The great undulating plains,
that would look burnt up, bare, and desolate, under the
blaze of the noonday sun, were now bathed in a soft
creamy light. Above the river and ravines, fleecy clouds
hung suspended, the light from the rising sun tinting
them and the shadows they cast with indescribably beautiful colours, which changed and changed again each
minute as the day grew older. Picturesque groups of
Turks, some on horseback, some on foot, moved slowly
from the town in all directions to their work in the fields,
while by the side of the road some score of men and
women, oxen and horses, were busy on a thrashing-floor—
the animals trampling out the corn, the men and women
tossing and sifting the grain from the chaff. Then, in mid
distance, emerging from the river mists, came a long string
of camels, with their bright trappings and heavy loads,
stalking along in their slow weird manner, the sound of
their pretty tinkling bells growing louder and louder,
while the cloud of yellow dust raised by their feet mixed
with the morning mists and enhanced the rich beauty of
the scene. But, alas! this beauty did not last long, or
rather our enjoyment of it was soon over, for on reaching

the summit of a steep rise, the sun shone painfully hot in our faces, and at the same time a breeze, coming up from behind, soon enveloped us in a thick cloud of dust that shut out the view. We felt that the pleasant but short morning was past, the world was fairly awake, and before us lay a long road and a weary journey. Soon human and animal life almost altogether disappeared, and we were the only moving things on the dreary burnt-up waste. Hour after hour we pressed onward at a brisk tripple, the day getting hotter and the country less interesting. Once, and once only, we had a small piece of excitement. We espied, some quarter of a mile from the road, a flock of big bustards, the first we had yet seen, and taking a Winchester from one of the zaptiehs, I stalked them to within two hundred yards, when, as they began to run preparatory to flight, I took a shot at them, and, I must confess, missed in a shameful manner, the ball kicking up the dust some fifty yards before reaching them. However, I made the best of it I could, and gave fifty reasons for my miss; while my companions made the worst of it, and declared that the ball did not get half way to the birds, and that I was a horrid muff!

On this day we made a good push forward, doing twelve Turkish hours, or, taking the hour at three miles, which is about what it is, we covered thirty-six miles. During all the day we only saw one village, a miserable poverty-stricken affair of some fifteen or twenty houses. Not a twentieth part of the land we passed over had ever been cultivated, and yet it was a rich alluvial soil that would

have grown wheat well. We saw a drove of some two
hundred brood mares feeding near a small brook, and
three or four flocks of Angora goats, and yet the waste
land on all sides produced a good nourishing grass, and
could have supported as many thousands of animals as
we saw hundreds.

The brook by which we saw the horses feeding was a
feeble little affair, and soon died a premature death. It
rose at the foot of some hills with rather a splash, but got
smaller and smaller the further it went, and finally lost
itself in the dry soil; and yet this brook and one fountain
was all the water we came upon during our thirty six
miles' ride. Doubtless many more fountains could be
made and water could in most places be procured from
wells.

Though we only saw one village, we constantly passed
cemeteries; some that had been used quite recently, and
others so old that it was only by accident we found fallen
headstones in the long grass. From this we inferred
that at one time, and since the Turks took possession of
the country, the population must have been very much
thicker than it is now; and, further, from the numberless
ruined villages and ruined houses in existing villages, it
may be supposed that this decrease is still going on, and
the population rapidly declining.

We stayed this night at the village of Kimas, and it
only needed one glance at the wretched hovels of which
it is composed to make us feel very thankful that we had
a tent with us, for though a tent is never a very com-

fortable residence, yet in summer it is far better than any village room in Turkey, and infinitely better than any khan.

Here, for the first time, we came upon the regular Eastern flat-roofed houses, and from this point we saw nothing else, not even in the towns. Nearly all the villages are built on the side of a steep hill. A wall about twenty feet long is run up, the hill behind cut away level, a retaining wall put up against the earth-face, and also side walls built. Strong poles are laid across and across this, and all covered with two feet of earth, which is trampled down hard to make it rain-proof.

The interior is divided by a low railing into two compartments, one smaller than the other. The human beings occupy the former, and the horses, cows, etc., the latter. Opposite the door there is an open hearth and chimney in the earth-face, and a slit in the wall eight inches square acts as a window. As there is no fence at the back of these houses, cattle and horses freely pass over the roof, until a day comes when the dry rubble walls give way or the timbers are so weak from rot that they fall in. Then it is said, "God willed it," and the house is repaired.

Looking at a village or town from the front, it looks like a series of irregular terraces mounting up one over the other, often so close that the roof of one house forms the courtyard of the one above it. The dirt of the villages is beyond belief. Huge heaps of manure are on every available spot, and often encroach over half of the road. Dead dogs and cats lie rotting within a few feet of the

doors, while open cesspools are everywhere handy. The
stable is never quite cleaned out. When the accumulated
filth of years has raised the floor so that there is not
sufficient head-room, the owner will clear out a foot or so
of the top surface, leaving the good old foundation reeking
beneath. Insects swarm ; and a night in one of these
rooms is death to sleep or rest. So disgustingly dirty
were these villages, that one of our chief difficulties was
to find a flat spot sufficiently clean to pitch our tent on,
and constantly, when we had just got it up, we found a
dead dog or some equally odoriferous neighbour close to
windward of us. The ground is always dusty, and nearly
always this dust is dry manure of various sorts. We soon
had a regular fixed plan for arranging the tent, and night
after night, at whatever village we had reached, our
arrangements were exactly the same.

Our tent was a circular one, ten feet in diameter, with
walls five feet high. Our baggage consisted of two pairs
of Russian leather saddle-bags, nearly a yard wide and a
yard deep, with flaps that folded over from behind, and
covered the entire front ; two camps beds that folded up
into a small compass ; a sack full of great-coats, and
mackintoshes, and rugs ; and two hand-bags for brushes,
towels, soap, tobacco, insect-powder, etc. Two of the saddle-
bags contained clothes, and the other two, pots, pans, etna,
tins of tea, biscuits, and other household, or rather tenthold,
goods. Directly the tent was pitched, the two saddle-bags
containing clothes were carried in and placed on their
backs close to the wall opposite the door, and the flaps

spread out in front. On these we sat, the bags themselves forming a back to lean against. Then the food-bags were brought in and placed close to my side of the tent, while the other things were arranged opposite. Pistols were strapped round the pole, and then out came the etna, and in ten minutes we each had a cup of tea. While this was brewing, our kitchen was being arranged; that is to say, all the food we carried with us, together with what we could induce the villagers to produce, was placed between my legs and the tent wall, in a snug corner between the bags. Iron plates, knives, forks, and spoons, put ready in the same place. Whenever we could get milk, no sooner was the etna off the spirit-lamp, than on went a saucepan of milk with a handful of rice in it, and as soon as this was cooked we went to supper.

For those who may be tempted to travel in Asia Minor, let me give a piece of advice. Carry all the food you can with you. Tea, tinned meats, ship's biscuits, etc.; and then, should you have a corner left, more ship's biscuits. Never mind, even if they are things you do not like; take my word for it, you will learn to appreciate them before you get through your journey, and if from what I am now writing you are induced to lay in an extra stock, I shall, I know, have a blessing bestowed on me from some out-of-the-way Turkish village.

The village bread in Asia Minor always consists of flat tough cakes, exactly like old dirty saddle-flaps. It is made of millet seed, sand, straw, and filth. It won't *eat*, but *churns* in your mouth; and is about as palatable as a

G

piece of soap, but not so digestible. In most villages a
little honey can be got; in one in three, milk is to be had;
in one in five, eggs. But in many nothing is forthcoming
but the "saddle-flaps," and then, if you have no food with
you, the *pièce de resistance* will be the buckle at the back
of your waistcoat. You may wash your hands, take your
place at table, say grace, and then fall to on the buckle,
and after pulling it as tight as you can, say grace again,
and dinner will be over, and dessert does not follow.

Generally we travelled all day, and reached a village
at evening, and at once looked about for a suitable place
on which to pitch the tent. The pack-horses (we had pack-
horses all the way after Angora) were brought up, and
their loads taken down. Usually a horse got away, kicked
its nearest neighbour, and then bolted in at the first open
door, and in doing so tore off his pack-saddle. By this
time half the men in the village would have lounged up
and squatted on their haunches around us; out came
baccy bags, and cigarettes were made whilst remarks on
our personal appearance, on our horses, our baggage, tent,
etc., were made in low voices.

We were asked what we wanted, and invariably were
told there was none of that special commodity. We all
worked, undoing pack-loads, pitching the tent, etc., but
rarely did a native put out a hand to help. If we called
to them to come and hold a horse, Mehmet ordered
Achmet to go; Achmet ordered Salih to go; Neuri ordered
Ibrahim, and so on all round, but no one stirred. Again,
when we asked for water, every one ordered every one to

fetch it at once; but not till the zaptiehs or Ali Agha had sworn at them all violently did any one move; then it was either fetched by the oldest man or the youngest boy present. Now and then the villagers behaved better, and all would lend a hand to put up the tent; and if an old soldier was present he always did so, recouping himself for his labours by swearing at the ignorance of his fellows.

It is well never to leave room in your tent for any one to sit down near you; fill up such spaces with the water-bottle, candle, teapot, etc., but leave a space near the door. As many of the villagers as can will visit you in the course of the evening, and as their hands have nothing to do while their tongues wag, they are sure to employ them in bringing to light a bosom friend or two, which they kindly liberate uninjured by their side.

All village Turks talk well for ignorant people, and when paying you a visit behave quietly and well. They will talk of horses, game, soldiering, farming, etc., and from them the traveller may pick up a good deal of useful information. But in these days, sooner or later, the conversation is sure to turn upon the iniquity of the ruling classes, and the Sultan, Grand Vizier, the provincial governors, great and small, all will come in for violent abuse; and as the same story is told in each village it becomes monotonous, and one is obliged to give a hint that one is tired and in need of rest, and the hint will be immediately taken.

CHAPTER VIII.

Departure from Kimas—Sirvi-Hissar (Pointed Castle)—Armenian hospitality—Armenian customs—En route again—A change in the
vegetation—The Sakaria—Tartars from the Dobrudja—Turcoman
tents—A row with the zaptieh—Hassan Bey's farm.

HAVING a short day's journey before us, we did not start
from Kimas till 8 a.m. (on Friday, 4th), and then we
mounted the hill immediately behind the village, and after
half an hour's ride arrived amidst some crags, which we
had seen in front of us all the previous day. They were
the first things we had come across to break the monotony
of the plain, and rising on the flat top of the hill in ragged
masses, covering about twenty acres, they really were
grand and interesting. We estimated them to average
from four hundred to five hundred feet in height, and they
were cracked and split up into a mass of blocks from the
size of a church to that of a cannon ball, some round,
some pointed, all more or less stratified, but the strata
never running far in the same direction. We got off our
horses to examine these stones more closely, and found
them to consist of rough granite of different colours.

Running all over the stones were numberless little
birds, I believe called " stone creepers," back and head
bluish-grey, throat and breast white, turning to rust colour

towards the legs. They kept up a continuous merry twitter, the notes being clear and something like the song of the robin, though faster and brighter. Besides these little fellows, we saw numbers of falcons of different kinds, and all over the rocks were white splashes denoting the nests of eagles and vultures, which must build here in vast numbers, as these are the only precipitous rocks within many miles.

This pleasant break only lasted for a few minutes, and then out we went once more on the burning, "howling desert," keeping the summit hills close to us on the left, and every half mile crossing small dried-up gullies that came down from them. It was a dreary ride, but fortunately only lasted five hours, when we arrived at a place called Sivri-Hissar (Pointed Castle), which stands in a semi-circular bay formed by the hills, the hills themselves here changing from rounded earth slopes to jagged granite crags which, like the crags we had passed in the morning, reminded us of Dartmoor tors. The semi-circle is about half a mile across, and in this are thickly clustered the houses, forming an irregular mass. Rather more than half belong to Turks, the rest to Armenians. Here, again, the houses are all built against the hillside, the hill forming the back wall, while the roofs are flat and covered thickly with earth. In front most of the houses are two storeys high, the upper storey being often one deep open verandah, in which the people live in summer, while on the ground-floor are a lot of small rooms.

Sivri-Hissar is a very picturesque, quaint-looking little

town, the houses built one above another on the steep slope of the rocks, and backed up by the bold crags, it is, however, quite a small place, containing but six thousand inhabitants. All are well off, and some (for this country) rich, having often a capital of £8000. The chief source from which they derive their wealth is the cultivation of the Angora goat, of which there are large flocks on the plain.

Mr. Thompson, of Constantinople, had given us a letter to his agent here, an Armenian, so we at once went to his house, and were most hospitably received. A large airy room, with eleven windows in it, was given us. Divans ran round three sides of it, and we were soon sitting curled up on deliciously soft cushions, drinking coffee, smoking, and feeling as if we had reached a perfect oasis in our desert.

We dined à la Turc with our host and a friend, all pegging away out of the same dish with our fingers. We had Angora goat's-flesh for dinner, as tough as india-rubber, and well it might be, as our host explained that he never killed a goat until it was so old it would not breed, or because it was sick. We asked no questions, but hoped the one before us was only aged! Besides this, we had good soup, cucumber chopped up in bad vinegar, water-melons, and grapes. The air of the place must have been very "hunger producing," for, though we ate like wolves, we seemed never satisfied.

Ten hours to the left of Sivri-Hissar is a forest of fir trees, which the villagers have to cut, so many to each

village, for the Government free of charge, and to transport it to Ismidt. It costs in labour about £10 a stick.
Our host told us that "the Armenians get on well with
the Turks. We are not like Bulgars and other Christians. When the Turk robs us we see nothing ; when he
thrashes us we say nothing, and so we have peace." Noble
people ! When a quarter of the town was burnt down
some years ago, the Armenians in England collected £300,
and sent it out to rebuild the school here.

The Armenians have greatly adopted the manners of
the Turks. The women live apart from the men in rooms
of their own during the day ; they cover their faces in the
streets, and wear a cloak (feredji) like that of the Turkish
women. The rest of their dress consists of loose baggy
trousers, tied in at the ankle ; round the waist is a
coloured shawl in three or four close folds, a linen shirt, a
short loose jacket, the head tied up in a rag, and the hair
hanging down the back in five or six plaits. As for shoes,
they scarcely wear them. Some of the girls are pretty,
but a woman of twenty-five is already a shrivelled hag.

The men wear loose baggy cloth trousers, drawn in at
the ankle, a close-fitting cotton waistcoat, over which is a
coloured cotton sack-like robe reaching below the knee,
and split up to the waist on either side. On their heads
they wear a fez, with a dark cotton handkerchief tied round
it, while on their feet would-be white woollen stockings
and stout shoes.

They look a poor, oppressed, melancholy set, without a
vestige of manly beauty ; but when one comes to talk to

them one is struck by the amount of knowledge they have
of the outside world, and it is quite refreshing to hear them
discussing the characters of Lord Beaconsfield, Lord Salis-
bury, and Gladstone, the latter of whom they appear to
think a perfect god. They all believe that England is soon
to govern Asia Minor, and look forward to that day as a
happy time.

We were so comfortably lodged and so hospitably enter-
tained at Sivri-Hissar, and, further, our Armenian host
gave us so much useful information, that we stopped on
with him over the 5th, and most reluctantly started once
more on our journey at 8 a.m. on the morning of October
6th. Thanks to a bridge over the Sakaria being broken
down, we were obliged to make a detour of six hours to
the south before we could pass the river.

Then, before starting, we had been told that as soon as
we were over the river we should find the tents of some
Turcomans, and be able there to get fodder for our horses ;
but after we had been on the road some three hours, we
heard the Turcomans were gone, and that if we passed the
village of Kutlu, some four hours only from Sivri-Hissar,
we should not find another for nine hours. So as the day
was getting on, we stopped at the said Kutlu, and very
disgusted we were at having to do so.

For the first two hours of our ride from Sivri-Hissar our
road wound round and among a number of tor-like hills,
barren and desolate in the extreme, with hardly a vestige
of herbage on them. We were constantly ascending until
we passed over the summit of a range of hills about eight

hundred feet above the plain, but over four thousand feet above the level of the sea. Then stretched before us a vast down-like plain, with here and there rounded chalk hills. All was waste, no life of any sort, human or animal, and we did not see a single sheep or head of cattle in our four hours' ride.

Again we passed deserted graveyards; and soon after we had gained the summit of the hills, we found the foundations of what must have been a considerable village, in which we saw a few finely sculptured marble columns, but without any sort of inscriptions. We observed near here three or four flocks of sand-grouse.

Directly we got clear of the craggy hills round Sivri-Hissar, we were struck by the great difference in the vegetation to that we had been passing through. From the forests round Brusa, all over the plain, till we reached Sivri-Hissar, the herbage was grass intermingled with wild thyme and familiar English weeds. Here the grass had almost entirely disappeared, except in the valleys, and its place was taken by bushy wild thyme plants, thickly interspersed with two descriptions of the gum tragacanth and other prickly plants. The gum tragacanth grows in round balls, and is as like a hedgehog as a vegetable can be to an animal, except that, if possible, the prickles on the plant are sharper than those on the hedgehog. The English weeds gave place to numbers I had never seen before, and almost all were prickly, making a loll on the grass an impossibility, and obliging one to carefully pick a spot to sit down upon. I once neglected this precaution, and the result was I sat down fair on the top of a fine tragacanth plant, which taught me a practical lesson I shall not easily forget.

With the change of vegetation, we noticed a marked difference in the soil, which had changed from a rich loam to chalk, in the lowlands mixed with earth, but on the hills almost pure. In all directions, as far as the eye could reach, great bleak white hills were to be seen, sparsely covered with vegetation, and utterly destitute of trees of any sort. Altogether, this country appeared to be getting worse and worse as we rode on, and we anxiously looked forward as we reached each summit, in the hope of some change to relieve the dull monotony of the scene.

The zaptieh we brought with us from Sivri-Hissar told us he had been with the Turkish army at Kars and its neighbourhood. He got his horse there, and if it is a specimen of the animals to be found there, I do not think much of them. Our friend had been a Bashi-Bazouk, and certainly was a proper-looking ruffian. He talked a great deal about the Russians, and I was astonished to find he did not speak at all bitterly of them.

We struck tent at Kutlu on the 7th, and, after three hours' ride, reached the main stream of the Sakaria. The country through which we passed was, as before, wild and desolate—one mass of big hills or little mountains tumbled about in all directions, with valleys and ravines between, but all alike, the highest hill and the deepest valley, burnt up to the palest straw colour, without a single green leaf to relieve the eye. In this three hours' ride, in fact, in all the twelve hours we rode on this day, we only passed one village; and I do not think we saw a hundred acres that had been under cultivation.

On arriving at the river, which is about twenty yards wide, deep, and rather rapid, we found an apology for a bridge. Stones had been heaped up in the river from each side, so as to lessen the width, and the centre was spanned by a few rough poles, over which were placed some rushes and earth, through holes in which we could catch peeps of the water beneath.

There was a small mud hut at the bridge, and when we arrived this was tenanted by some dozen Tartars. Poor creatures, they told us they were refugees from a village near Kustendji, on the Dobrudja, and they quite brightened up when I told them that I knew that part of Turkey well. I did not, however, talk to them long, for I saw one being buried hard by, and another carried out of the hut on a rug by four men, and I was told all were ill; so, dreading a bout of small-pox or typhus, I wished them a happy end to their troubles and continued my journey. Just over the bridge we came upon a dozen tents of the nomad Turcomans, and were disappointed to find them such poor shelter; in fact, they were much after the fashion of gipsy tents in England, bad both in hot and cold weather. Half an hour further on we met three or four Turcomans, accompanied by their ladies, all riding astride. They were fine, wild, brisk-looking people, as dark as the darkest gipsy. We were struck by their energetic bright manners and cheerful way of speaking, and one old lady quite shouted out her greetings to us.

After riding nine hours, we reached a village, and there commenced a grand fight all round. *We* wished to put more road behind us, Ali Agha was indifferent, Anton melancholy, the zaptieh was furious, and the arabaji sided with him. The zaptieh swore there was not another village on the road for nine hours, but on asking a villager he told us there was one but three hours further on. Upon this Ali Agha in the plainest terms told the zaptieh he lied; the battle of abuse waxed hot and strong, and in the midst of it G—— and I rode on, leaving the others to follow.

We had not gone far before we met a three-horse araba, and were almost scared at being addressed in English by some one from the inside. It turned out to be a Mr. Binns, an Englishman from Angora, who there carries on business as mohair merchant. He told us he had heard we were coming, and had left a letter with his clerk to offer us his house while we stayed at Angora. He was himself on his way to Eski-Shehr, but hoped to be back by the following Saturday. What the village Turk had told us proved correct, and at the end of three hours we came to the village of Hassan Bey Keui, or rather to the farm of Hassan Bey, for the village was half an hour further on. Here we found some three or four tumble-down cottages and a deserted farmhouse, sadly out at elbow and looking very insecty ; so we pitched our tent, and in half an hour were drinking a cup of tea, our one luxury.

CHAPTER IX.

Sand-grouse—Entering Angora—English consulate—Said Pasha —
Difficulties of a governor—Municipal legislation—More emigrants
—Consular influence.

AT 7.30 next morning we were again on our road, with
a twelve hours' ride before us. Again the same dreary
treeless waste up and down, down and up, a village, or
rather a few huts, about once in four hours, a few large
flocks of Angora goats, hardly any cattle or horses, and
not a soul to be seen for hours together. The only
incident on the road was a shot I had with Ali Agha's
old gun. At a low part of the road, near a small brook,
we came upon a small flock of sand-grouse, and jumping
off my horse I crept up, hidden by some rushes, till within
twenty yards, when they rose. The first barrel missed
fire, but with the second I brought down a bird.

We were much disappointed during this ride at seeing
no game, and at the great dearth of both animal and
insect life. We had only seen two flocks of big bustards, and some dozen flocks of sand-grouse. No other
game of any sort, and very few birds, except larks and
wheatears. Near Sivri-Hissar I heard a few coveys of
French partridges calling in the early morning, and a Pole
we met there told us he had shot in a day ten or twelve

brace over dogs. Again, at Angora, we were told there
were "lots of birds," but we could not hear of a heavier
bag than six brace.

Just four hours before Angora, we reached the summit
of a high hill, and there in front of us was the town
itself. A few white houses dotted about among their
numberless dark brown companions looked like *eyes*, and
had the effect of making the town appear quite near.
This last part of the journey was got over very slowly, for
all the horses, except those G—— and I were on, were
pretty nearly "through," thanks to the bump, bump style
of riding of those upon them; but even a Turkish journey
comes to an end at last, and after fording a small stream
we found ourselves in the six-feet-wide streets, twisting
and turning at every few yards, and all the while clambering up the steep cone-shaped hill on and around which
the town is built.

At last Ali Agha halted before a house, and the next
minute we were greeted by Mr. Gatheral, the English vice-
consul, who told us that the Bulgar merchant, by name
Matteo Bishof, to whose house we were bound, was living
out of the town, at the vineyards. However, this was
of no consequence, as we were invited by the hospitable
consul to take up our abode with him.

Our first stage in Asia Minor was over, and very thankful we were, for a more uninteresting, dreary country could
not be found than that through which we had ridden.
We had fared roughly, and had gone through much discomfort and some fatigue, and therefore all the more

appreciated the nice, clean, airy, well-furnished, and well-conducted house of our host, and when he ordered in "five-o'clock tea " we felt at home again, and could hardly believe we were in one of the most thoroughly Eastern of all Eastern towns in the middle of Asia Minor. The only drawback to our perfect contentment was hearing there were no letters for us, as there should have been ; but we did not know whom to abuse, our forwarding agent in Constantinople or the Turkish post, probably both were to blame.

In one respect our visit to Angora was well timed, as we had the good luck to find Said Pasha installed there as vali; and though he had only been there a short time and never previously acted as the governor of a province, and therefore, perhaps, could not give us as much information on local subjects as other pashas might have done, yet we found in him a clear-headed, intelligent, clever man, with vast experience of the ways of the Sublime Porte, of the Sultan, and of the chief persons of notoriety in Turkey. Besides, he spoke English perfectly, having been twelve years in England, at Edinburgh and Woolwich, and had profited by the good education he had there received. He is middle-aged, but, unlike most of his contemporary pashas, he is an active man, and now at his prime. Unless those who know him best have been greatly deceived, he is an honest, honourable man, whose fondest hope is to see his unfortunate country recover from its troubles, and who is desirous to do his utmost to bring this about; but, anxious as he undoubtedly was to devote himself to the service of the State, I fancy despair had begun to fill his mind, and that he had almost given up hope.

He had held high office at different times at Constantinople, had been Capitan Pasha (Lord High Admiral or something like it), and under the present Sultan had been Chamberlain of the Palace. He had held this post ever since this Sultan had reigned till a short time previous to our visit to Angora, and I believe for a time was a prime favourite, and one of the few men in whom the Sultan trusted, and whose advice he sometimes asked for and acted on.

Said had stood by the Sultan through the Conference at Constantinople, had seen Midhat Pasha's short-lived constitution born, and I fancy had never had the slightest hope in it. He had heard at the palace war proclaimed, after he had worked with all his might to prevent it, assuring his master that, come what might, Turkey must in the end come off second best ; and that the reed he was leaning on, namely, England's active assistance, was, if not a broken reed, at least a bruised one. Ministers were taken into favour and sent to outer darkness in rapid succession. Grand vizier followed grand vizier, general followed general ; and, lastly, on Said devolved the duty of pouncing upon Midhat Pasha without warning, and seeing him put on board the Sultan's yacht and despatched to Europe.

Then came Said's own turn. He left the Sultan one evening, feeling he was liked and trusted, and was doing

good both to the Sultan and the country; next morning,
before he left his house, he had a visit from an officer
bearing an order from the Sultan that within twenty-four
hours he was to be out of Constantinople and across the
Bosphorus on his way to Angora as vali. With him fell
also all who had through his influence obtained posts
under the Government, besides several who were known
as his friends, and yet no one knew what offence he had
given, and he himself could only make a guess. So
sudden was his dismissal and departure, that he arrived
near Angora before it was possible for the superseded vali
to wind up his affairs; and so, as it is not etiquette for a
new governor to enter a town before the old one is out of
it, the man, who four or five days before had been a
sultan's high chamberlain, had to be the guest of a poor
villager, and spent days in a dirty grubby cabin.

He had now shaken into office, and was trying to do
his duty, but as yet had only discovered how wretchedly
the business of the vilayet was conducted without being
able to see how he could better it. His task was made
all the more difficult by his being honest. In the eyes
of all his subordinates this was a crime, and therefore
every man's hand was against him. Let him propose
what he would to his council, his council were all sure
to oppose him, and instead of any question being settled
on the spot, both sides had to refer the matter to Constantinople; but as Said was in disgrace, no one there would
back him, and invariably his opponents gained their point
or else the question remained unanswered. The natural

H

consequence was, Said was a governor-general in name only, and in the very smallest matters was powerless.

A few days before we arrived at Angora, a Greek baker, at the request of the English consul, had made some bread a shade or two lighter coloured than the universal black stuff. To do this he had to use finer flour, and at the same time, to make a profit, he had to charge a trifle more for each loaf. Now, in all Turkish towns, the municipality regulates the price of bread, which is put so low that, to make any profit, the bread must be of the commonest description. At once the baker was pounced upon, taken before the council, and told he must either sell the white bread at the same price as the black, or, better still, give up making it. "For," said the wise men, "your shop is in the giaour quarter, they will buy your white bread; and is it to be endured that Christians are to fare better than Osmanlis?" The baker appealed to the consul, and the consul appealed to Said Pasha, who at once, on his own responsibility, authorized the man to make and sell white bread as before. He did so, and the next day the municipality sent zaptiehs to the shop, and they quietly turned out the baker, shut up the shop, and locked it. Said was again appealed to, and though he gave repeated orders that the shop should be opened and the man allowed to continue his business, nothing was done, and so it remained up to the time we left Angora.

Again, winter was approaching; provision of charcoal had now to be laid in. Therefore the municipal council, in anticipation of this, promulgated a law that the price

of charcoal was to be so much—a few piastres less than it
was then selling for. The charcoal-burners, who bring
the charcoal into the town on pack-horses, remonstrated
but in vain, so they finally appealed to the pasha, who
told them to sell it at the usual price; but the municipal
council was not to be thus beaten. They sent zaptiehs
to seize the pack-horses with their loads, and then they
sold the charcoal to themselves and their masters at the
reduced rate, and handed over the proceeds to the owners.
I am glad to say, in consequence of this, the charcoal-
burners brought no more charcoal to the town; but
secretly opened a market a few miles away, where they
sold it to their *friends* as of yore, these friends being all
Christians. I cannot say I grieve much at the thought of
these councillors shivering through the cold minus their
mangals (charcoal braziers).

While we were at Angora, all were busily arranging for
the settlement of the emigrants from Bulgaria. Hundreds
of both Circassians and Tartars had arrived, and more
were coming; and the trouble and confusion the former
caused was beyond belief. The Governor-General of Brusa
would despatch, say two hundred of them in arabas to
Angora, and then telegraph to say how many were
coming, and what quantity of bread would be required for
them on a certain day. But he counted without his host.
The Circassians would start, but having on the road heard
something about Angora they did not like, they either
returned to Brusa or went on to some other town, and
then raved like madmen because on their return or arrival

bread was not ready for them. Meantime the bread at
Angora was all spoilt. Those who did come on had
villages allotted to them, but after having been sent to
their destination, and after the old villagers had built
them their houses, they were pretty sure to return to
Angora, and quietly state that they did not like their new
homes—there were no mountains and no forests there; or,
as in one case I heard of, because the village was off a
main road so was dull.

They behaved as if they were lords and masters of the
country, and kicked up a row with every one, from Said
Pasha to the zaptiehs, if all was not exactly to their taste.
It was quite useless being harsh or severe with them, they
did not understand it; and it would have been about as
reasonable for a master of hounds to storm at foxes for not
settling in just the woods he wished.

With the Tartars it was very different. They went
where they were told; and, what is more, took themselves
in their light waggons. The old men and women set
to work to build houses and till the ground, while the
young men drove to the nearest forest, and in a few days
appeared in Angora again with wood for sale. In some
way all worked hard, and it would have been better for
Asia Minor if, for every Tartar that arrived, there had
been a hundred, ay, a thousand.

Our host, Mr. Gatheral, had been asked by the pasha to
sit in the council that was arranging for the settlement of
emigrants, as an *ex-officio* member, and it was owing to the
prompt way he did business and grasped the real position

of affairs, insisting on work being done, and not only
words wasted, that some sort of method was established,
and that little by little the miserable emigrants were
drafted to different villages. Men were sent all over
the vilayet, from village to village, to inquire into their
capability for receiving these people in small numbers,
and on their reports the council acted.

Mr. Gatheral accompanied us on our forward journey,
partly on private business of his own, and partly to hear
for himself what the old inhabitants of the villages had to
say about this forced addition to their small communities,
and we often had opportunities of hearing what was said.
It invariably was, "Send us Tartars, we will help to support them till they can support themselves; but send the
Circassians to the next village. We like Tartars, but we
don't like Circassians." In one village the mudir went
even further, and said, "If you send Circassians here, we
will shoot the lot at once. We know the animals; some
were sent here years ago. We supported them for a year,
we built them houses and gave them land, and all the
time they were here they never did an hour's work; but
at night they prowled about, stole our cattle and sheep
and that of our neighbours, and treated us as if we were
dependent on them. At last we kicked them out, and if
more come we will shoot them."

Mr. Gatheral is a splendid specimen of what an upright,
honourable, energetic Englishman, when acting as consul
in Turkey, may do for the general good; that is to say, if
he has tact, for without it his other good qualities would

be of little service. Not only was Mr. Gatheral consulted about the emigrants, but day after day his opinion was asked and his advice acted upon by the pasha and megliss, and little by little abuses of long standing were disappearing, and a more healthy state of things being established. Through his influence, personal security for all classes was better in Angora than in any town we saw, and even in questions pertaining to property his influence was making itself felt, and now and then a rayah actually obtained justice against a Turk; but, as Mr. Gatheral told us, there was yet a fine field for reformation whenever a rayah was pitted against a Turk in the local law courts, and it might be said that no one, except Turks, held property (never mind how long it had been in his possession) except on the sufferance of his Mussulman neighbours. Should this sufferance fail, and should a Turk claim the property, invariably the Christian had judgment given against him, or had to buy the claimant, or oftener buy the judge. According to Mr. Gatheral, the two great causes of complaint among the people of this country are, first the insecurity of property, and next the hideous robberies committed in the collection of taxes.*

* Not many months after we left Angora, we heard, with great regret, of the death of Mr. Gatheral.

CHAPTER X.

Angora—Ruins—Temple of Augustus—Angora goats—An outrage by soldiers—Tortures—Superior zaptiehs.

ON the morning after our arrival in Angora, I took a struggle (it cannot be called a walk) through the town, inhaling foul smells and wringing my ankles on the detestibly badly paved streets, till I found myself at the old fortress, on the highest point of the cone-shaped hill. There is very little to admire in the fortress itself, for the original building had, during various sieges and assaults been all destroyed, and the present one is of Turkish construction, the old stones being again used to make the walls. Ancient statues might be seen worked into the walls, some feet upwards, all mutilated; and intermixed with the granite cubes are fine marble pillars, cornices, etc. The view from this point is very extensive, but looking over dreary wastes is not edifying, especially for those who have just traversed them. The town of Angora extends over the face of a rounded hill, which on its north side is severed from a corresponding hill by a ravine only twenty or thirty yards wide, with steep precipitous cliffs, at the bottom of which runs a small brook. Immediately in front of the town to the west is a considerable plain, rich and well watered, but in every other direction it is surrounded by hills, some as much as fifteen hundred feet high. Those nearest to the town are covered with vine-yards and gardens, but beyond all are barren wastes, only affording a scanty pasturage to a few sheep and goats.

In all parts of the town, but chiefly at the foot of it, where the hill merges into the open plain, are masses of ruins; but so well have the Turks here followed their usual plan of destruction, that hardly one stone remains upon another. The smaller dressed blocks have been carried away, to be used in building the hovels of the town, while others have been used by Turks, Christians, and Jews as gravestones, and afford an illustration of the difference there is in the three races. In the Turkish graveyard, which is far the largest and is the nearest to the town, the smallest stones have been used—those that took the least trouble to move; next in size come the gravestones of the Christians, and lastly those of the Jews, which invariably are formed of the heaviest and largest stones to be found, laid flat on the top of the grave. All the graveyards are dirty, rubbishy places, but owing to the stones in the Jewish grounds being placed flat in the first instance, it is neater than the other two, where the stones originally were stuck up on end, and have since fallen about in all directions.

Just as one enters the town of Angora from the Eski-Shehr side, one passes the remains of what must have been a considerable building, probably an amphitheatre, but nothing now remains but the stones of the foundation. Some of these stones exceed six feet in length, four deep, and as many wide, and therefore were too heavy to remove, and being composed of granite were too hard to break up. Here and there a marble cornice of great size, or fluted marble column reclined half in and half out of the ground, whilst in the town itself in almost every courtyard handsome capitals may be seen used as horse blocks, or, having had a round hole cut in the flat surface at the top, are converted into mortars to pound corn in.

On the summit of a low hill on the north side of the town, half-way between the amphitheatre and the river, stand the walls and entrance gate of a noble marble building of which I have just seen so good a description in a book called "Travels in Armenia," by Mr. Kinneir, that I shall take the liberty of copying it. The book was published in 1818, but as far as I can remember the building appears to be in the same condition as it was when visited by Mr. Kinneir.

"We now bent our steps towards the Temple of Augustus. We gained admittance by bribing the Iman of a mosque, who gave us the key of a wicket that introduced us into a small court, at the upper end of which stood the object of our curiosity. This ancient edifice is built entirely of white marble, and consists of a vestibule, a large oblong hall, and a small apartment or rather alcove behind. On the right and left side of the wall of the vestibule as you enter is an inscription, recording the principal actions in the life of Augustus Cæsar; but part of it have been intentionally effaced, and even pieces of marble forcibly removed. I was upwards of seven days

copying this inscription, but as I have since discovered
that it is already known to the world, I do not conceive it
necessary to insert it here. The gate leading from the
vestibule into the saloon is a masterly piece of workmanship, about twenty-five feet in height by nine in breadth;
the supporters of the lintel are beautifully decorated, as
well as the whole of the moulding and entablature. Like
the rest of the building, it is formed of ponderous blocks
of white marble, and, considering its great antiquity, is in
a wonderful state of preservation. The saloon is twenty-
nine paces in length and twelve in breadth. The roof has
fallen in, but the walls I should guess to be still about
forty-five feet in height, and exhibit the remains of a
beautiful cornice. This interesting monument of antiquity
is so much concealed on one side by a mosque, and on the
others by old houses which rest against the walls, that it is
impossible to form any idea of its exterior appearance. It
is generally believed to have been a temple erected in
honour of Augustus; but to me it seemed rather intended
as a basilica or public hall of audience."

The glory of those days has departed, and the Angora
of to-day can be little like the Angora the Turks found
when they became masters of the country. Unbaked mud-
brick buildings stand on the foundations of marble temples
and palaces. Decaying mounds of filth and rubbish fill
every vacant space, while the steep, tortuous, narrow streets
are little better than open sewers. Two-thirds of the
population had suffered from ague and typhus fever the
summer before we were there, and yet the land and the

climate must be the same as in the days of its greatness,
and doubtless as Angora and its district fell and went to
ruin with the coming of the Turks and the departure of
people of the West, so it might revive and become rich if the
Turk disappeared and the Western took his place once more.

What coals are to Newcastle the goat is to Angora.
Almost every one directly or indirectly lives by it, and
two-thirds of all the conversation in the town is on the
subject. Two or three English houses have agents established in Angora for the purchase of mohair (goats' hair), and
these again have native agents under them in the smaller
towns of the districts where the goat flourishes. Almost
every oke of the hair finds its way to England, and is
manufactured into alpaca stuffs at Bradford, Norwich, and
other places.

Times were bad in Angora when we were there, owing to
the present fashion for ladies to wear soft clinging materials
such as bège, cashmere, etc., and the stiffer mohairs being
for a time neglected. The hair fell to one-half its usual
price, and those who had large stocks in hand could not
find a market even at this reduced figure. But mohair does
not easily spoil, and by holding on till fashion changes
again the merchants hope not to lose much in the end.

As we were at Angora in the autumn, the goats, though
very pretty, had not got their full coats, which towards
the end of winter hang down to the ground on either side
of them in the softest wavy white curls, the staple often
being five or six inches long, and apparently incapable of
becoming dirty as the wool of the sheep does. During the

famine years of 1873 and 1874, two-thirds of all the goats
perished, but now they are as numerous as ever, and the
traveller constantly sees flocks of one hundred to a
thousand animals grazing by the roadside.

We were told that by crossing the common goat twice
with the Angora the pure breed could be obtained, but if
removed from the few places in different parts of the world
where it flourishes, it soon deteriorates, and the hair
becomes exactly like that of any other goat. Of late years
several flocks of these pretty animals have been sent from
Angora *viâ* Constantinople and London to the Cape of
Good Hope, but though they lived and thrive there, the
breed has constantly to be renewed by goats sent out from
Angora and crossed with those bred in the country, and
even then I believe the hair of the Cape is never as fine
as that from Angora.

Mr. Matteo Bishof, the Bulgarian merchant I have
before mentioned, pointed out to us a curious fact
connected with the Angora goat, namely, that it lives and
does well only in countries situated within a few degrees
of forty north and south latitude. Thus it thrives in
California, Spain, Asia Minor, and Persia, north latitude,
and in New Zealand, Patagonia, the Cape, and parts of
Australia in south latitude. At the Cape it deteriorates,
perhaps because the forty degrees south latitude passes
rather south of it. Others have attributed the excellence
of the mohair of Angora to the excessive dryness of the
climate during the greater part of the year, and also to
the extraordinary amount of electricity there is in the air.

Our cavas, Ali Agha, had twice been to the Cape with
goats for his master, Mr. Thompson, of Constantinople,
and one of his oft-repeated boasts was that he had started
from Angora with a hundred goats, and arrived at the
Cape with a hundred and one,—one old goat having died
at sea, and two having been born in its place.

In the month of October, 1877, just two months after
the Battak massacres were known in England, an agent of
Mr. Gatheral's, an Armenian, came in from Yuzgat and
told him of the following outrages that had been committed
at an Armenian village eight hours from that town. A
band of recruits arrived there one evening on their way to
Constantinople. They took possession of the place, and
then ordered the villagers to bring them everything they
had, money, food, etc. The people in a panic obeyed,
except a few who, having a lot of raki, and dreading the
effect of it on the soldiers, hid it; but the men so rummaged
about the village that they soon found it, the result being
that in a short time they were all drunk. "Then," as the
consul expressed it, "they made a hell of the place."
Every woman, young and old, was insulted and outraged
in presence of husbands, fathers, and brothers. All the
cattle, horses, and sheep were either stabbed or shot; and
finally the village burnt to the ground. The ruffians then
departed for Yuzgat, forcing the men of the village to
accompany them as porters, the soldiers even riding on
the men themselves; some of the old and feeble soon
broke down, but were forced to continue by being pricked
forward by knives and bayonets. One old man actually

died on the road, and thus added murder to their other
crimes.

On hearing this, and having assured himself it was true,
Mr. Gatheral telegraphed to Sir H. Elliot and Sir P.
Francis, and was instructed by the former, through the
telegraph, to see the pasha and make further inquiries,
and, if necessary, go himself to the village. Mr. Gatheral
had hardly received this order before the governor, Suriah
Pasha, sent for him, and on arriving at the konak, he
was received in private by the great man, who was suffering from an acute attack of rage mingled with fever. He
insisted on seeing the Armenian who had first brought the
news, but was unable to make the man waver from his
first statement; so, turning to the consul, he said, "See
what you have done! I have to go to this vile place at
once!" And indeed he was off in his carriage in half an
hour. The end of it all was that the soldiers were caught,
and as all was proved to have occurred as stated, the
officer in command *was degraded,* while some of the men
were sentenced to prison for five years—not a very severe
punishment for wholesale rape, arson, robbery, and murder!
But every cloud is said to have its silver lining, and in
this case Suriah Pasha found a *gold* one. The inhabitants
of Yuzgat, who are all Turks, took advantage of the pasha
being there to lay before him the fact that Yuzgat is the
central town of the province of Angora, and that therefore
it would be much better it should be the seat of the local
government. The pasha saw and acknowledged the force
of their arguments, and promised to push the matter at

Constantinople, but pointed out that, to be successful, a large sum of money would be required at Constantinople as bakshish. At once the people of Yuzgat subscribed £1800, which they handed over to the pasha, and, it is hardly necessary to say, that they have heard no more of the seat of government being moved, nor have they seen one para of the money they subscribed.

I forgot to mention that the village was rebuilt for the destitute inhabitants, and their cattle and flocks restored. I asked how this was done, and was answered, " Oh, the neighbouring Christian villages were forced to give and transport the necessary material, and from their own flocks and herds to replace those destroyed."

I asked Mr. Gatheral whether he had ever heard of "impalements" in this district, to which he answered, "No, never; though doubtless impalement was usual formerly from the word being so frequently used as an oath by the Turks. Bastinado, too, is quite done away with. The last case I heard of took place here four years ago, but I made such a row about it that it is a thing of the past."

I asked if people were ever tortured to extract confession, to which he replied, "No, not now. Two years ago Abdul Rhaman Pasha, who was governor then, had an Armenian chained up under the public cesspool for some days to make him confess to having stolen some government moneys. I telegraphed as soon as I heard of it to Sir P. Francis, who at once instructed me to interfere. I did so, and got well snubbed by the pasha, who told me he was doing what he considered right, and that it was no business of mine. However, Sir P. Francis was not the man to let such a thing drop, and a telegram came from Constantinople ordering the man's release. The man got over it, though for some time he was at death's door; and the worst of it all was, that soon after his release it was clearly proved that he was innocent, and another man was found guilty and imprisoned. Through this the pasha was removed in disgrace; but, as is usual when we English interfere, he was *promoted*. He was sent direct to Bagdad, where not only was his pay higher, but he was made commander-in-chief of the troops as well as governor."

While we were at Angora, Mr. Binns (the gentleman who had taken us by surprise on the road by addressing us in English) returned from Eski-Shehr. Among other things, he told us that the two zaptiehs who had escorted us to Sivri-Hissar, and with whose soldierly, clean appearance and pleasant civil manners we had been so much pleased, had, on their return journey to Eski-Shehr, taken upon themselves to reform one of the greatest evils this unfortunate land is suffering from. They commenced liberally paying the police! To do this they stopped and robbed three Turks. From two they took considerable sums of money, and from the third a cow and calf, which they drove into Eski-Shehr and sold openly. The victims, or rather one of them, hating reform like a true Turk, followed the zaptiehs into Eski-Shehr, and called on Mr. Binns, who he imagined, being an Englishman, must have something to do with us. Mr. Binns took the man before

the governor, who promised to inquire into the case. But
as it was well known that the governor had himself taken
the zaptiehs' pay, it was a little difficult for him to complain of their taking from others ; and so our civil, well-
mannered friends will probably continue to relieve the
Government of the difficulty of paying the police.

CHAPTER XI.

Country houses—A round of visits—A Bulgarian merchant—Tax-
collecting—Pack-horses—Preparing for the road—The start—A
night in the strangers' room.

WE were much surprised to learn that during the summer
months all the Christians who can afford to do so quit
Angora itself and live in small detached houses about
five miles out of the town. We were not surprised at
their *liking* to quit the crowded, dirty, smelling place for
the fresh open country, but at their being *able* to do so—
all our previous knowledge of Turkey leading us to suppose that there was no safety except in towns.

We rode out one morning to these vineyards, accompanied by the consul, and paid a series of visits to many
of the chief Greek families living at them. Though burnt
up, wild, and comparatively barren-looking, yet there is
something rather taking in this colony of country villas,
dotted about as they are on the slopes of a considerable
hill, and surrounded by low vines and fruit trees. Origin-
ality is rare in Turkey, and the construction of these
houses confirms this. They are all nearly alike. The
bottom storey built of stone, with stables under it, where
the cellars should be, and on this stone erection a much
bigger wooden house, the whole having the effect of a big

box standing on a smaller one. The windows often project
out some feet, and bays, angles, balconies, etc., jut out
where least expected. There is the universal large salaamlik upstairs, with divans all round, and small rooms opening into it. Though they are, I know, insect-infected
places, yet they are *very nearly* nice, and would be quite
so if all were kept clean and tidy. As it is, there is a
dusty, littered, untidy appearance in and around the
house, and anything but pleasant odours.

One or two of the houses were better; for instance, one
had a flower-garden all round it on terraces, with marble
basins and fountains playing, of deliciously clear water,
while overhead waved the shady ball acacia and willow,
with vines creeping over trellis. The flowers were very
poor—not so good nor so well looked after as what one
sees in a labourer's cottage in England, marigolds being
the chief thing to be seen.

On opening the front door, we found ourselves in a large
entrance hall, about thirty feet square, paved with flag-
stones, and surrounded by divans, while in the centre a
small fountain threw its waters into a marble basin.
This all sounds very charming, but just see the owner—a
fat puffy man of sixty years of age, dressed in a mangy
great-coat, dirty linen, no collar or necktie, and his feet
thrust into slippers. Then his wife, huddled up in a bundle
of fusty-looking dark clothes, after the European style of
a hundred years ago, her head tied up in a greasy old
rag, whilst one foot dangles from the divan on which she
sits, clothed in coarse cotton stocking, evidently minus

garter, and with ample ventilation at the heel, which is nowhere.

Three or four attendants, men and women, loll about on familiar terms with the master and mistress—dirty, untidy, flabby, and whining! The owner's two daughters are rather pretty, but owing to their having wound a long sash a dozen times round their middles, they look as if they had considerably run to waist.

Hardly any of these Greeks speak their own language, but use in their family intercourse that of their master the Turk, and this we were told is even more universally the case with the Armenians.

The proprietor of the house and family above described is a man who has made a fortune in Angora goats' hair and opium, and to prove that he has not fared badly in business, we were told that his house in the vineyards, together with his gardens and the cost of bringing water in pipes from a fountain on the hills above, cost £5000, and his town house is equally comfortable.

We found one half of the population in the vineyards suffering from ague, and all had a cadaverous, sickly expression; but if they indulge every day as they did when we visited them, I am not surprised at it. When we entered the house, every one hurriedly rose from the divan, and salaaming, requested us to perch ourselves thereon. This done, we all salaam again, and then we are put through a fire of questions. Where do we come from? Do we live in England—in London or Bradford? (Bradford being the place where all the goats' hair goes to.) Do we

know Mr. Foster of Bradford? Where are we going to?
What is our business? And as we answer all *truthfully*,
no one believes us! Meanwhile we are all smoking
cigarettes, and the busy little fleas are migrating from the
divan up our legs and backs. Then in comes a slipshod,
big-waisted, fuzzly-headed handmaid with a tray, on which
is a glass of very sweet jelly, generally made of cherries;
right and left of this are two glasses, one full of spoons
and the other empty, and two or three glasses of water
stand about on the tray. The first guest takes a spoon,
dips it in the jelly, and reverses it as he puts it in his
mouth, so as to give full play as a scoop to his tongue,
and down it goes. Then, putting down the spoon in the
empty glass, he gulps down some water, and the tray
goes on to the next in rank. (When going through this
ceremony, I am always carried back in thought to the
days when I was in the nursery, days on which I had
shown temper and fretfulness, and a little grey powder
was thought to be necessary.) More cigarettes, then
Turkish coffee, followed by a glass each of sherbet, which
is fruit syrup mixed in water. After this a turn at water,
melons and grapes, finishing with raki and rahathlecoon.
Three or four visits of this sort were trying to one's
digestion, and we fully expected to have fever or some
other ailment.

On another occasion we paid an afternoon visit to Mr.
Matteo Bishof, the Bulgarian merchant I have before
mentioned, and I must say I was astonished to find a
man with such enlightened views and liberal opinions in

Turkey. He had kindly put his house in the town at our disposal, and after spending a few days with our good-natured countryman the consul, we moved into it, taking our servants with us, Matteo being away meanwhile at his house in the vineyards. On entering the rooms prepared for us, we were surprised to see a large bookcase containing nearly all Dickens's and Thackeray's works, besides several standard works in French and English.

Matteo is about twenty-eight years of age. He was educated at Roberts College, in Constantinople, and is become one of the richest men in Angora. He was going to be married, a few weeks after our visit, to a Greek child thirteen years old, and expected to get a considerable "dot" with her. I saw and spoke to the damsel, and I must say I felt glad Matteo was to be her future husband, and not I; for besides being a complete child in figure, face, and manner, she was far from pretty. Being quite the cleverest man in the town, Matteo has a very good time of it, and instead of his fearing the Turks, they fear him! He has never been in England, but he speaks English grammatically and well, and the information we received from him was good, and always proved to be accurate.

A young Englishman, a Mr. ——, lives with Mr. Gatheral to assist him in his business. A few days after our arrival, Mr. Gatheral sent him to a small town eight hours from Angora to collect some money due to him from the local government. Nothing was heard of the lad for

some days, but at last a letter came from him begging
Mr. Gatheral to send him a few bottles of maastic without
a moment's delay, as "the kaimakam asked me directly
I saw him if I had any, and was much disgusted at finding
I had not, and all business was at a standstill. At last
I remembered the bottle of spirit I had for heating my
etna, and this he has now just finished, sweetened with a
little sugar. I have got on well, and have collected two-
thirds of the money, but the bottle is empty, and I shall
not get a paras more unless you send me some raki.
I have greatly missed my tea, but the kaimakam drank
all the spirits of wine."

One morning a young Armenian called on us at the
consulate. He had been lately employed travelling
through the neighbouring vineyards estimating the value
and assessing the tithe. The consul persuaded him to
produce the paper he had drawn up. There was so much
to pay for vineyards, so much for garden, so much for
honey-bees—in all about £25. To collect this there were
employed, first, our acquaintance, the Armenian ; then a
Turk to see that he did not cheat; a man to measure the
land, etc., and a clerk to revise the accounts ; and when
all these were paid out of the £25 collected, there was
£3 2s. for the Government !

From Brusa to Angora our luggage had been transported in a light Tartar araba, which had got on pretty
well, only coming to grief on an average about twice
a day. But we were told that the roads we should now
have to pass over were only fit for pack-horses, news that

we did not regret, as up to this time we had abused the
araba for its slowness, and fancied that with pack-horses
of our own, our journey would be much quicker; but in
this we soon found we had made a mistake, and we often
regretted the despised araba, especially when the pack-
horses were being loaded and unloaded morning and night.
Before quitting Angora we purchased three new horses,
which brought our stud up to six, all good useful animals,
but, like most of the Turkish horses, full of fight and
mischief. We had grave doubts about the last one we
bought, fearing it would not stand work, as it was as fat
as a pig; but, contrary to our expectations, instead of
knocking up, it got into condition with our slow work,
and turned out so well that if I had to make another
journey in Asia Minor or anywhere where one does not
ride fast, I would have all my horses as fat as possible
at starting.

When we first arrived at Angora we had intended, after
a rest there, to push on to Yuzgat and Sivas, but we altered
our plans when we heard that the dreary plains we had
passed over continued almost the entire distance; and
after much poring over Kiepert's map, and collecting
information from everybody we met, we settled to proceed
to Kaiserieh *viâ* Kur-Shehr, hoping by doing so to get
sooner into a fresh and more interesting country.

We were all up early on the morning of October 19th,
intending to be on the road by 10 a.m., but first one thing
and then another stopped us until it was 2 p.m. before we
were fairly under way. A parting visit had to be paid

to Said Pasha. First one and then another of the chief
men of the town came to take leave. Then saddle-bags
had to be arranged with care, so that each pair had their
contents equally distributed to ride well on the pack-
saddles. Then Anton our cook was found to be so drunk
he could not move, and had to be dismissed, and an
Armenian lad of eighteen who had been a hanger-on of
Mr. Gatheral's hired in his place; and when all was
thought to be ready, it was discovered that the spirits
of wine we had brought from Constantinople for our etna,
had all found its way into the drunken Anton, and half
an hour was lost before more could be procured. At last
the order came to start, and a few steps were taken, when
two of the new pack-horses set to work kicking and
plunging, and each succeeded in getting rid of its load
before we reached the first turn of the street. The packs
were disentangled from their cords, and the cords from
the horses' legs, and once more were bound on the pack-
saddles, this time so tightly that they could not shift, and
to get rid of them the horses had to kick themselves clean
out of the pack-saddles, a feat they accomplished about
every two hours for the rest of the day.

For the first few hours our road ran by the side of the
Angora river, through gardens and vineyards, with steep
hills on either side seamed and intersected by water-gullies.
The low lands by the side of the brook were clothed with
the withered remains of the summer crops, but the hills
were barren wastes of stone and dust. Little by little as
we ascended the brook the valley opened out, till just at

sunset we came upon the open country, and found stretching before us a repetition of the same hilly, dreary, barren expanse that we had left on the other side of Angora. The hills were higher and steeper, but still bare and treeless, and as one of my companions remarked, the scene before us was like the mountains of the moon as depicted in old school maps.

It did not tend to cheer our spirits when Ali Agha informed us that we had come all wrong, and had lost our way, and that we must turn from the line we had taken and hunt over the hills for the road we had missed, and the village at which we hoped to sleep. This we did, and at the end of an hour came upon a collection of mud huts that rejoice in the name of Oda Bashi.

By that time it was too dark to see to pitch the tent, so we were obliged to put up in the strangers' room, which was a filthy place opening into a stable some three feet deep in manure. Here, for the first time on our journey, G—— and I slept in net hammocks, and were delighted to find them most comfortable; but we found that it is hardly worth carrying them in Turkey, first, because not one room in a hundred is large enough to swing them in; and secondly, when the room is sufficiently large, the mud walls are so rotten one cannot get the hammock-hooks to hold in them.

On the night in question there were three posts in the room supporting the roof, so by fixing the head-lines to separate posts, and the foot-lines to the third, we managed pretty well, the only drawback being, that as the post

at the feet was a feeble one, each time one of us moved
we set the other swinging and woke him up with a start.
At first we kept a candle burning, but hearing a suppressed
titter, I turned towards the narrow open slit in the wall
that does duty for a window, and there discovered all the
children of the village taking turns to peep in to look at
the quaint way the mad Englishmen slept in the air, and
long after I had extinguished the candle I heard roars of
laughter in the courtyard, and I have no doubt that we
and our hammocks will be remembered by some of those
youngsters when they are grandfathers and grandmothers.

CHAPTER XII.

Disobedient Yuzgat—Killidghar—A coal-mine—An afternoon's sport
—The Kizil Irmak—Agricultural prospects—Cotton—Silver
mines—Village boors.

HAVING been told by different people in Angora that some
very rich coal-mines had been discovered near a village
called Killidghar, and fancying that it might be an out-
crop of the Heraclea coal-field on the Black Sea, we determined to visit it, though by so doing we should have to
leave our direct route for some twenty miles.

On the morning of the 20th we were off in good time,
and in six hours reached the village of Killidghar, having
passed but one village on our way, which is called Assi
Yuzgat (Disobedient Yuzgat), and is inhabited by Turcomans. We halted there to water our horses at a fountain,
round which stood a number of gipsy-looking women, who
entered freely into conversation with us, and on my
proposing to buy a pretty Persian greyhound one of them
had with her, they indulged in a little chaff, asking what
I, a traveller, could want with a dog; was it not a wife I
wanted, and how much would I give for one.

Before reaching Killidghar the country became very
broken, the hills almost amounting to mountains; in fact,
I see I mentioned them as such in my note-book, but in

those days I had not seen the Taurus, and now that I have faced them, the former, though abrupt and steep and some thousand feet high, appear to me only hills.

Perhaps I may here remark that in describing a country, a writer must always have a difficulty about hills and mountains. Where does a hill end and a mountain begin? Does not our language want some name to describe a small mountain, or a big hill? Could we not get a few more words manufactured for us in the workshop for words belonging to our cousins across the Atlantic? They have given us the word "cañon" for a cleft through a mountain, and it works well.

Our stay in Killidghar was quite one of the bright spots in our journey, for on our arrival we were at once taken to a fresh two-storied house on the outskirts of the village, and shown into a room on the upper storey, with boarded floor and clean divans, cool, fresh, and sweet, the windows looking into a vineyard filled with fruit-trees, and on beyond across the valley some quarter of a mile wide, to the steep, rugged hills. Not only were we well lodged, but we were well fed, the villagers bringing us bread, chickens, milk, eggs, youatt (a sort of sour curds), and last, but best, a splendid comb of virgin honey.

The owner of the house was a young man, the last of a long line of Deré Beys, the only landed or hereditary aristocracy of any kind in Turkey. Doubtless his ancestors had been a great power in the land, and had looked upon themselves as very great people; but times were changed, and our host was apparently a very humble, quiet, civil young fellow, and treated us, his guests, as if we were the proprietors of all we saw and he the stranger. On our mentioning the object of our visit, he sent for the elders of the village, and from them we gathered that some years ago a man sinking a well had found a vein about nine inches thick of black soft stone, and in showing this to a soldier who had seen the wonders of the outer world, he pronounced it to be coal. It burnt when mixed with an equal quantity of wood, and further, made a disgusting smell. The well soon after fell in, but the news of the discovery reaching the Pasha of Angora, he ordered the villagers to reopen the well and send him some of the coal. This was done, and cost in labour £73, which the pasha forgot to pay. The coal was sent off, and some Frank, seeing it in Angora, pronounced it useless. From what we were told we came to the conclusion it was lignite. The well, which was some three hours from the village, was filled up and would take three days to reopen. The bey offered to have this done for us if we would pay for the work, but the chances of finding coal appeared to us so slender, and the vein originally found was so shallow, that we determined to continue our journey on the morrow and leave the mine alone.

In the course of conversation, the bey told us that the neighbourhood of the village was renowned for the quantities of red-legged partridges, and pointing to the hills opposite, he said, "there they cover the face of the earth." I do not often let my hopes be raised by what natives say as to game abounding, but so confidently did the Turk speak, I thought for once I was sure of an hour's good sport; so taking Ali Agha's old gun I started for the hills, with a village urchin as guide to show where the coveys were thickest. The hills were little short of precipices, barren, burnt up, and covered with stones. Up and up we went, across and across, and then up again, my hopes getting lower as I ascended higher, till at last in despair I tucked the gun under my arm and turned downwards. No sooner had I done this than up jumped a big hare, and before it had got out of sight I rolled it over, to the intense joy of the young sportsman, who first cut its throat with a knife a foot long, and then broke both its front legs. The first proceeding I could understand, but the last was a puzzle to me, and the Turk, when asked why it was done, could only give "custom" as a reason. I reloaded, and proposed looking for more game, but the lad said, "What! not satisfied? Is not a hare enough for you? Well, it is for me; so I shall be off to the village to show it." On second thoughts I determined also to give up, and together we returned to exhibit our splendid bag!

The next morning, directly after quitting the village, we began to ascend a steep hill that took us an hour to cross; the road, which had been fairly good at first, becoming soon nothing but a mule-track covered thickly with loose stones from the size of a man's head to that of a bushel, so that we could only creep along, and often had to get off and lead our horses.

After passing over this hill we came upon a wide

valley, down the centre of which the river Kizil Irmak (Halys), here some fifty yards wide, poured its muddy waters. This river and the Sakaria (Sangarius), which we had passed after leaving Sivri-Hissar, are the only two rivers that descend through the central plains of Western Asia Minor and empty themselves into the Black Sea. The former rises near Sivas, runs south-west till near Kaiseriah, then west and north-west till within thirty-five miles of Angora, where it turns north-east, and finally enters the Black Sea about half way between Sinope and Samsoon. Its entire length is somewhere about six hundred miles, and the valleys on either side of it are the richest part of all the great central upland. Unfortunately the feeders to this stream are few and short, so that they enrich the country very little.

The other river, the Sakaria, rises on the hill near Bey Bazar, some forty-five miles west of Angora, and flows west till near Eski-Shehr, there turns north, and empties itself into the Black Sea ninety miles east of the mouth of the Bosphorus.

Neither of these rivers are navigable for anything but small craft, and even these cannot ascend far from the coast. Yet these two rivers, properly managed, might be an inexhaustible source of wealth to Turkey. The immense tracts of rich soil, that only requires water to make it produce enormous crops of cereals, might be irrigated by them at a comparatively small cost, and if the rich valleys thus brought under cultivation were connected with the Black Sea by tram roads, or even well-maintained

macadamized roads, Western Asia Minor might compete
in the grain market with the fertile provinces of the
Danube, and would, besides, yield other produce which
those countries could not. I have often seen it stated in
books and newspapers that the various mines and forests
of Asia Minor were some day to pay off the foreign debt,
and make Turkey one of the richest countries in the world;
but if ever Turkey is to attain to this happy state of things,
or anything approaching to it, I think *water* and not
minerals or wood will do it, and this water will have to
come chiefly from the Kizil Irmak and the Sakaria.
Besides the land immediately under irrigation, other land
in the neighbourhood would be benefited. Trees would
quickly follow the irrigation canals, and with the trees
would come rain and dew, and these falling on the
mountains and barren plains would in their turn produce
more trees, so in time the whole land would be fruitful.

There are, however, two evils to contend with which
places this source of wealth almost beyond the region of
hope. The first is fever. That extraordinary disease that
searches out every corner of Asia Minor, from the low-
lying plains of Cilicia to the highest village in the rocky
Taurus, and from there over the burnt-up tracts of the high
central uplands to the hilly shores of the Black Sea, to
the Mediterranean, and the Archipelago. Some districts
suffer rather less than others, and some years are freer
from it than others; but it is found everywhere, and has
been since the days when the Crusaders, under Godfrey de
Bouillon, were victims to it throughout their long marches.

K

The other drawback is the Turk. Without foreign assistance he will do nothing; ay, more, without foreign *coercion* he will do nothing. The country, as it is, did for his fathers, and it will do for him; and as for his posterity, they must look out for themselves. A barren and unfruitful land; a miserable, half-starved peasantry; an empty exchequer, and the steady periodical loss of provinces is better than the active assistance of Europeans in any shape, except that of loans. And further, like a wild, untamed, savage animal, his instinct is to destroy and not to create. See what he has done for the noble towns of the old Greeks and Romans, the roads and canals, the palaces and temples that he found in all directions when he first swarmed over the country! Not one stone stands upon another, the canals are filled up, and the remains of the marble temples lie scattered about as horse-blocks and tombstones. In the place of these what do we find? Towns of mud bricks, mule-tracks for roads, the rich irrigated lowlands scorched up deserts, and from end to end of Asia Minor not one building with the faintest pretensions to architectural beauty. To the last the Turk will resist all interference; but should a strong European power find its interests so compromised by the present state of affairs as to make it worth its while to coerce him, and insist on good government, the task will not be so difficult as may be supposed. The Turks, as soon as they realize the fact that they cannot resist longer, will succumb to fate, and even often lie on their backs and enjoy the blessings others produce—blessings which they of themselves are incapable of reaching out a hand to grasp.

There is one other thing I should like to mention here, and that is the false hopes that seem to exist both in the minds of native Christians in Turkey and also among Europeans as to the *speedy* benefits to be obtained by European interference. Doubtless the former would obtain justice, together with security for person and property, and so at once be bettered; but materially to reform the country must be a long and weary operation, the fruits of which will never ripen in the lives of those now in existence.

Before Western Asia Minor shows a return for labour spent, the population must be increased *tenfold*, whereas at the present day it is melting away rapidly ; but the tide might be turned, and if once the land was exempt from wars, famine, and sickness, a happy state of affairs that might be brought about by a good government, the inhabitants would begin to multiply.

Then emigrants might be invited, and encouraged to settle; but owing to the ague, I fear many would not do so, unless some tempting bait, such as a new and profitable industry, could be established special to the country.

Perhaps in the next few years the Turks of Europe will leave the giaour-infected lands in the west of the empire, and settle in Asia; but so vast is the country, and so empty, they would be a mere drop in the ocean. People point to the great strides Wallachia and Moldavia have made in the last twenty years, and from this argue that Turkey may do the same, forgetting that the former

country started rich in arms and legs, and further, that
these arms and legs belonged to and were worked by an
active energetic people, greedy for wealth, and not fearing
to work, whereas the inhabitants of Turkey are just the
opposite. The Turk is only active when he is destroying,
as when he is at war, and the Christians (Armenians) are
as a race more given to working with their heads than
with their arms and legs; and, besides, taking the two
countries, there are per acre in the former country from
six to ten persons where there is one in Turkey.

After passing the river Kizil Irmak, we found the
country less hilly, but as burnt up and desolate as ever,
and during the twenty-five miles we rode on this day, we
only saw two small villages. It was at this stage of our
journey that we first came upon the cotton plant. We had
never before seen it under cultivation, but during the rest
of our ride eastward we constantly met with it growing
in the valleys and on the hillsides; but whether the plant
thrives in Asia as it does in other countries I must leave
others to decide, contenting myself with noting what we
saw. On the best-cultivated lands around Adana, where
the soil is the richest, the plants were the finest, and
produced most. They were planted in rows two feet
apart, and grew from nine to eighteen inches high, and
each plant produced about ten pods of the size of a big
walnut. When we first came across the cotton plant, the
pods were just bursting open, and the villagers were
beginning to pick it.

Our halting-place on this night was the village of

Madan, celebrated a few years ago for its mines of argentiferous lead-ore; but these are now unworked, owing to
the want of fuel, all wood within fifty miles of them
having been consumed in the smelting furnaces. We
inspected the old workings, which were to be seen near
the village on the slope of a rocky hill, the mines themselves being empty pits from twenty to thirty feet deep,
with rough steps cut in the sides, up which the ore was
brought to the surface on men's backs. We also saw in
the village huge mounds of slag, the refuse from the furnaces, and as we were told that when the mines were
worked only the silver was saved and carried away,
these mounds must be excessively rich in lead.

From Madan to the sea, following the valley of the
Kizil Irmak to the mouth of that river, is about two
hundred miles. Forests, as I have said, are to be found
at fifty miles distant on this route, but I doubt the mine
ever being worked at a profit, unless coal were discovered
in the neighbourhood.

G—— and I pitched our tent in a deserted garden close
to the village, while Mr. Gatheral occupied a room near
us. Of all men I ever met, I think Mr. Gatheral is the
best fitted to be a traveller. Nothing ever seemed to
come amiss to him. Bad roads, stumbling horses, scorching sun, inefficient servants, dirty lodgings and detestible
food, failed to upset his equanimity, and he always appeared
after the longest day as fresh as at the starting, good-
tempered, ready to eat a bad supper and sleep well. Then
his knowledge of Turkish was great, and his knowledge

of the people greater, and from him and by his help we obtained a great deal of useful information, and gained hints that stood us in good stead when he was no longer with us.

I wish here to remark, for the benefit of any one who may follow in our track, that the villagers of Madan were the greatest bores we had yet met with, from the kaimakam, who was half-drunk, down to the smallest child. Whenever we appeared outside the tent, crowds surrounded us, others came and gazed in at the tent door with a vacant expression of countenance, and we were jeered at and insulted again and again, till at last we could stand it no longer, and Mr. Gatheral came forward as consul and made the kaimakam place a man to guard our tent and drive away the crowds, a duty our own zaptiehs should have performed, but they were a couple of useless ruffians, about as intelligent as the street dogs that spent the night barking at us.

CHAPTER XIII.

Kur-Shehr—Universal hospitality—Armenian hosts—Chances of emigration—Deré Beys—Immunity from fever—A Turkish bridge—
The end of the plains—Kaisarieh.

FROM Madan we rode on two days, reaching on the afternoon of the 15th the environs of the town of Kur-Shehr
(City of the Desert), a name that shows that this hideous
district was not much better when the Turks first settled
there. We were all struck with the resemblance of the
approach to this town to that of Khiva, as described by
MacGahan in his admirable book. For the last two hours
before reaching the town, we rode down a valley watered
by a clear rapid little stream, covered with gardens divided
from each other by high mud walls, and thickly planted
with luxuriant fruit trees—peach, apricot, plum, pear,
apple, quince, etc.; while the rich soil beneath was covered
with flourishing vines. All along the road were detached
houses inhabited by settled Turcomans, the men a fine
race with much savage beauty, but the women flat-faced
and very ugly. The houses, which were flat-roofed box-
like buildings, all faced away from the road, and were shut
into yards by high walls, but, for Turkey, all looked clean
and prosperous, and from the outside we began to form

favourable hopes of the town; but these hopes vanished directly we got into the narrow streets.

It was just like all the other towns we had seen—mud houses massed together — unpaved, undrained streets, miserable open shops, the entire stock of which could not be worth many pounds, and finally, the market place one huge manure heap. We went at first to a small khan, which was full of travelling merchants, occupying all the rooms with their goods; but by dint of bribery we induced a Greek to induce the khanji to induce one of these men to turn out, a work of considerable difficulty, as he had to move some hundred packages. No sooner had he done this, than an Armenian who knew Mr. Gatheral arrived and insisted on our going to his house and becoming his guests.

Let me here remark that, as far as my experience goes, and it extends over thirteen years spent in Turkey, hospitality is a virtue possessed by *all* the inhabitants, and not, as has been asserted by some travellers, confined to the Osmanlis. The Turk is naturally most hospitable to the Turk, and the Christian to the Christian, but it often happens that the Turk receives the Christian as his guest, and the Christian the Turk. We have reason to be grateful to both, for both came forward at different times, both did their very best for us, and this without any expectation of our being able to make them any return. In one Armenian house the very servants refused to take the bakshish we offered them when we were leaving. Should a respectable traveller find a want of hospitality on the

part of either Turk or Christian, I can but think it is his
own fault. Perhaps he has been heard by his servants cry-
ing down one nationality, speaking well of the other, and
the servants mentioning this to outsiders, it soon spreads
all over the country in the rapid way that tittle-tattle
always does in the East, and the people he has defamed
naturally do not feel very hospitably inclined towards
their defamer.

Our host or hosts, for there appeared to be two or three
masters in the house, gave us the best they had—a clean
room, soft divans, a good supper and breakfast, and clean
beds spread on the floor. Except when we were in bed,
the room was always full of guests, asking us questions
and telling of their grievances; but it was the old story
over and over again, so I shall not repeat it. All asked
when the English were coming, and all evidently thought
we had something to do with that happy event; indeed,
later on, our host told us it was so, saying, "It is being
said of you in the bazaars by the majority of the population, Mussulman and Christian, ' Please God these Englishmen are the forerunners of others who are coming to
govern the country properly.' Another strong party say,
' Let them come, let them go, we are too old and too wise
to hope for better days. Nothing ever improves our condition, but everything works for our harm, be the inten-
tion good or bad.' While the remnant say, ' To hell with
them and their government, we don't want to be interfered
with!'"

Somehow the subject of emigration cropped up, and we

were discussing the advantages of it, and mentioned the fact that a considerable community of Armenians were settled in Liverpool, and were all doing well as traders and merchants, also that a number were in Calcutta, and were prospering there. All present agreed that it would be a fine thing to emigrate, but said that it was impossible to do so; first, because the Turkish Government would not allow them; and, secondly, because it was not the "custom." One sturdy black-bearded fellow, between thirty and forty years of age, said he had often wished to try his fortunes in America, and that having no wife and children he could do so, only his papa would not let him go! We asked him if he did not consider himself a man, old enough to judge for himself; but he assured us it was the "custom" to obey a father in all things, without venturing to offer an opinion—that is to say, a man of sixty, if his father is alive, must obey him.

Most said they had not the means to emigrate, but when one came to inquire, all had more or less property, some in cash, lent out at interest, and others in houses, but at any rate ample to carry them to one of our colonies and fairly start them in business. All agreed that life under the Turk was unendurable, and that if England did not soon stretch out a helping hand they must help themselves—this idea not running in the direction of revolutions, but in begging some one else to help them. One old fellow preached us quite an eloquent sermon upon the *duty* of England, as a Christian nation, to help their fellow-Christians the Armenians; but when we asked if *his*

people had in the slightest degree helped their fellow-
Christians the Servians and Bulgars in their late troubles,
he assured us that Servs and Bulgars were quite different
to Armenians, and that it was not a Christian duty to
help them.

The real fact is, it is the " custom " to be misgoverned
by Turks, and so they put up with it, and look upon it as
their natural condition. Emigration or self-help of any
sort is beyond them; and even if the men would quit the
country the women would not, and would use their irresis-
tible powers of tears and entreaty to bind their menkind
under the Turkish yoke. Poor creatures! hundreds of
years of oppression have stamped out all manly feeling,
and made them what they are, a fit people for slavery,
whose noblest ambition is to cheat and outwit their
masters, an operation they perform with great skill.

The greater part of the land in the neighbourhood of
Kur-Shehr is owned by a few Deré Beys, who let it to
the peasants on the half-profit system. These Deré Beys,
we were told, are all-powerful, and virtually the real
governors of the district, for should a governor or other
official refuse to obey them in the smallest particular, or
give judgment against them in any case, they unite to pay
a bribe in the proper quarter at Constantinople, and the
man is at once recalled.

In one respect Kur-Shehr is superior to any other town
we visited throughout our whole journey. Fever is unknown there, though *why* it escapes this scourge, which is
to be found everywhere else in Western Asia Minor, no

one could tell us. If we ever interfere in the government
of Turkey, possibly this immunity from fever may lead to
Kur-Shehr becoming the residence of an English official.
Poor fellow! I shall pity him, for a more complete "living
tomb" cannot easily be found. Again, should it ever be
our misfortune to have to send an army into Western
Asia Minor, Kur-Shehr would be a good central spot for
hospitals, where fever patients would have a chance of
recovering, if they did not die of monotony.

After saying good-bye to our late host and travelling
companion, Mr. Gatheral, who was about to return to
Angora, G—— and I started once more eastwards on the
morning of October 24th. The country we rode through
on this and the following days was an exact repetition of
that we had past over on the journey from Angora, except
that the villages appeared to be further apart, and more
wretched looking, the people more uncouth, and, if possible, the land more burnt up.

Twenty-five miles from Kaisarieh we reached a rough
rocky ravine, and after winding down this for a quarter of
an hour we once more came upon the river Kizil Irmak,
over which we passed on a stone bridge—a modern
Turkish erection, pronounced by Ali Agha and our zaptiehs to be a work of great beauty, but which we, with
our poor European notions of engineering, thought the
most ridiculous thing we had ever seen. The road leading
to it on each side mounted up so steeply to the bridge
that it had to be made in paved steps. The bridge was
only ten feet wide, with no parapets, supported on one

pointed stone arch some sixty feet above the highest point
the river ever attained. I say one arch, for I do not count
the two little ones that pierced and weakened the abutments. The entire span was only forty feet, just a third
less than the height from the water to the crown of the
arch.

After passing this our road wound along a narrow
valley, down the middle of which flowed a rapid stream.
An hour further on we reached the summit of some small
hills, and there before us lay the plain of Kaisarieh, backed
on the south-east by Mount Argæus, with its conical peak
of perpetual snow, and flanked right and left by the spurs
of the Taurus. All day we had seen the grand old mountain peak shining before us in the sunlight, but it was
only now we had an uninterrupted view of the whole ;
and though both it and the surrounding mountains were
treeless and barren, yet our spirits revived at the grandeur
of the scene, and we both exclaimed, " Thank God, we
have done with those dreary plains ! " I verily believe
even the horses rejoiced at the change of scene, for they
cheered up, trotted on briskly, even kicked a little, and
finally one bolted up a side path amidst rocks and crags,
and had to be fetched back with some difficulty from a
narrow ledge overhanging a precipice.

Between the hills on which we stood and the foot of
Mount Argæus, extended a flat plain some five miles wide,
running north and south, all rich and cultivated, while
the foot of the hills on either side were for miles clothed
with vineyards belonging to villages that were dotted

about at a few miles distance from each other. All was watered by innumerable little streams that descended from the perpetual snow, and the whole panorama appeared richer, prettier, and pleasanter than anything our eyes had rested on since we had quitted the immediate neighbourhood of Brusa.

Kaisarieh itself stands on the plain in a recess formed by the mountains, and is by them sheltered and protected on three sides; but it seems strange that people should choose to live down on a damp flat plain, almost in a swamp, when within half a mile of them are beautiful hills, affording the best possible site for a town. For this, however, the Turks are not responsible perhaps, for they inherited the town in its present position, and in those days it possessed fine buildings and houses that made it worth retaining. Now it is simply a rookery of hovels, and nothing could be a greater blessing to the inhabitants than if one of the fires that often take place there were to destroy it all, and thus force them to migrate to the villages that are thickly dotted over the slopes of the hills.

Doubtless in the days of its greatness the present town was only a suburb or business quarter, for even now may be seen on the neighbouring hills foundations and massive blocks of stone, marble, and other building materials. Besides, history tells us that in the day of Valerian, when it was plundered and pillaged by the Persians, the inhabitants amounted to four hundred thousand, and therefore, to contain them, the town must have been very much

larger than it is now with its population of only twenty
thousand. Tradition says the town was founded by one
of the sons of Japhat. This may or may not be true;
but anyhow Kaisarieh plays an important part in the
history of Western Asia Minor. Herodotus states that the
first inhabitants were of Syrian extraction. The Medes
and then the Persians conquered and possessed it, together
with the entire country of Cappadocia. It was annexed
to the Roman Empire in the time of Tiberius, and then
in his honour its ancient name of "Muzaca" was changed
to that of Cæsarea. Temples were built and consecrated
to the emperor. It possessed an amphitheatre, baths,
and other public buildings, and maintained its greatness
until the Eastern savages came in, destroyed all, and left
it as it is to-day, a collection of decaying hovels containing
a population of savage, bigoted, ignorant, corrupt Turks,
with the poor, cringing, unmanly Armenians as their
subjects, and with only a few scattered stones lying
prostrate and broken, together with the traces of the
foundations of the once-splendid buildings, to show what
the old town had been in the days before them.

CHAPTER XIV.

Sixty brothers—A mission-house—Religion a nationality—Talas—An American host—Missionary work—Armenian gratitude—A native pastor—Vicarious liberality—Hospitality bordering on brutality.

WE had sent on Ali Agha early in the day into Kaisarieh, that he might if possible find us lodgings somewhat better than the dirty khan rooms; but our hopes of his doing so were small, and as we drew near the town, and saw what a miserable place it was, our spirits sank to zero, and we felt quite sorry for ourselves. But just as we reached the entrance of the town we espied a young gentleman, prancing about on Ali Agha's horse, who galloped up the next moment, and with many salaams addressed us in what he fondly believed to be English, but what really was a conglomeration of that familiar tongue, with American slang, Turkish, and Armenian. " You sares two brodders ? yes ; oh, me werry, werry glad. You many brodders here, I guess. Come long; come to your brodders."

Now this was all very astonishing, and our surprise increased when riding on a little further we found some sixty persons—old men, middle-aged men, boys, small and great, and even quite little children—all drawn up on the roadside, and our first friend presenting them to us as our " brothers " ! We were much flattered; but for the honour

of the family at home stated our conviction that our
father's children, all told, did not amount to half a score.

Our acquaintance then with some difficulty explained
that the gentlemen before us were no blood-relations, but
only "Christian brothers"! Greatly reassured by this,
we inquired how it was we were so highly honoured by
all turning out to receive us. Little by little we gathered
that two American missionaries with their families lived
in a village near; that Mr. Gatheral had written to them
to say we were about to visit Kaisarieh, and these gentlemen had most kindly told the brethren to look out for
us, and take us on to the village as soon as we arrived.
"But," added our informant, "it is now late, and the
village is five miles off, so you must put up in the mission-
house till the morning." Agreeing to this, we made a
move as if to enter the town, but our friend stopped us,
saying, "The brothers will accompany you. If we go by
the direct way to the house we must pass through the
town, and probably the Turks will fall upon us and hurt
us; come round here and slip in quietly." But this we
declined to do, and rode straight on, the band of sixty
slipping and sliding, dodging and twisting after us, all
showing plainly by their scared looks that they expected
to be kicked a little by every Turk they met. All passed
off well, without either the brothers or ourselves being
assaulted, though we did hear from all sides growled out,
"English!" "Giaours!" etc.—the etc. being better left to
imagination.

At the mission-house a clean room was given to us,

L

the only piece of furniture in it being a large bookcase fairly stocked with English and American books; but we were used to sitting on the ground, and had our camp-beds, so were independent, and felt that we had fallen into good quarters, and we should have been quite happy were it not for the large family of brothers we had found. No sooner were we squatted in the corners than the sixty who had accompanied us entered thick and fast and shook hands; then one-half squatted on their haunches round the walls, and with mouths open, the lips turned back, and a vacant expression on their faces, stared at us without speaking. The other half, I believe, dashed out and squandered themselves over the town in pursuit of every Armenian in the place, who were all fetched in to shake hands with us, till what with the shaking, and what with the closeness of the room packed thickly with the living mass, we felt inclined to make a bolt of it; but for two miserable hours the torture continued, at the end of which our servant appeared with some supper, and our gaping friends took their departure, leaving us to digest with our dinner one piece of information that we had picked up from them, namely, that the Armenians of Asia Minor divide themselves into three different peoples—Armenians, Catholics, and Protestants. To them religion is a nationality, and one constantly hears a man say, "No, I am not an Armenian, I am a Catholic, or a Protestant;" in fact, they fall into the error we do when speaking of Jews. How often one hears it said, "So-and-So was a Jew, but he is not now, he is a Christian"!

After supper we clambered up a ladder on to the flat roof of the house, which, being a two-storied one and standing on a piece of raised ground, gave us an extensive view of the town, and it was hard to believe we were in an inhabited place. The houses were all flat-roofed, and to us looked as if the real roof had been destroyed or carried away. The walls were composed of rough stones set in mud, but not one could be seen that had not crumbling broken places in it. The doors and window-frames were all unpainted, and most of them broken and decayed. A river of mud some foot deep ran down the middle of each street, over which projected the stained and warped wooden shutters of the open shops; and all looked exactly as if the place had been sacked and destroyed about a year ago and no one had entered it since.

While looking at this, the "brothers" attempted to storm us again in our new position, but we pretended to come down the ladder each time they started to come up, and so kept them at a distance; but if we kept them out of sight they kept themselves in our minds, for they all gathered somewhere below, and with dismal nasal intonations poured out a string of old familiar evangelical hymns. We, however, made no response to this; so, disbanding, they scattered themselves about, and from all directions the hymns were levelled at us—from neighbouring house-tops, back-yards, balconies, the streets, and one small boy was just going to begin one into the keyhole, when I opened the door suddenly and so scared him that his hymn stuck in his throat and half choked him.

By the time we crept into our beds, we had made up
our minds that one clear day in Kaisarieh was all British
human nature could stand, and after that we would push
on over the mountains; but our determination was shaken
when we awoke next morning and found a young, pleasant,
good-looking American clergyman standing at our bed-
side, inviting us to hurry up, mount our horses, and be off
with him to his house in the neighbouring village of Talas.

Having for the sake of warmth gone to bed in our
clothes (there was no glass in the windows of our room
and the door would not shut), we were soon ready for the
road; so leaving Ali Agha and the boy to pack up and
follow us, we started off, and in an hour's time arrived
at the foot of what looked like a precipice with a mass of
houses clinging to the sides of it one above the other, so
closely packed that the top of one house formed the
terraced garden of the one above it, with the narrowest
little streets zigzagging up and up between them on
natural ledges of rock.   It is more than a village, containing about six thousand people, most of the rich Armenians
and Turks of Kaisarieh residing there, and only going
into the town to transact their daily business.   Our
friend's house was the highest of all in the town, thereby
possessing the rare advantage of overlooking its neighbours, and not being overlooked in return; besides, what
is far more important, it had the water fresh from the
spring just above it, before it had trickled down an open
street in a little stream, from which all the rest of the
houses are supplied.

Thanks to the houses being built of dressed stone, the
town had a neater and more prosperous look about it
than any place we had yet seen, and we were told that
many of the merchants were, for Turkey, very rich; but
in spite of their riches, the famine of 1873 and 1874 was
very severe here. All who depended on the land for support suffered more or less, and hundreds in the surrounding
villages actually died of starvation.

Our new friend, Mr. Staver, having piloted us safely up
the hill, past several unprotected precipices, showed us
into a clean cool entrance hall, where we were met and
heartily welcomed by his most charming wife, who at
once conducted us into an exquisitely clean bedroom, and
so great was our delight at this wondrous contrast to the
filthy hovels we had been reduced to, that for the first
few minutes we could only stand and stare at the snug,
homelike, comfortable American furniture, and above all
the beds with their snowy sheets. I veritably believe,
had it not been for our keen hunger and the prospect of
breakfast, we should have undressed as fast as we could
and taken a roll between them. As it was, we contented
ourselves with a good wash and brush, and then hurried
downstairs to revel in the further luxuries this most
comfortable house afforded, and enjoy the delight of
having once again clever, intelligent, pleasant companions
to converse with.

In the drawing-room was a large organ that had come
from New York, and had been brought all the way across
these dreary plains on the backs of camels. Under Mrs.

Staver's skilful hands this organ was made a means to humanize and instruct the members of her husband's flock. She also accompanied Mr. Staver in his songs, he having a fine baritone voice such as one rarely has a chance of hearing. We stayed some days in our comfortable quarters, enjoying the rest, and feeling much interested in the simple but hard-working lives led by our missionary friends, admiring the noble unselfishness that had led them to devote themselves to the work of teaching the Gospel to the natives of these parts, educating them and trying to raise them to a higher state of civilization. I sincerely wish their work might be crowned with the success it merits, but from all I learnt it seemed to me a thankless task, and I cannot feel hopeful of great results.

The whole of Asia Minor, Syria, and I believe part of Persia, is divided into missionary fields, and each field is divided into districts, the centre of which is some big town, such as Kaisarieh. In America there is a Board of Directors of these "Congregational Christians," who collect money for carrying on the work, appoint secretaries and ministers, and allot the "fields." Again, there is a Board of Directors with a secretary at Constantinople, who do the lay part of the work, such as the financing, receiving and forwarding Bibles, school books, etc. Nearly all the missionaries are married, but beside their wives there are a number of single ladies who devote their lives to teaching in the schools. Periodically, delegates from the different fields meet in one of the towns and consult and arrange for work. Each resident missionary holds

services every Sunday in the place where he lives, and
besides this, as soon as he can speak Turkish, he goes on
tours, preaching in every village. Then there is a large
staff of Armenian pastors, supposed to be " Gospel men,"
and under them are Bible readers, both men and women,
and also school teachers. All these are paid salaries.

It is marvellous to see the intense earnestness of
the missionaries. Their work is everything to them.
Home, with its comforts, family ties, intellectual intercourse, and even self-respect, give place to " the work,"
and a man once launched in it, relinquishes all hope of
returning to his country or friends except for a short visit
once in about ten years.

The schools are fairly well attended, but the children
are excessively slow at learning, and it often takes a year
to teach an Armenian child to spell out words of two or
three syllables. The Turks are the best friends the
missionaries have, for they simply leave them alone.
They find that the missionaries do not try to proselytize
among them, and they have not the smallest fear of the
Mussulman voluntarily becoming a Christian. To do so
would be to recede, and it would be as likely for a Turk
to become a Christian as for an Englishman to worship
a fetish, with this addition, the Turk would become an
outcast from his nation, and utterly lose all social standing, in fact, be something worse than a giaour. This
being so, the Mussulman leaves the missionaries alone,
caring as little whether one sect of Christians goes over
to another as he does if a dog leaves one street for another.

No, the real enemies to the mission work are the Christians, and they carry their enmity so far that the missionaries and their wives cannot go out into the streets without being abused in the vilest language, mobbed or stoned, and it is a constant occurrence for these ladies as they pass through the streets to have dirt thrown upon them, or some woman or child spit in their faces. The missionaries literally turn the other cheek to the smiter, and so low and mean are these Armenian creatures that they derive rare sport from their doing so.

I have said above that the missionaries in their zeal for their work even lay aside self-respect, and I think I am justified in saying so, for a man such as our host, Mr. Staver, must have lost much of his before he could patiently submit to seeing his pretty refined young wife subjected to such indignities. In 1873 and 1874 Asia Minor was suffering from a famine. The missionaries then came to the fore as no one else did, and early and late worked like slaves, relieving distress and distributing to all who required it the help sent out by England and Scotland. I asked, " After that, did not the people treat you better ? " And the answer was, " Not one jot; gratitude is unknown. When a man says ' thank you,' it is for favours to come. Another famine is not expected, so they think it useless to say ' thank you ' for past help."

Now, I may be wrong, but I cannot help feeling that these men, with their great determination and powers of self-sacrifice, are being thrown away. It is like a man with a rich farm of a thousand acres neglecting to cultivate nine hundred and ninety-nine because one acre is a barren rock, and devoting all his time, brains, and money to making that one acre bear a miserable stunted vegetation. The sower who went out to sow the seed did not *purposely* throw a portion amongst thorns and briars, or in stony places. Are not these people doing so? I sadly fear the missionaries lend the cloak of religion to these Armenians, who accept it to hide their swindling, lying, cheating, and other mean vices, and also because they think, and truly, that they may get a little protection from the missionaries, and through them sometimes have justice done them.

During our stay at Talas we received many invitations to visit Kaisarieh "just to show ourselves"; but remembering the "brothers" we had already seen there, and also the way they had stared at us, we refused to be exhibited. We had, however, the honour one evening in Talas of meeting the native Armenian pastor, "an honourable man," which means, in the language of Kaisarieh, a man of some social standing. We were evidently expected to be greatly impressed by him, and I do hope we succeeded in showing a sufficient amount of intelligent interest, though I cannot say either his appearance or manners were very prepossessing. He was a short, dark man, with bushy whiskers and beard that were pushed forward in a fringe in front of his face by high though somewhat flabby stand-up collars; his dress was a parody on that of an English clergyman, and would have looked better had his white choker been tied under his chin instead of his left ear, and moreover if collar and said choker had not been separate from the unstarched shirt, showing about an inch of throat between them each time he looked up. He told us he had visited Scotland for the purpose of collecting money for a church, and had been very successful there, obtaining sufficient, not only to build a church, but also a house for himself. He abused the Turks a little, but he abused the Catholic and other Armenians very much more, rolling his eyes in a terrible manner when expressing his opinion that they all required severe chastisement. Altogether his conversation did not make any lasting impression on us beyond a general conviction that if the Turks were removed out of the way for a short time, the three denominations of Christians would cut each others' throats. I am not quite sure that it is not to be desired that the Turks were removed!

We accepted one other invitation while at Talas, to the house of a rich Armenian merchant who lived near. It was for a *feed*, but as it was too late for breakfast, too early for dinner, and too heavy for lunch, I have a difficulty in giving it a name. Here we had repeated what we had already heard again and again, the long, and I fear sadly true story of Turkish misrule, injustice, and corruption, finishing with the usual question, when were the English coming, and were we the forerunners of those who would be in authority when that happy time arrived? One intelligent creature, with a considerable exhibition of temper, stated his opinion that we as a nation were disgracing ourselves. "You are," he said, "notoriously the richest people in the world, therefore,

if you do not come to govern us as you ought, you are at
least bound to assist us Christians by spending, say twenty
or thirty millions in making roads, railways, bridges, and
other useful public works." It is curious how liberal
people in Asia Minor are with other people's money!
Our Armenian boy, whom we had engaged ten days before
at Angora for three liras a month, and who had already
received five liras in advance, and a suit of clothes, came
to us here at Kaisarieh, saying, "Tchellaby, give me three
liras, I require them!" Probably he had never in his life
before seen three liras altogether, but he spoke quite like
a Rothschild, and his astonishment when he found we were
not good for any amount he might choose to ask for was
most comical.

But to return to our "feed." It was hospitality bordering on brutality. We sat squeezed tightly together at a
round table, six of us, the table crowded with plates,
dishes, glasses, etc. Dinner was served à la Russe and
consisted of twelve courses. I noted them down as they
were served, and here they are: 1, cream with honey;
2, soup; 3, mutton chops and sliced potatoes; 4, a thick
flat flaky pastry, saturated with melted sugar; 5, a large
freshwater fish covered with oil; 6, another thick slab of
pastry with cheese in the middle of it; 7, a mixture of
chopped meat and vegetables; 8, rice-flour pastry, very
sweet; 9, some small cucumbers stuffed with meat; 10,
roast chicken; 11, more chopped meat and vegetables;
12, pilau. We had besides, as dessert, apples, pears, sweet
melons, water-melons, and grapes.

CHAPTER XV.

Products of the district of Kaisarieh—Roads—Good-bye to Talas—
Mount Argæus—Visiting a kaimakam—Armenian agriculturists
—Lahore sheiks—A revolutionary leader—In the Taurus.

THOUGH the actual town of Kaisarieh is, as I have said, a miserable tumble-down place, the large vale in which it is situated is rich and productive, growing wheat, barley, rice, and cotton; while the slopes of the hills are covered with vineyards and thickly planted with fruit-trees, such as plum, apple, quince, and almond. Nearly all the fruits of the soil are consumed in the town and neighbouring villages, export being almost an impossibility, as Kaisarieh is some two hundred miles from Samsoon, the nearest port on the Black Sea, and one hundred and sixty miles from Mersin on the Mediterranean. High mountains have to be passed in both directions, and the roads are mere mule tracks. Since the days when the Turks first overran the country, no road has been made or repaired in these parts, and hardly a vestige of the fine roads inherited from their predecessors now remains.

Cotton, being light, is the chief article of export, and it finds its way to Mersin, and the camels that carry it to the sea return laden with groceries, Manchester and Swiss cottons, American mineral oil, and a few other

luxuries. The corn grown in the district is exactly calcu-
lated for the yearly wants of the tithe-collector and
villages, and should a bad harvest come, which does
happen every now and then, the people simply starve,
having no store in hand to carry them over the bad time.
Owing to the excessive dryness of the climate, macadamized roads are not greatly needed during eight months
of the year—the existing track would serve even for
wheeled carriages, if only a few small bridges were made
over brooks, a few swampy spots filled up, the road
widened in the passes over the hills, and some rocks and
boulders removed. The whole road over which we had
passed might be made excellent for carriages all through
the summer at a very trifling expense, perhaps about
£2000, and I do not think it would cost much more to
put the road between Kaisarieh and Mersin in the same
condition; but then, money is money in Turkey, and
every penny that can be collected is required by those in
authority and finds its way to Stamboul.

Besides, the inhabitants are not sufficiently civilized to
feel the want of carriage communication. Their fathers
rode on horseback and carried their goods on pack-
animals, and what was good enough for the father is
good enough for the son. They know that if they could
export their corn at a profit they would grow more, and
so would have a supply when a year's crop failed; but
the periodical famines are one of the things they are
accustomed to, and so they are content to bear with it;
besides, a man must die some day.

Between the town of Kaisarieh and the neighbouring village of Talas there is a mountain torrent that cuts the road, and often in winter and spring makes communication between the two places impossible; yet it never strikes the people to bridge it over. Often we came upon villages that were shut off from the main track by a muddy brook only a few yards wide, that had to be forded with great difficulty each time a man quits the village, and which might easily be made fordable by casting in some of the loose stones that are close at hand; but it is no one's business, and it is always pleasanter to the Asiatic mind to squat hour after hour behind a wall, than to work in any way.

All over the plains of Asia Minor bullock-carts are used, two-wheeled affairs something like the old Roman chariots, the wheels, which are discs, being fastened to the axle, so that the axle has to revolve with the wheels, instead of the wheel revolving on it; but these carts are only used in their respective villages, the roads near being quite sure to have some grip or hole in them that makes them impassable for anything but horses and other pack animals. There are no forests within two days of Kaisarieh, and for fuel the people use dried manure, and the before-mentioned hedgehog-like plant of the gum tragacanth. I am not likely to forget this latter fact, for once while standing talking in the streets in Talas, a small donkey buried in its load of this prickly fuel came upon me from behind, and gave me a brushing that reminded me strongly of the days when I suffered from the twigs of the birch.

When we first arrived at Talas we had intended continuing our eastward journey to Albistan, but hearing there were two revolutions going on in that direction, and not being desirous of being robbed or murdered, we altered our plans and determined to turn south, so as to cross the Taurus by the old historic road through the Cilician Gates, and descend into the rich plains of Adana.

So comfortable had we been, and so kindly had we been treated by our good friends at Talas, that it was with great reluctance we gave orders for all to be in readiness for a start on the morning of November 2nd. We had by this time learnt quite to dread the start from any place where we had stopped more than one night. No matter how early we ordered the horses, or how carefully we had arranged everything over night, we never could after a long halt get away in good time, and on this occasion our departure was delayed well into the morning. The two zaptiehs we had ordered to be in readiness never appeared, and as we were told the road swarmed with robbers, we thought it just as well to take a guide who could protect us. Mr. Staver had just had £70 worth of goods carried off whilst on the way from Samsoon. Disbanded, destitute soldiers swarmed all over the country, and the hills were full of men who had taken refuge in them to escape the conscription.

At last an old Turk, whose son was the leader of a gang of robbers belonging to the latter class, offered to show us the way; so, judging that his paternal authority would be sufficient to protect us from his son's gang, we

engaged him. An hour was wasted while he was gone to
borrow a horse, but at last we wished our friends good-
bye and started away round the Allah Dagh, over a plain
that lay between that and the big mountains, and then,
after an hour's ride, we entered a narrow valley that led
up in the direction of Mount Argæus. Up and up we
went, on a track only a few feet wide, often with a
precipice on our right, and great overhanging crags on our
left. Now and then we caught a glimpse of the Taurus
in the distance, through ravines and valleys that joined
ours at right angles.

Four hours' ride took us out of the gorge, and then
opened out before us a wide expanse of moorland, bounded
on our right by Mount Argæus, and on the left by a
lower range of hills. Climbing up these last for two
hours more (thus making six hours in all from Talas), we
reached the watershed, and as we were then only some
thousand feet below the snow, we must have been over
nine thousand feet above the sea. After this the road
descended steeply, and in three hours more we were safely
over the mountain and out on a plain. Nowhere could
the scenery we had passed through be called pretty or
even grand, at least those acquainted with the Alps
would not think so; for even Mount Argæus, with its
thirteen thousand feet of elevation, is a quiet, unassuming
old fellow with smooth slopes and rounded sides. He
looks as if he had originally been a monster volcano with
a huge crater on his summit, the east rim of which has
been carried away by the melting of the snow, leaving

the top of the mountain in the shape of a shell or saucer standing on end. Our friends the Stavers told us they had ascended this mountain by the edge of the saucer, experiencing little difficulty until within two hundred feet of the top, when it became precipitous, and not being accustomed to mountain-climbing, and having no hatchets, rope-ladder, or alpenstocks with them, they gave up the attempt to get to the top. This is not, however, a maiden mountain, previous travellers having, much to the astonishment of the natives, reached the summit without much difficulty.

Just before sunset we arrived at Everin, a small town situated at the edge of a considerable plain, and there, refusing the invitation of the governor to become his guests, we pitched our tent in a little garden that was shut in by high walls, and by keeping the door shut, had the luxury of settling down without half the inhabitants gaping at us. "A cat may look at a king," and "Hard words break no bones," but I confess the being treated as a dancing bear at a fair is by our village boors at home, makes my toes itch; so does the being called "Giaour" by Turks, and "Protestant" by Armenians, knowing as I do that these names are considered by them as the worst and most insulting in all the language.

While the tent was being struck in the morning, we paid a visit to the governor, who we found in filthy clothes, sitting on a dirty divan in a dirty room. He pretended to be much hurt at our preferring our tent to his house, and explained that he was quite up to the ways

M

of Europeans, having been kaimakam of some place near
Philippopolis, where he had seen no end of Europeans,
among others Mr. Blunt, who was consul there, and Mrs.
Blunt, who, he told us, was "a very good lady, nearly as
good as a man." The fact of the padishah having lost the
greater part of his European possessions seemed to affect
him little. "What does it matter, there is plenty left
here?" But what he *did* care for was having, through the
depreciation of the paper currency, his salary reduced to
a quarter of its nominal value. We did not feel for him
much, as he looked as if he could take good care of himself, and we had no doubt he would make all square by
screwing the difference out of his people. He sent a lot
of zaptiehs to escort us out of the town as a guard of
honour, and he told the two who were to go through with
us to Adana to inquire in each village they passed whether
the roads were clear of robbers, and if there were any
doubt about this, they were to take a guard of twenty
men, well armed, from village to village, and finished by
saying, "Please God, you will see no robbers," a prayer we
readily said "Amen" to.

Two hours from Everin, we came upon the first Armenian village we had yet seen. Up to this time all the
Armenians we had met with lived in towns, but here they
were tillers of the soil. The village was placed out in the
middle of the plain, which was here nearly a swamp, the
water being obtainable only a few inches below the surface even after the long dry summer. In winter and wet
weather it must be under water; but in spite of these

drawbacks no one could have passed the village without
noticing how much superior it was to any belonging to
the Turks. The houses, built of mud bricks, were larger,
higher, better thatched, and had more outhouses, stables,
etc., round them, and for the first time we here saw
quantities of hay stacked ready for winter.

The whole population turned out to have a look at us,
and a more miserable fever-stricken set I never saw; but
they were civil and obliging, and volunteered to send a
lad on with us to show us the way across the remainder
of the plain, an offer we fortunately accepted, as our
onward road lay through boggy swamps and innumerable
stagnant ditches that would have been impassable without some one who knew the best tracks. As it was, it
was more by good luck than management that we got
through without being bogged. At each muddy hole the
pack-horses made a fight to have a roll, and had to be
whacked to keep them up, and when this was done they
rushed forward floundering and staggering about, their
feet sinking deeper and deeper the faster they went, so
that by the time we got to the hills, both the horses and
their loads were splashed all over with mud that smelt
enough to breed a pestilence.

A ten hours' ride on this day took us to the village of
Dum Daghle, situated in a sheltered valley between considerable hills, where, having refused the headman's kind
offer of the village manure heap to pitch our tent upon,
we retired to a garden in which was a beautiful spring of
icy cold water, and after a good deal of manœuvring we

succeeded in pitching our tent between the stems of a lot of small plum trees and close to the windows of a hovel, in which lived two Indian sheiks from Lahore, holy men, who were much respected and venerated by the villagers for their great powers of sitting up all night, and howling out without any intermission, "Allah, Allah!" for an hour, then after a howl changing it to "Allah, la il Allah!" going on with these or like repetitions till daybreak. These devotions at first kept us awake, but after a time they acted as a lullaby and soothed us to sleep.

The village of Dum Daghle is in the district formerly under the sway of a Deré Bey, whose stronghold was a neighbouring mountain called Kozanli Dagh. Some years ago the descendant of these beys, one Kozanli Achmet, revolted against the Government and gave a lot of trouble. Regular soldiers were sent against him, and his band of Kurdish mountaineers were dispersed. Kozanli Achmet himself accepting a pashalik and a pension as a reward for the trouble he had given the Government. One condition was made, namely, that he should not quit Constantinople, and this he had kept till a few months previous to our visit, when he stole back to his hills, called out his men, and attempted to start as an independent ruler as his ancestors had been.

Various reasons were assigned for Kozanli Achmet's having done this. One, that receiving his pension in paper, it was not worth behaving well for. Another, that he was jealous of the Bulgars, Russians, and English, all getting territory out of Turkey's late troubles, while he, a

good Mussulman, got nothing ; and a third was, that the
Government itself had sent him home to make a row to
serve political ends.   Anyhow, whatever the reason may
have been, he appeared at the head of a gang of mountain
gentlemen who, having nothing, could not lose by the
venture, and who, besides, enjoyed murder and rapine as
a tiger does blood.   For a month or so they had a good
time of it, stopping travellers, threatening small unprotected towns, levying blackmail, and generally behaving
in the fine manly way common to ruffians.   At last the
Government sent troops against him, when, like snow
before the sun, his followers melted away, and once more
became honest men, loyal to the padishah, and living in
the paths of virtue, leaving their heroic chieftain destitute
and surrounded by the troops.   Remembering, I suppose,
how he had been rewarded on a previous occasion, he
threw up the sponge and surrendered, hoping, no doubt,
to be further rewarded ; but in this he was disappointed,
for on reaching Constantinople he was first shut up in
prison for awhile, and then exiled to Tunis, where doubtless he will remain till he sees a favourable opportunity
of once more leading his followers to robbery and murder.
He had just surrendered when we arrived in his country,
every one was talking about him, and in each town we
entered we heard a new version of the affair.

Each official who had had anything to do with the
suppression of the revolt shook his head when talking
about it, and said it had been a very grave affair.   From
two thousand to twenty thousand mountaineers had been

in revolt, the number being fixed to suit the fancy of the narrator, who always finished by saying that he and he alone had done all for the suppression of the row and capture of the greatest and most dangerous enemy the country ever had; but he had only done his duty, and looked for no reward. Then those who had had nothing to do with it said the whole thing had been a mere storm in a teapot, magnified by pashas and generals for the sake of getting a greater reward for their energetic conduct, and that really Kozanli Achmet had never had more than five hundred men, and these were almost without arms or ammunition, and never intended to do any fighting. I am inclined to believe these latter, for what they told us as to the number of the insurgents was confirmed by villagers, such as those we saw at Dum Daghle, men who had nothing to gain or lose by telling the truth. Throughout all the rest of our journey there was always a revolution going on in our neighbourbood; but I will take them as they come in their proper districts, only mentioning that the knowledge of there being bands of marauders all over the country lent increased interest and excitement to our long rides.

For the first three hours after leaving Dum Daghle, we passed over high open moorland country, and then entered a valley, down which flowed a considerable stream, which, winding its way through the rocky defiles of the Cilician Taurus, enters the plains of Adana, and finally empties itself into the Mediterranean, a little to the east of Mersin. The scenery now began to be really grand.

The valley, which in no part was more than a mile wide, held a pretty nearly straight course to the eastward, bounded on the right by high, rounded mountains, but on the left by a range called the Allah Dagh, that rose precipitously from the valley, the face of the uninterrupted cliff being in many places four and five hundred feet high, while, above this, again rose a perfect mass of rugged peaks and precipices, many of which appeared quite inaccessible. This lofty range of mountains extended as far as the eye could see. At first they were bare and barren, but, as we got further on, they began to be covered with trees—first small juniper-bushes, then cypresses, and lastly, pines; and, as these were the first trees of any sort, except a few we had passed in gardens, that we had seen since we left the country round Brusa, we welcomed them with delight. Our enjoyment of the scenery was, however, sadly spoilt by a cutting cold wind blowing up the narrow valley as through a funnel, and carrying with it clouds of dust that got into our eyes, mouths, noses, and the pores of our skin, and we were very glad at last to pitch our tent in the garden of a solitary roadside khan, and get under its protection. Later on in the day the wind dropped, and it became quite pleasantly warm, and I think I shall never forget the loveliness of the night, when we went out for a few minutes' stroll before going to bed. Just over the summit of the Allah Dagh appeared the full moon in a sky so clear and free from vapour that it looked like ink, while the mountains, with their caps of snow, the opposite hills, and the valley, were bathed in a soft clear light that made everything as visible as at noontide. The only sound to break the perfect stillness was the rippling of the rapid brook that went dancing away past our tent, winding and twisting like a living belt of silver.

CHAPTER XVI.

A highway to the East—Camping on a housetop—Cilician Gates—
    State of the pass—Sudden change in vegetation—An unwelcome
    visitor—A happy hunting-ground—The grey mare *not* the better
    horse—Plains of Cilicia—Cotton crop.

LONG before daybreak innumerable strings of camels,
mules, and donkeys, began to pass our tent, most of them
returning to the interior with bales of merchandise or
loads of planks and timber, and the valley resounded far
and near with the cries of the drivers and the jingling of
the numberless bells, small and large, that the poor beasts
carry.

We were now on the main route from the Mediterranean to the interior—the road that connects Western
and Eastern Asia, and by which, for centuries past, all
traffic between them has been carried. We were told
that just then an unusual amount of movement was going
on, as winter was approaching, and in these high regions
snow might be looked for at any moment ; therefore all
were hastening to get out of the mountains before the bad
weather should set in. We made a rough calculation the
next day of the number of beasts we passed, and in the
evening amused ourselves by making out the quantity of
goods imported by this road, the result being that we cal-

culated that one train per day, on such a line as the Great
Western or Great Northern, worked for two months,
would carry the year's traffic, even supposing that the
same amount of pack-animals passed with their loads
every day. We afterwards checked this by returns given
us by merchants and others, and found that we were very
near the mark in our reckoning. Were the roads made
sufficiently good for wheeled carriages, the traffic would
doubtless be greatly increased; but even then it would
not amount to anything great, owing to the excessively
thin population and their contentment to live like semi-
savages and dispense with what we of the West consider
as absolute necessaries.

Such as the traffic was, we wished it anywhere but on
our road; for, owing to the narrowness of the track, our
pack-horses were always being shoved off it by long
strings of camels, and it took all our time to prevent
their being jostled over into the river that for the greater
part of the way ran at the foot of an unprotected perpendicular cliff at our side.

By noon on the next day we were fairly into the pine-
forests, and were disappointed to find the trees poor,
stunted, twisted old fellows, hardly ever more than two
feet through at the butt, but all looking ancient and
poverty stricken, as well they might be, for the soil they
grew out of, a loose blue stuff looking like semi-decom-
posed slate, was absolutely barren except for these trees,
not even a blade of grass or a thistle growing upon it,
even in spots where the forests did not encroach.

In the afternoon our river suddenly left us, turning away to the left through a crack in the big wall of mountains, and we, after passing over a few hills, came down upon the direct road that leads from Koniyeh to Adana. Here, also, we hit the line of telegraph posts that leads from Stamboul to the eastward, and we were amused to see three Turkish officials repairing the line by fixing the wire to a tree by means of a big iron spike, which was turned down to hold it!

Every few miles along the road we found khans, nearly all of them new large square blocks with flat roofs, the interior being one big stable, except that in one corner or at the side of the entrance there was a small café that answered also as a sleeping-room for the numerous travellers who stop there nightly. Our road lay through a gorge so narrow that we passed khan after khan without stopping, because there was not sufficient room near them between the steep hills on either side whereon to put up our tent, and finally we had to use the flat roof of one of them as a camping-ground, much to the disgust of the owner, who greatly objected to the tent pegs being driven into the earth roof. The top of a khan offers several advantages; it is clean and dry, and the smell of the disgustingly filthy surroundings is a little diluted before it reaches you; and then, if one has the luck to find a khan the roof of which does not run into a bank at the back, one is in a kind of fort where cattle, dogs, and humans are not for ever falling over the tent-lines. Yes; by choice I prefer the top of a khan to the neighbouring

ground, and far before the interior with its reeking odour
of animal and human, to say nothing of insect-life.

We were up early on the morning of November 6th,
and after continuing to ascend the narrow gorge for an
hour, we came out upon an oval-shaped space some five
miles long by two wide, shut in on all sides by high hills
covered with pine trees, and forming a sort of large basin
with apparently no outlet. After crossing this we passed
between the great stone forts erected by Ibrahim Pasha in
1832, when he and his Egyptians invaded the country,
and which remain to this day in fairly good repair, some
of the guns he abandoned still remaining in the forts,
while all around may be seen big cannon balls that were
too cumbersome to be carried away either by the retreating Egyptians or since by the Turks. We passed between
the two forts, and then turning a little to the left, between
two shoulders of the mountain that overlapping each other
had concealed the exit, we entered a narrow defile and
began quickly to descend, recognizing as we did so the
fact that we were at the celebrated Cilician Gate, a pass
that in the year 333 B.C. was trodden by Alexander and
his army on their march eastward, and in 1097 by
those of the first Crusaders who had survived the slaughter
of such battles as that of Doralæum (Eski-Shehr), and the
devastations of the fever that was then, as it is now, the
scourge of the country. Besides these, wave after wave
of advancing and retreating invaders had flowed along
this road and spread their forces over the open land
beyond. Assyrians, Medes, Scythians, Persians, Romans,

Greeks, Saracens, and Osmanlis, had each poured to and
fro, to say nothing of the innumerable followers of semi-
independent chieftains belonging to each dynasty, who
spent their time raiding either on the rich plains of Adana
or the open uplands of Western Asia.

Through this pass, too, marched Cyrus to attack his
brother Artaxerxes, accompanied by the ten thousand
Greeks made immortal by Zenophon, doubting lest he
should be attacked, "the road being only broad enough
for a single carriage, very steep, and impracticable for an
army to pass if any one opposed them." Such is the
description of the pass as it existed 2279 years ago, but
bad as it was then it is worse now, and unless the road
were repaired Zenophon's single carriage would come to
grief upon it.

The road, which descends rapidly, follows the course of
a torrent, now on this side now on that, crossing it
constantly by high-arched stone bridges which are so
dilapidated that often there is only room for one horse to
pass at a time. In two places the bridges have altogether
given way, and the traveller has to plunge through the
brook midst huge loose boulders, risking a fall and a bath
at every step. Nowhere is the road more than eight feet
wide, and in some places this has been washed away by
the torrent to only a foot or two, and in others stones and
large rocks have rolled down and lodged upon it, making
a climb up the steep face of the hill necessary to pass
them. Nature made it as bad as she could, and has been
at some time assisted by man, who took it into his wise

head to pave the track with round boulders from the
brook as big as the largest cannon ball, over which a goat
might, if not very careful, fall and break its neck. Never
before had I seen such a road, or even dreamt of one like
it, and to ride down was more than my nerves would
stand; so I jumped off and, together with my companions,
trudged the historic way on foot, dragging my poor horse
slipping and stumbling from one stone to another after me.

On each side rose mountains, in places precipitous
and everywhere very steep, while at every few yards
were inaccessible positions which, if occupied by a few
determined men, would make the road below impassable
to an enemy. Bad as the road was, our men, by their
masterful stupidity, added to the difficulties of it. When
a narrow place had to be passed, one or other, in spite of
all remonstrance, was sure to make a rush at the pack-
horses, drive them close together, and then begin to whack
them. Horses that were given to fighting were allowed
to stop and have a kicking-match, where the road was but
a foot or two wide, with unprotected precipices down to
the water below. Where for a bit the road was fairly
good, the animals were allowed to crawl along, but when
we came to places, as we often did, that looked like steep
stone staircases which had had all the steps rummaged
out of place by crowbars, down would come the stick, and
blunder went the horses. It was a wonder we ever
reached the bottom in safety, and a miracle we had not
one or more horses lamed; and I take credit to myself
that on that lonely mountain, in a land where murder is a

cheap luxury, I did not shoot a servant or two. But I
think now that I was right not to do it. One horse did
get pushed down a cliff side some ten feet, but just saved
itself from falling over a precipice twenty feet below by
hanging on to a narrow ledge; two others lost their
shoes, and we all lost our temper.

What with the abominable roads, fighting horses, and
idiotic servants, we had not much leisure to look about
us; but I did notice that on rounding a point the vegetation
entirely changed, or rather fresh vegetation suddenly
appeared, all within a few hundred yards. Figs, vines,
myrtles, bay trees, and evergreen oaks lined the way,
getting thicker and more luxuriant as we descended, till
on the lower hills they became a thick jungle; and here
many other shrubs appeared, conspicuous among which
was the hydrangea that even then, late in the year as it
was, had a few pink flowers left. In two hours' time we
came out upon open rounded hills, and here the road
divided, one to the right leading to Tarsus and Mersin,
the other to the left leading to Adana. We took the
latter, and after continually descending these foot-hills for
three hours, we arrived at a poor little village called Yeni
Keui and pitched our tent. Besides the change in the
vegetation we had become aware of another. We had left
the cool, not to say cold air of early winter behind us on
the mountains, and were once more back at midsummer,
and the clothes we had but the day before been abusing
for not keeping out the cold were now oppressively hot.
We had succeeded in cramming three summers into one.

The first in England, the second at Brusa, and here in the plains of Cilicia the third; the result being that our complexions were irretrievably spoilt, the skin being here actually burnt off our faces, necks, and hands, and if it had not been for our à la Franca clothes we could have passed muster very well as Kurds or Turcomans.

The villagers at Yeni Keui seemed delighted to see us, and did their best to show it by offering us first a fairly good room, then the roof of a house, and lastly a noble dish of sour curds, and as we had not been more than a quarter fed each day since we left Kaisarieh, we accepted the last readily and gratefully. As a further addition to our repast, I started the etna and made some tea; but when, after finishing this operation, I turned round to get the curds, I found, to my intense disgust, a monster toad half-buried in the middle of the dish making faces at me, but evidently enjoying his nice cool quarters, and in no mind to quit them. I ladled him out with a big spoon, and started him on his travels outside the tent; and then, setting fancies aside, we fell to and finished up his bath!

The headman of the village paid us a long visit in the evening, and the accounts he gave us of the game to be found near here made us long for a few days shooting. The country was for miles round a succession of low hills, cut up and intersected by ravines, with patches of scrubby bushes from two to four feet high all over them. In these, according to our friend, were wild boar, fallow deer, wolves, hyenas, leopards, jackals, foxes, and hares;

while on the higher slopes of the mountains, in addition
to most of these animals, red deer, ibex, and lynx, are to
be found. Then, for winged game, there were red-legged
partridges, and franklin, and quail, and I fancy also black
cock, but of this I am not quite sure. The old fellow
pressed us to stop a few days in the village and have some
shooting, promising, if we did, to take us to the mountains
and put us face to face with a stag. We were obliged to
refuse this tempting offer, but the villagers said they
would willingly take in and assist in all ways any English sportsmen we might send out to them; and I have no
doubt any shooting-party that made this village their
head-quarters would be well treated and have great
sport. Yeni Keui is but two days' easy ride from Tarsus,
and but one from Adana, and in the same time, pack-
horses, with tents, food, etc., could reach the village. In
the early autumn there is fever, but after the beginning
of November that is past, and there would be little danger
of getting it.

Then, again, Yeni Keui must be a paradise for an
ornithologist or a botanist. Late in the year as it was,
I saw many flowers quite unknown to me; and I was told
by the American missionaries and others that, in the
spring, the whole country is like a well-tended garden
covered by innumerable bright-coloured flowers. I shall
not, however, myself touch upon either ornithology or
botany in these pages, but leave that task to my good
friend Mr. Henry Elwes, who, from his knowledge of the
country and his deep study of these subjects, is so well

N

qualified to give a correct description of all that is known
of both throughout the districts I visited. Two chapters
emanating from his pen will be found at the end of this
volume, which, I venture to assure the reader, are better
worth reading than all the rest of the book.

Soon after leaving Yeni Keui, on the morning of the
7th, we overtook a quaint family party travelling in the
same direction as ourselves. It consisted of a newly
appointed kaimakam on his way to take up his residence.
First and foremost rode the great man, a fat, soft, white-
faced, unhealthy-looking individual on an Arab horse
that jogged lightly and gaily along. Then came his
major-domo, an Armenian, on a diminutive jackass, carrying, besides its rider, a bundle of bedding and some dozen
pots and pans. The jackass was followed by a poor, lean,
raw-boned, melancholy-looking grey horse, on which was
perched Mrs. Turk, her saddle consisting of some half-
dozen mattresses tied on the top of the pack, and so arranged that the lady lay upon them in almost a horizontal
position, her two feet, in ragged stockings and heelless
slippers, sticking out and wagging over the horse's ears.
The "grey mare" was not the "better horse." Being
on a journey, the lady had dispensed with a veil, so we
were able to see that she was very fat, very pale, and
very unwholesome-looking, and that at every step of the
horse she shook and vibrated like a huge shape of blanc-
mange. On either side ran a young Turk, to keep the
beds and their fair burden from toppling over, whilst in
the rear of the procession was an old negress, on another

small donkey, riding man-fashion on a high pack-saddle. As we passed, our pack-horses pranced and neighed, the lady screamed, and her attendants as well as ours shouted and yelled, but the great lord and master jogged on in perfect indifference, never once turning his head to see what was the matter.

Early in the afternoon of our sixth day's ride from Kaisarieh, we reached the summit of some low hills, and there directly in front of us we saw the town of Adana, placed on a dead level plain that extended in the direction of the Mediterranean Sea as far as eye could reach, while in all other directions it was only limited by hills and mountains in the far distance. It reminded us of the Cambridgeshire fens, and, like them, was treeless, but unlike them (as we could note from our elevated position) it was only partially cultivated, and had no made roads, and no watercourses, except the rivers Sethoon (Sarus), and Jaihan (Pyramus), both of which rise in the Taurus, the former to the north, not far from the source of the Kizil Irmak, and the latter near Albistan. The two rivers run almost parallel, the one on the west and the other on the east of the large valley, the average distance between them being about forty miles, while the length of the valley, between the sea on the south and the Taurus on the north, is about eighty miles.

A few days later we journeyed over this plain, and found it to be the most fertile part of Asia Minor we had yet seen. With its almost tropical climate and deep rich loam it is most fruitful. Wheat, barley, millet, lentils, cotton, and many other crops are most productive, yielding rich harvests under the simplest and roughest cultivation, the plough and the hoe being the only implements of husbandry used. Then figs, grapes, sugar-cane, oranges, and date-palms grow well, and, were it not for fever, which is always rife in spring, summer, and autumn, and, moreover, if the population had a little more "go" in them and were better governed, all might be a perfect garden—a second Lombardy—and not only support all its own people, but those who live in less-favoured regions among the mountains that surround it on three sides. Cotton alone might be a source of great wealth, even now it is the most paying crop, and its production and preparation constitute the chief industry of the people. It had been a bad year for this, owing to the small amount of rain that had fallen, but the yield of the district was valued at over £160,000, and we were told that in good years this was doubled. A small part is sent into the interior, to towns that cannot produce it, but the greater part is shipped for Marseilles and other European ports. There are several factories in Adana, owned by Armenians and Greeks, where the cotton is separated from the husks, but the same operation goes on in a less extensive way in almost every courtyard in the town.

With the help of the two rivers (Sethoon and Jaihan) almost every inch of the plain might be irrigated, and thus become independent of rain; but we were told that this was not done for fear of fever. This is a lame excuse of the idle, for the fever cannot be worse than it is, every one having it as badly as they can for three parts of the year, a fact made patent to all by the cadaverous, yellow, hollow-eyed faces one sees everywhere. Much has been written and said about the prevalence of fever in Cyprus, and perhaps it may be worth observing, when seeking a cause for this scourge there, that the mouth of the Adana valley opens on the sea just opposite that island, and as the distance across is less than eighty miles, I think the birthplace of the fever may be the mainland, and that it migrates to the island in search of victims.

The gum-tree would grow quickly and well round Adana, but it is hopeless to expect the Turks to plant it, and even if they did the inhabitants would soon destroy it, timber being in great request.

CHAPTER XVII.

Adana—Dearth of news—Scorpions, hornets, etc.—A land of milk and honey—Missis—The Kaimakam—Dying Circassians—Gazelles—Old castles.

ADANA is like all other towns in these parts, no worse (it could not well be that) and no better. A collection of tumble-down dilapidated houses and hovels, dirt heaps for streets, and streets for drains. Each morning, while we were there, a market was held, in which the villagers disposed of their cotton to the merchants, and this was presided over by a government official, who got a percentage on all sold. He was appointed by Government to see the cotton made up into bales, as lately complaints had come from Marseilles that old boots, shoes, sand, and various other commodities were found in the bales that arrived there. The local authorities were glad to get such a piece of patronage, for owing to the fine field for roguery it opened, it was a place much sought after, and the applicants paid well for their appointments.

We had hoped to see a European paper or the *Constantinople Messenger* here, and so learn what the rest of the world was doing, but in this we were disappointed, no one in the town caring to go to the expense of having one sent them. Even the governor-general did not get one, and the only way outside news reached the town was by the word of mouth of some chance traveller.

We were here obliged to put up at a khan, but were fortunate enough to secure a room that was almost all windows, built on the flat roof over the café. Most known insects swarmed in it, and we had an active life day and night; but we reduced our misery somewhat by hanging up our hammocks, and so getting out of the way of all those that had not wings. Having work to do during the daytime that prevented our swinging continually between the floor and the ceiling, we were then at the mercy of all, and were attacked by perfect armies; and though we fought manfully, and the slaughter of the enemy was great, yet we only succeeded in just holding the field. To this hour the thoughts of the battle gives me the creeps. We were told that scorpions were very plentiful, but though we often saw them in other places, we were not troubled by them here, perhaps because our room was high up and dry.

As for hornets, the town from end to end was as thick with them as a pastry cook's shop in England is with flies in the dog days; but they seemed to be a good-tempered lot of fellows that if not interfered with would not sting, though they constantly came buzzing in at the open windows. During all the day there must have been many hundreds flying about the eaves of our room, going in and out under the flat rafters, and every house in the town had its little swarm round it.

Far, far away in the corner of some distant land of the

East there must be a spot that contains all that mortal
can require; if there is not, the people tell stories, for the
traveller, directly he sets foot in Asia, is told, whenever he
asks for a thing, that it is not to be had where he then is,
but will be found a few days eastward, and on asking for
it again at the end of that time he is told he must go yet
further east. Thus at Constantinople we were told that
we should find good servants, good horses, good greyhounds, good sheep, good fowls, good food, and good men
at Brusa. On arriving there, all these good things and
many others were promised us at Angora. From Angora
they were moved on to Kaisarieh, from there to Adana,
and so on, always eastward to the end of our journey,
when we were assured three more days would have taken
us into the promised land. These hopes are held out to
one as the historic thistle was to the donkey to tempt
him on, and I firmly believe are, like the thistle, "only
a plant." Anyhow, we never came up with them.

Before reaching Adana, old Ali Agha would cheer us on
our way by telling us of the milk and honey that flowed
there; but on asking for some sort of food for supper, we
were told that we arrived too late, the shops were shut,
and nothing to be had. The cows would be milked at
night, and the milk sold in the morning, when also meat,
bread, honey, and a dozen other good things could be
bought, all of the best. The morning came, and we awoke
half starving; but on asking for breakfast, we were assured
that though the cows had been milked as promised, the
owners had drunk all the milk. The butchers had not

killed any sheep, the bakers had not baked any bread, and
so there was nothing to be had except a piece of black
bread and a small jar of honey, in which all the bees that
made it had committed suicide by drowning. We kicked
up a row, stormed and threatened, but had to finish by
eating the stale bread, honey, and bees, finding the last,
if not pleasant, at least strong flavoured. All the villages
ahead of us were full of good things, and the padishah
himself would do well to visit Aintab, just to taste the rich
food to be found there.

What with the stupidity of the inhabitants, the badness
of the food, and our poor accommodation, we were not
sorry, after resting our horses three days, to take to the
road again, and thus exchange a dirty hard wooden bench
for the saddle, and our garret for the tent. During our
stay we had collected all the information we could respect-
ing our future route, and finally determined to make straight
for Aintab, thus passing through a part of the country
little travelled over, as proved by Keipert's map, which
represents it as almost entirely one big plain, whereas, as
will be seen, it is nearly all of it mountains.

We left Adana on the morning of November 10th, and
after passing the Sethoon by a good strong bridge at the
edge of the town, we turned eastward over the great flat
plain. G—— and I rode on in front, and after a time, on
looking back, we saw in the distance that something was
wrong with the pack-animals, but supposing it was only
a load shifted, and that they would soon come up, we
went slowly on. An hour passed, and there was no sign

of the horses, so getting off we waited for them under the shade of a bush, and after a while they turned up, and then we learnt that one of the pack-horses, when half an hour out of the town, considered he had gone far enough, so bolted past Ali Agha and Kevok, and never pulled up till he was at the stable door in the khan yard at Adana. Kevok had to ride back after him, and then, having no one to stir up the beast from behind, had dragged him at foot's pace all the way back.

Twenty-five miles from Adana we came upon the river Jaihan, at a place called Messis, that in olden times was a strongly fortified town, as the ruins of massive stone fortresses plainly show, but which we found to be now a dilapidated village without a good house or building in it, but still holding rather an important position, being situated on the main road that leads round the head of the Gulf of Iskenderoom and to Aleppo, etc. Besides, there is here a good stone bridge, the only one over the Jaihan throughout its whole length; and as the river is deep, and averages from thirty to sixty yards in width, all the traffic between the two banks has to pass here. In any other country Messis would, from these circumstances, have maintained its former prosperity, even if the old fortifications had been allowed to disappear; but having for years been the head-quarters of a race of Deré Beys and their Turcoman followers, these gentlemen had, by robbing and murdering travellers and merchants, first forced traffic into different channels, and then, as a consequence, poverty and ruin had followed.

Barker, in "Lares and Penates; or, Cilicia and its
Governors," says that "Missis, anciently called Mopsuestia,
is said to have been founded by Mopsus, a celebrated
prophet, son of Manto and Apollo, during the Trojan war.
It is now (1853) a ruined village, about twenty-five miles
north-east of Adana, and through it flows the Jaihun
(Pyramus). . . . The Pyramus springs from the other side
of Marash, whence it passes winding along the plain to
Sis and Missis, and finishes its course in the Bay of Ayass,
which is opposite Alexandretta."

Having to change zaptiehs here, we rode direct to the
konak, a tumble-down building consisting of two small
rooms, a stable, and a prison, the latter being simply an
open shed with wooden bars in front, through which we
could see some half-dozen unfortunate wretches squatting
on the ground. The place was just like a kennel; and as
the bars were old and rotten, and there was no guard outside, I cannot conceive why the prisoners do not discharge
themselves by breaking a bar and walking off.

On making known our wants to the kaimakam, a
little, bright, active gipsy-looking fellow, he told us we
had come at the right moment, for he was about to start
for Aintab himself. He would at once pack up and be
ready by the time we had drunk our coffee; a promise, it
is needless to say, he did *not* fulfil. But as we could not
with decency refuse his company, we had nothing for it
but to bide his time, whereby we were detained two
hours. First he had a letter to write to the Governor of
Adana, just a few words that a European would have

written while he was directing the envelope, but which occupied him for half an hour. Then he wanted his servant to give him money for the road, and the servant wanted money for the house, till words waxed high, and at last the big man made a forced loan on a chance visitor. Then came the packing or, rather, the bundling up of beds, which took another half hour, then dressing, and his only pair of socks could not be found. The room was searched again and again, the bedding all unpacked, and, finally, a messenger sent to call a friend who lived in the other side of the village, for, as the kaimakam said, "He may have got them on. He was here this morning, and may have fancied them." But no; the friend arrived, his trousers were pulled up, and his feet discovered to be in his boots, minus the socks. Finally the servant took off the pair he was wearing and lent them to his master. Then orders were given to start, but at the last moment the zaptiehs were not forthcoming, and, from what we could gather, it seemed they refused to turn out as they had not been paid for a year.

At last we started unattended, the great man himself being our guide and escort, and as his horse when near ours, pranced and jumped, and if held in ran away and kicked, I am afraid he had not a pleasant time of it. He was very communicative; said he was the last of a long line of Deré Beys who had been independent chieftains in the neighbouring hills. Times were greatly altered for the worse, as owing to the thinness of the population an independent chief could no longer be supported, and so he had had to exchange his hills for the town, and now earned his livelihood as a governor, supplemented by a small pension given by the Government, when they had it to give, in exchange for his lands. He also told us he was first cousin to Kozanli Achmet, and that it was entirely owing to his daring and energy that the would-be chieftain had been captured. All the great men had tried their best to entrap the chief, but had failed; when our friend "just put his foot down and it was done." His harangue, and the way he delivered it, convinced us that it was the report *verbatim* that he had sent to Constantinople, and that by blowing his own trumpet thus loudly he hoped to be rewarded.

Besides the Kozanli Achmet affair, much trouble had been given in the neighbourhood by the Circassians. These gentlemen some year previous had made their old homes in the Balkan peninsular so hot for themselves, that on the Russians crossing the mountains they thought it advisable to decamp. By thousands they flocked into Constantinople, and from there had been shipped off to all parts of Asia Minor. Sixteen thousand had been settled on these plains by the Government, and so fatal had the country proved to them, that it would have been kinder to have sent them back to the Russian lines with halters round their necks. Out of the sixteen thousand there only remained five thousand, and of these there was not one woman to thirty men, not one child to a hundred men! Only the exceptionally strong had survived, and this small remnant were dying off rapidly. The Government had lately consented that these people might leave the fever-steeped plains and migrate to fresh spots on the hills; and as we rode along on this day and the two following, we met parties of them on the tramp. Such objects!— great tall gaunt men dressed in filthy rags, but retaining their silver-mounted pistols and knives, staggering and tottering along in the dust; others, in even a worse plight, were clinging on to a lot of worthless household goods on the top of camels or miserable ponies. Fever was written on the faces of all, but, besides this, hunger had left its terrible mark. "The Government," our Deré Bey told us, "allowed each adult twenty-two ounces of black bread per day, and half this quantity for each child ; but," he added, "they wanted this every day, and often we had not got it to give, so they starved."

From what we saw and what we heard as to the unhealthiness of the plain, we could but suppose these poor savages had been sent there to get rid of them. Anyhow, so awful and overwhelming had been their sufferings, that a Bulgar could not have wished them a worse fate. Long will the Circassians be remembered in the East, and their name reviled for their deeds in Bulgaria; but never again will their name be a *terror*, for, scattered as they are, starving, and incapable of working (as the Tartar emigrant does), and with every man's hand against them, they must soon die out, and when that takes place I do not believe a creature, either Mussulman or Christian, in all Turkey will regret them.

Soon after leaving Missis I saw gazelles for the first

time in my life. Three of them were feeding about a
quarter of a mile from the road, but they were so shy
there was no getting nearer them, for they hurried off in a
jaunty trot the instant I turned my horse's head in their
direction. I afterwards often saw the beautiful little
creatures at various places before we reached Aintab, and
once or twice they were so near I could note their little
curved horns and prettily mottled sides though it was
only for a minute, for directly they saw us they ran off at
a surprising rate, so fast that I doubt the assertion of
the inhabitants that Persian greyhounds could run them
down.

Cultivation may be said to end at Missis, for during the
rest of our journey over the plain we only came upon a
few fields near two or three villages that showed signs
of the plough, though doubtless in the days when such
towns as Missis were large places, the corn that fed the
inhabitants was grown here; besides, in later years there
must have been a considerable rural population, or the
Genoese would not have built fortified trading stations all
over the country. In all directions on the plain there
are small cone-shaped isolated hills, and on the summit of
nearly all there are the ruins of massive stone castles,
which we were told belonged formerly to the Genoese;
but of this I am uncertain, as the Turks and other natives
believe that *every* ruin in the country was the stronghold
of these enterprising people. Besides, we know that ever
since the days of the Turks, independent Deré Beys have
divided these lands, and I think it is likely some of these

old castles may have belonged to them. Anyhow, whoever
they were owned by would not have lived in them if
the country had then been as depopulated as now. The
former would have had no one to trade with, and the
latter no one to plunder.

The kaimakam's horse was so restive and behaved so
badly when near ours, that its rider held it back, allowing
us to get some miles ahead. Thanks to this, we escaped
the nuisance of having him with us all the evening, for
just at sunset, espying a village a quarter of a mile to
the left, we abandoned the direct track and made for it,
our friend the Deré Bey riding on in happy ignorance of
our halt.

CHAPTER XVIII.

Yilan Kalé (Snake Castle)—Nogai Tartars—A Tartar engineer—Good
    shooting and hunting—A Circassian settlement—A Turcoman
    village—Cattle-lifters—A Turcoman wake—Insolent villagers—
    Fever and ague—A Turkish breakfast.

WE pitched our tent in the village of Yilan Kalé (Snake
Castle), belonging to some Nogai Tartars, who settled here
just after the Crimean war. The village took its name
from a castle on a hill close to it, which had been so-
called from the fact that the barren rocks on which it
was built were alive with snakes of the most poisonous
description. It was so late, and we were so tired and
hungry that evening when we arrived, that we did not go
up to the castle, nor had we time to do so in the morning,
as we had to hurry off, having a long day before us. But
even from the village we could see it must have been a
very strong place in days of yore, built as it was on
precipitous crags, with only a narrow ridge by which it
could be approached, the ridge further being protected by
a deep ditch across it, over which there had been a draw-
bridge. The walls appeared perfect, and the villagers
told us it only wanted a roof to make it habitable.

In the evening the villagers sent Ali Agha to request
us to allow them to come and have a talk with us, and

o

we consented to receive three, all our little tent would
hold.   The first was an old man, about the stupidest and
most stolid creature we had seen.   He with some difficulty
informed us that he had been to Mecca, and therefore
was a Hadji, and then he lapsed into an imbecile lump
of humanity, and we concluded the Mecca journey had
proved too much for his brain.   His stupidity was made
up for, however, by the sharpness of his companions, two
quick-witted clever young fellows with whom it was a
pleasure to talk.

Unlike all the other races we had mixed with, they put
straightforward questions, never for a moment beating
about the bush, and answered us in the same frank
manner, and though we quickly discovered that the English
were out of favour for not having helped the Osmanlis in
their late troubles, and for grabbing Cyprus, yet they
were throughout polite and well mannered, unlike many
of the Turks, who when speaking to us on the same
subject had been most rude.   On telling the Tartars that
England, though friendly with many nations, did not consider it her duty to rush into war whenever two of her
friends fell out—as, for instance, when Prussia and France
had a turn up, and that when we were fighting a neighbour,
the Osmanlis did not assist us, they at once owned there
was reason in what we said ; but as regards Cyprus we
did not escape so well, not knowing ourselves why we
had taken the island, or what good we hoped to get
from it.

In spite of this our nation's wickedness, the Tartars,

like all others in Turkey, expressed a hope that we should soon come and govern them ; for, they said, " We have no government of our own, all is bad, and day by day getting worse." On asking them if they expected to get off paying taxes if the English came, or what good they expected, they assured us they quite understood that taxation was necessary, but added, "We want to have Englishmen here that we may see what they do, how they work, how they trade, that we may be able to do the same. Then we want to have some of the wonderful machines you have for tilling the ground ; and, beyond all, we want schools. As it is, we have nothing and cannot improve our condition, and as we are, so must our children be, tillers of the soil and nothing more." They spoke most bitterly of being forced to live out on the great plains, with no towns near enough to trade with, and always suffering from fever.

Whenever we have had the good fortune to fall in with Tartars, we have been struck by their intelligence, and I am convinced, if Europeans ever are their masters or con-duct the government of Asia Minor, the Tartar will be found to be the most helpful and the most capable of improvement of all the races—in fact, the only one with energy, brains, and ambition. Then, they are honest and industrious, that is to say, they seldom or never take to robbery ; and if there is work to be done that will enable them to make money, the Tartar is sure to find it out as quickly as a vulture does carrion.

Soon after leaving Yilan Kalé the next morning, we had

to cross the river by a ferry which belonged to one of the villagers, and had been constructed by him. It was a rough affair, but yet it showed how the Tartar would learn from and imitate Europeans if only he had the chance. The man told us that when he first worked the ferry he did so by using a rope, but finding this soon wore out, he went to Alexandretta and bought a lot of nail-wire rods, and with them had as nearly as he could imitated the wire rope he had seen in the rigging on board the steamer that brought him from the Crimea, and had succeeded in making a rope a hundred and fifty yards long that worked fairly well. We examined it, and though here and there a wire end stuck out and prevented its free run round a revolving bar in the ferry's bow, yet it was strongly and well twisted, the joints of each of the six strands being generally hidden in the centre of the rope. We had at that time intended to return home *viâ* Iscanderoom, and on telling the Tartar this he asked us to inquire if there was any merchant there who would get him a wire rope out from England, saying, " if there is one, write me a line to say how much it would cost, and I will ride to Iscanderoom and pay down the money." Unfortunately, we afterwards altered our plans, and did not go to Iscanderoom, so could not execute the commission of our go-ahead friend.

The Tartars told us that game of all sorts was most plentiful on the plains and in the mountains bordering them, and they, like the villagers at the mouth of the Cilician Gates, offered to do their best for any sportsmen

who would visit their village; they would give them a
house and the best food they had got, and would turn out
all the lads and young men as beaters. I am sure, that
were a party of sportsmen to visit this village in the
winter, they would be well repaid for their trouble, and
though the life would necessarily be rough, yet there
would be no real hardships to put up with. Three days'
ride from Mersin would bring them to it, and then on all
sides game would abound. At every mile of our ride we
saw the fresh routings of wild boars, and these might be
shot or stuck as in India. The plains are good riding, with
here and there a thicket, in which the boars hide during
the day; but as these are low and not thick, the game
might be easily started. There are also in these thickets
fallow deer, and these the natives ride down and spear in
the winter, when owing to the softness of the soil a horse
can overtake them. All the game I mentioned as being
found at Yeni Keui abounds here; but to do any good, it
would be absolutely necessary to take out dogs, as there
are none except the Persian greyhound, which is excellent
for coursing, and the useless masterless street dog.
Pointers, spaniels, and one or two well-trained lurchers
are the dogs I should prefer, and if one had a few couples
of active harriers or fox hounds grand sport might be had
with them. The ponies of the country would, I fancy,
answer all purposes, but if they should not be fast
enough for pig-sticking, good Arab horses can be bought,
costing about £25 each. A tent should be taken, and
also a large provision of ships' biscuits, preserves, sugar,

tea, etc. As for meat, the guns would provide that in abundance.

Half an hour's ride after crossing the river by the old Tartar's ferry, brought us to a village—a place that had been intended for the head-quarters of the Circassians had they been able to live there. It stands on the left bank of the river Jaihan, only a few feet above the water, and the greater part of the houses were in ruins, although the rafters and beams were still green, their owners, the Circassians, being all either under the sod or on their road to find more healthy quarters.

At the konak in this village we found our friend again, the Bey of Missis, who pretended to be much hurt at our giving him the slip the night before, and exclaimed, " Just see what you have lost by it! Had you come on with me, you might have enjoyed perfect comfort on these divans instead of sleeping in a tent. The kaimakan would have fed you on the best of everything; and, besides, what a talk we might have had." As he spoke, I felt an army of fleas attacking me, and thanked my luck that I had been spared this " perfect comfort." The bey then tried to persuade us to rest for a couple of hours, and then go on with him; but this we declined, as we said, and truly, that we were anxious to get over as much road as we could so as to pass the mountains between us and Aintab while the fine weather lasted.

Leaving the plain on the left, we skirted along at the foot of the hills on our right, and just at sunset arrived at a Tartar village, where we had intended to sleep; but on

seeing the squalid, miserable place, we quickly changed
our minds, determining to risk a night out in the open
rather than spend it there. There was one dilapidated
two-storied stone house, probably once the residence of the
head of a tribe, and around this were a few pits roofed
over, from which, as we rode up, peeped out the heads of
sundry women and children. In front of the stone house
was a small willow tree, beneath which lay a tall, thin
young man, apparently dying, while a friend sat beside
him brushing the swarms of flies from his face. No one
took the least notice of us, and though we succeeded after
a while in hunting up the headman, and in learning from
him that there was a Turcoman village an hour further on,
he refused us a guide, saying that no one in the place was
well enough to travel so far on foot, and there was not a
horse in the village. However, there was fortunately a
pretty good track, and we managed to hit off the village
of Toprak Kalé just before dark.

The Turcomans to whom it belonged had lately arrived
from the high mountains, where they always spend the
summer, on account of the pasture to be found there, and
they were now busy erecting their winter quarters, sowing
a few patches of corn, collecting fuel, and making all snug
That the winters are not very severe may be seen from
the style of the houses, which consist of a reed roof over
an oblong shed, the walls being made of stout reeds
placed in an upright position and laced together top and
bottom, but with the space of an inch between each reed.
The front of the shed is quite open, and the only

furniture consists of a few carpets and some pots and pans. We pitched our tent on a piece of flat ground, just in front of the village, and tethered our horses close to us by head lines, but no sooner had we done so than an old greybeard came to say that they were not safe "Every one in these parts are robbers, and though you should sleep with your eyes open, your horses will all be stolen. I will take them to my house, and be responsible for their safety. It is better for me to do so, for we get into trouble with the kaimakam if every horse that comes to our village disappears, and several have done so lately." We allowed him to take the horses, but I don't think we should have felt much surprised had we found them and their protector gone in the morning. Appearances are deceptive, and we may have misjudged these people, but certainly more villainous looking savages could hardly be found ; and I quite believe, when the old man said " all were robbers," that he included his own neighbours. The villagers were evidently awake to the danger of having their own cattle stolen, for apparently all kept on the move throughout the whole night ; and, besides, there were four or five savage, wolfish-looking dogs to each house that kept running about, howling and barking all night, and making sleep out of the question.

During the night we heard a noise from a house close to us that at first we thought was a woman convulsed with laughter, but as it went on hour after hour without intermission, I at last got up and took a peep out. Some half dozen men sat about at the open end of the house,

smoking and chatting, and paying no heed to the row
going on within; while the moon, which was at the full,
lighted up the entire village, and showed various groups
squatting round, and apparently watching the large herd
of cattle belonging to the village that was collected near.
In the morning, Ali Agha told us that the noise we had
heard was made by a woman whose husband had died in
the night, and that what to us sounded so much like
laughter, was a correct form of wailing.

The only food we could get at this place was the usual
flat cake of half-baked dough, rather more dirty than
usual, very sour, and very tough.   No milk was to be
had, in spite of the large herds of cattle, and chickens
there were none.   Hunger made us turn out early next
morning, and while we were packing up and loading the
horses, the young men of the village, to the number of
about twenty, lounged around, and inspected the operation.   They criticised all we did, sneering and jeering at
everything, besides discussing our personal appearance in
anything but flattering language.   We thought it advisable to take no notice of them, for so insolent was
their behaviour they appeared to court a row, and I think
we were fortunate in getting off without one.

Two hours' ride over what must be in winter the bed
of a lake, brought us to the small town of Osmanié, which
is presided over by a kaimakam, a poor unfortunate who,
unless his plunder is exceptionally rich, must lead the
tristest of lives.   On riding into the courtyard of his
house and sending Ali Agha up to his room with our

firman and a request for a zaptieh, we were invited to
pay him a visit. We found him a bright, intelligent
little fellow, full of local information, civil, and hospitable.
He told us that this town had been the headquarters of
the Circassians, but that the last of them had either died
or emigrated, and that now he was left in peace with the
old inhabitants. "Look there," he said, pointing from
his window, "that will show you what a nice spot this
is!" And close by we saw a piece of ground, about
two acres, dotted thickly over with graves, all so recently
filled that grass and weeds had not begun to grow on
them. We asked how it was that *he* did not die, to which
he replied that he and all the others in the town
migrated each spring to a village on the high mountains
where, though there was fever, it was not of so deadly a
type. "Here," he said, " *all* is bad, except the soil. Air,
water, and food—all are bad. Look at this boy of mine,"
calling up a poor little creature of about seven years of
age. "See what this place has done for him, how swollen
he is round the body, and how shrunk are his limbs! It
is killing him, but what is to be done?" He further
said that the whole district was almost depopulated, only
a few Turcomans living in it during the winter; adding,
"It is a great pity, for there are great riches about here.
On the hills are splendid forests of pine and oak, besides
mines of various kinds, and the soil yields splendid crops.
Go home to England, tell your people how rich it is, so
that they may come and settle, and make us a railroad to
the sea. What does land cost in England?" And on
our telling him that in places such as London it some-

times fetched £1000 an acre, he said, "Well, come here, and you shall have a thousand acres for a pound ! "

Osmanié being close to the eastern slopes of the Kozan Dagh, the kaimakam could give us a lot of information about the late outbreak there; and he confirmed what others had told us of its having been a very tame affair, not more than five hundred armed men having taken part in it. After chatting awhile, we asked permission to continue our journey, but the kaimakam said he could not allow us, as strangers, to leave without breaking our fast, and that some food would be ready in a few minutes. Important as it was for us to push on, we were so intensely hungry we could not refuse his hospitality, and in a few minutes we were enjoying the first real meal we had had since we left Kaisarieh. We ate it à la Turc, squatting round a trencher placed on the floor, and using fingers for forks, but having large wooden spoons provided for the liquid dishes. There were about six courses, all good, but one super-excellent. It consisted of the milk of a cow that had lately had her first calf, and it was as rich and thick as cream, only far more delicious, and into this our host stirred a quantity of highly flavoured honey. On my saying how good I thought it, he pushed the dish to our side and insisted that we should finish it all, a task we willingly performed. As we finished with the dishes, they were sent out to our servants, and I could see, through the open door, Ali Agha and the Armenians eating like wolves, showing thereby that they, like their masters, were about half-starved.

CHAPTER XIX.

Up the Giaour Dagh—A drunken official—Wanton destruction of forests—Where robbers rob—A soldier from Kars—A country gentleman—Fertile plains—Aintab—A superior khan—Armenian college—A generous Osmanli—An obstructive governor—Armenian students—Want of self-respect.

BIDDING farewell to our kind entertainer, we mounted our horses, and passing through the town, which was more than half-deserted, we soon entered the hills, and bearing southwards our road led us by the side of a rapid stream, now following along its banks, now passing over a spur covered with old stunted pine. Now and then, on the summit of some precipitous, craggy hill, we saw the ruins of an old castle, but no inhabited dwelling appeared in sight for hours, and it was quite dark before we reached the village of Baghtche, and the tent had to be put up by candle light. While I was helping to do this, G—— went to call at the konak, but he found the kaimakam had retired to his private residence, and his vikil (lieutenant) reigning in his stead. This gentleman was already a little more than half drunk, but fortunately he proved friendly in his cups, though his friendship proved somewhat embarrassing when he wanted us to put up in his little den of a room, and join him in making a night of it. Excusing himself as best he could, G—— made his escape, but was soon followed by the drunken Osmanli, who settled himself down in our tent as if he meant to spend the night there. He insisted on seeing our firman, which he slowly read, or rather hiccoughed, out; he then crumpled and dirtied it, and finally tore it. After telling us he always respected the orders of the Sultan as given in the firman, he proceeded to abuse him and all in authority, calling them names that it will not do to translate. He said he had only been a civilian a short while, that he had fought through the late war as yuz-bashi (captain), that the Russians might have been all annihilated if it had not been for the stupidity of the generals, and when we said this was doubtful, as the Russians had three soldiers for every one the Turks had, he said, "Well, what of that; can't one Turk thrash three of any other nation?" A piece of swagger I think I have heard used by Englishmen when speaking of themselves and when, unlike this Turk, they had not the excuse of being drunk.

We were at last relieved of his odious presence by his being summoned to attend upon the kaimakam, and he took his departure, saying he would soon return, but when he did so, Ali Agha stopped him outside the tent and told him we were tired, and were about to go to bed. But he kept the fact of his existence before our minds by retiring to his room close by and singing in drunken strains a doleful Turkish ditty till after we had fallen asleep. We saw him again next morning before we started, looking

very woe-begone, for, as he explained to us, "he felt very
poorly as he was very drunk the night before, and was not
yet quite sober!" Neither the man himself nor those
about him, the kaimakam included, appeared to think
there was anything to be ashamed of, all speaking of
his state much as one would of a man with a sick
headache.

The kaimakam came up to us in the morning and
asked to see our passport. We explained that, travelling
as we were with a firman, we did not require one; but
this he denied, and said he was thinking of stopping us
and turning us back, orders having been sent from Constantinople that no one was to be allowed to pass without
a passport. We laughed at him, and asked how he proposed doing this, and he said the plan was to hand us
back, guarded by zaptiehs, from town to town on the road
we had come, thus giving us the chance of revisiting all
the places we had just passed till we reached Constantinople again. I suppose he feared getting into trouble if
he carried out his threat, for he gave us a zaptieh and
sent us forward; but we had not much to thank him for.
The zaptieh was mounted on a poor colt only two years
old, that could not go out of a walk, and proved a heavy
clog to us all the way to Aintab. On leaving Baghtche,
we again followed up the brook—the road narrow and
bad and covered with blocks of stone, and nowhere more
than three or four feet wide, the hills rising abruptly on
both sides of us and covered with stunted pine-trees. We
were assured that a little distance off this road there is

some really fine timber that has been left uncut and undestroyed, as it grows in inaccessible places. Wherever man can without much trouble get at it, as on this road, wholesale destruction takes place. Huge tracks are purposely burnt to allow the villagers to sow a little corn on small portions of the so-cleared ground. At night we saw in the distance long lines of fire where the forest was burning. A villager may not want to clear more than half an acre, but when once the trees and shrubs are well ablaze, they create a breeze which carries the fire forward, clearing thousands of acres that will never be required, and leaving the country barren and desolate-looking, and the rain of the district becomes less and less each year as the trees are swept away. The slope on the western side of the Giaour Dagh, up which we rode from the plains of Osmanié, was gradual, taking us in all about five hours to reach the summit, but when once that was passed, the hills were much more abrupt on the eastern side, and the descent was made in an hour and a half. I believe, however, a workable railroad could be made over this pass by tunnelling the summit, and then descending along the face of the mountains, which is pretty regular; but in this I may be mistaken, for it is most difficult to judge of gradients on a winding road by just riding over it.

Every now and then, during our ride over the mountain, our zaptieh, who was leading the way, would halt, unstring his carbine from his back, and tell us to look out, for we were about to pass "a bad spot," that is to say, where robbers might be expected. Old Ali Agha would bring

his old cap-gun to the fore, and then peeping carefully
behind each rock or bush we would ride on perhaps for
a quarter of a mile, at the end of which distance the
zaptieh would return his carbine with a jerk to his back,
Ali Agha do the same by his gun, and both proceed
making cigarettes and chatting, for "the bad spot" was
passed. And yet perhaps we were riding through a gorge
from behind the great rocks of which a single man might
have kept the whole lot of us at bay without our having
a chance of seeing, much less harming him. The fact is,
"custom" rules the robberies of Turkey just as it does
all else. It had been the "custom" to rob on this crest,
from behind this stone, on crossing this brook, and it
being so established by "custom," nowhere else would
a Turk think of stopping a traveller, and I have no doubt
we were perfectly safe when the zaptieh put his carbine
on his back. The only drawback to our satisfaction in
finding we had safely passed "the bad spot" being that
probably there was another just a little further on. If
we believed half we were told by kaimakans, merchants,
zaptiehs, and peasants, we stood a better chance of being
robbed on this day than on any other we spent in Asia
Minor, the Giaour Dagh having been celebrated for
generations past for a race of men who were fond of their
neighbour's property, and who made it their "custom" to
take all they could from chance travellers, not even ex-
cepting their lives.

The zaptieh who rode with us on this day told us that
he had but lately returned from Erzeroum. He had been

with Muchtar Pasha in the great fight near Kars, had
from that fled to the town, and when the town was taken
by the Russians had retreated to Erzeroum. Like his
chief, the drunkard we saw at Baghtche, he attributed the
defeat of the Turks to the want of good officers, who,
he said, were all either old fools or beardless children.
Muchtar was no soldier himself, and did not know how
to manœuvre his army. Then all the officers, from the
highest in rank, robbed the soldiers of their pay and
rations, till the soldiers were so discontented and disgusted,
that they would not fight as of old, saying, "What did it
matter who is victorious, we cannot be worse off than we
are now?" Our friend had belonged to that deservedly
ill-reputed force, the Bashi-Bazouks, that is to say, an
untrained, self-horsed volunteer, whose object in appearing
in the field was to amass all the portable plunder he could
for his private use. He told us he had lost two horses—
one by a Russian bullet, the other by starvation, the poor
beast only getting the Government allowance of 1¼ lb. of
corn per day, without straw or hay ; and as the country
was covered knee-deep in snow, it could not supplement
its meagre fare by grazing. Altogether, I think the man
had failed to make the campaign a profitable one, and had,
like many others, learnt a lesson that he would not forget
in a hurry as to the folly of fighting for the padishah.

    After descending from the Giaour Dagh, we were about
two hours crossing a plain, and then again began to
mount lofty hills that barred our way in front, the only
name for which that we could discover from the people

was Jerrid, which is also the name of a large Turkish village situated in the midst of them. When half way up these hills we arrived at the house of a Deré Bey, the grandeur of which our zaptieh had been greatly extolling, but which we found to be a small four-roomed stone house, very dilapidated, and with a general out-of-elbows appearance. The owner turned out on our riding up to his door, with, I suppose, the remnant of his clan, two lean young men, very dirty and but half clad, and one small boy. If the house was a disappointment, so was its owner, for instead of the noble chieftain, half soldier, half robber, and wholly ruffian that we had expected to see, he was a fat, phlegmatic, middle-aged, muddle-headed fellow, in no way distinguishable from an ordinary peasant.

Ali Agha and the zaptieh made a great fight of it to induce us to make this the end of our day's journey, but as it was doubtful whether we should reach Aintab the next day if we did not get over more of our road to-day, we insisted on going forward, and in this the bey backed us, assuring us that the village of Jerrid was only an hour and a half further on, where we should be treated like princes. He did, however, invite us to stop with him, but seemed greatly relieved when we wished him good-bye and rode on. Jerrid proved to be a good three hours distant, and we did not reach it till after dark, but it was a comfort to feel we had made Aintab within easy reach for the morrow.

Throughout the whole day we had seen only one small village on the Giaour Dagh, and an encampment of Turco-

mans on the plain. Not one acre in a thousand had been
cultivated, and yet much of the land was rich and fertile,
and it struck us as strange that the people of Jerrid
should prefer living on the top of an almost barren soil-
less mountain, when such much better land might be had
close by. But on mentioning this to the villagers, they
said they lived on the hills so as to be out of the way of
the Turcomans, who during the winter made the plains
their headquarters, and who would steal every head of
cattle they possessed if the village were not so inaccessible. We were begged to see the great pashas on our
return to Constantinople, and tell them that during the
past year the Turcomans had lifted just a quarter of all
the cattle belonging to the village, and that the people
dare not resist even when the cattle were driven off in
broad daylight; for if they did, they were sure to have a
spear or a ball sent through them, and all their remaining
cattle taken. These villagers were Turks, but were so
harassed by their more pugnacious neighbours that all
their usual bounce was gone, and they were more like the
poor cringing Armenians than the lords of the soil as
found in more favoured spots.

Continuing our journey the next morning over the
uplands of these hills, which were all the way one great
jumble of rocks and stones, destitute of trees and almost
of earth, we reached, after three hours, the edge of a
hill that descended abruptly to a tract of country that
extended eastwards to the horizon, and which from our
elevated position looked almost level, but on reaching

it we found it to consist of wave after wave of rounded
hills, the summits stony and barren, but the vales and
slopes composed of a rich red earth, producing good crops
when cultivated, and covered with a fair amount of vegetation everywhere. Even the Turks have appreciated this
fruitful land, for we saw considerable villages dotted
about in all directions, and surrounded by vineyards and
gardens, the valleys cultivated, and the sides of the hills
affording pasturage to large flocks of sheep and herds of
cattle.

In the distance to our left, the zaptieh pointed out a
thick veil of mist that floated in the still morning air, and
told us that it covered Aintab, our destination on this
stage of our journey, at the sight of which we all, men and
horses too, brightened up, and after jogging along for four
hours we reached the town, and established ourselves in
the best khan the place afforded. Aintab stands well out
on the plain on low ground, and is thirty-six miles from
the Euphrates, and a long day's ride from Aleppo. It is
the capital of a great corn-growing district. All round
the town the hills are composed of a fine-grained, soft
limestone, that is easily dressed, so easily that even the
Turks make use of it—and the houses are built of square
blocks, giving to the whole town a substantial clean
appearance, far more civilized than any town we had yet
seen. Immense vineyards extend for miles down the
valley, the grapes from which, when pressed into a sort of
cake or dried whole in the sun, form the chief food of the
inhabitants.

Our khan was on the usual pattern, a square courtyard surrounded by stables with a lot of rooms over them, with a rickety wooden balcony in front, facing into the square which is entered by a narrow gateway that can be closed at night. In the centre was a large stone basin of water, and around the accumulated filth of years. Our room was about fifteen feet long by nine wide, an unglazed window with a grating over it at one end, and a shaky door at the other, while the ceiling was a solid stone arch,—the whole being rather like the dry arch of a railway bridge, and about as comfortable to live in.

Ali Agha, directly he had unloaded the horses, went to market, quickly returning with some pieces of meat an inch square spitted on a thin stick, on which they had been a little roasted and a good deal burnt over a charcoal fire; besides these, he brought us bread and grapes, so we fared well and congratulated ourselves on lighting on so rich, not to say luxurious, a place.

As we were riding into the town we passed on our right a really fine block of buildings standing on the summit of a low hill, which we at first thought must be barracks, but on inquiry we learnt it was a college for young Armenians, that had been erected and started by the American missionaries, after the plan of the Robert College at Constantinople. Besides the building itself, there was a good European-looking house near for Dr. Trowbridge the principal, both houses standing in some twenty or thirty acres of ground surrounded by high stone walls, the entrance to which was through a gateway with a lodge over it. All the buildings were good and substantial, being built of the soft stone quarried close by, but at the same time were simple and businesslike. The money necessary for them had been collected in America and England, and expended, I should say, most judiciously by Dr. Trowbridge, who had conceived and carried out the whole thing.

When Aintab was chosen as the fittest place for this establishment, Dr. Trowbridge paid a visit to the town to select a site, and at once fixed upon the present one as the most desirable; but he had little hopes of obtaining it, as the land was cultivated and belonged to a Turk of the old school, who would not be likely to smooth the path for the improvement of such Giaours as Armenians. Doctor Trowbridge, however, called on him, explained his plans, stated his wants, and finally asked if he would sell the coveted site. The old Turk listened attentively without saying a word, but when Dr. Trowbridge had finished, he chucked up his head, gave a click of his tongue and said, "No, I won't sell." But then, to the intense surprise of Dr. Trowbridge, he went on to say, "As you, a stranger, are doing all this for the improvement of the people, gaining and hoping to gain nothing for yourself by it, I should be doing a shameful thing if I took money from you. No, I will not sell; but I will give you the site for nothing, and may your work prosper." The old fellow was as good as his word, and quickly had the proper deeds of transfer made out. It was a noble, liberal-minded thing to do; just one of those flashes of generosity that

every now and then the Turk exhibits, and which has
made him a favourite with those Europeans who, being
generous themselves, remember such acts as this, but
refuse to hear, or if they do hear at once forget, anything
that shows the dark side of his character. Such occur-
rences are I fear very rare, and far oftener one hears of
such mean, small-minded acts as the following. Dr.
Trowbridge, having secured the land, set to work through
his ambassador, backed I believe by ours, to procure a
firman allowing him to build. Months were wasted before
this could be obtained, but at last it arrived, when at once
the building was pushed forward and soon was sufficiently
advanced to receive students, who were clamouring to
be admitted. Then came another hitch. The governor,
hearing the college was about to start work, rode up,
attended by a lot of zaptiehs, closed the doors, and affixed
his seal on them, saying, "It is true you have a firman
to build, but it says nothing about opening, and opened
the college shall not be if I can help it." The affair had
to be referred to Constantinople, and a month was wasted
before Dr. Trowbridge was authorized to break the seal
and start to work. We were shown the seal, with string
attached to it, and I hope Dr. Trowbridge will adopt our
suggestion and deposit it in the museum he has opened,
as a specimen of Turkish obstruction to anything that is
for the improvement of the people.

Dr. Trowbridge, in addition to being president and
managing the finances, etc., lectures in the college, reads
prayers to those of the students who wish to attend, and

works as a missionary in the town. There is besides another American missionary who assists him, and under these is an Armenian head-master, who was trained in America, and several native assistants. A young Armenian doctor, who was educated in America and who practises in Aintab, takes medical classes in the college and instructs the students in chemistry, using a capital laboratory there is in the college for this purpose. In connection with the college a hospital has been built, or nearly built, nearer the town; but for want of funds this has not yet been completed.

At the time of our visit to Aintab there were about seventy students living in the college, ranging from the age of fourteen to twenty, and others attended the classes from their lodgings in the town. The internal fittings of the college were not finished; when they are, three times this number will be entered on the books, applications for admittance coming in fast from all directions. Each scholar pays £9 yearly, finds his own bedding, and caters for himself; black bread, cheese, grapes, and perhaps a water melon, being his ordinary fare. Some few youths, whose friends cannot afford to pay the £9, are admitted at a lower rate, but are obliged to make up the difference by working in the grounds during play hours at a fixed rate of wages, and we saw gangs of these quarrying stone, levelling in holes, and making themselves generally useful, apparently quite as jolly and happy as their richer companions who were lounging about, or playing a sort of rounders, or the newly imported game of croquet, which

latter seemed to have found great favour in the minds of
the somewhat effeminate youths. Dr. Trowbridge assured
us that the students were mostly steady, industrious, and
anxious to acquire information, but from what I gathered
here and in other places I do not think the Armenians
are a clever race, and they are so satisfied with themselves
directly they know a little, that they cannot resist trying
to turn it to profit, and therefore leave their colleges when
too young and only half educated.

My readers must not picture to themselves a lot of
lads such as.form the students in European schools and
colleges. The Armenians, in appearance, are totally
different, and the difference unluckily all against them.
Their usual dress is a sort of long, wadded, cotton dressing-
gown, slit up at the sides so as to make it form an apron
behind and before, old baggy-kneed trowsers, very short
and very dirty, a fez, or oftener a bare shaggy uncombed
head, and to finish all, feet thrust into slippers the heels
of which are nowhere. I have said this is the *usual* dress,
but even among these lads one now and then sees a
dandy who has taken special pains with his costume and
evidently believes it to be quite correct. I have one of
these strongly impressed on my memory—a youth of
nineteen or twenty, short in the leg, long in the back,
and very long in the neck; head, covered with thick
black hair some three inches long, which is so stiff it all
stands straight up on end, minus a parting and sadly in
want of hair wash; complexion lead coloured, features
thick and coarse, mouth invariably gaping open, with lips,

upper and lower, well turned back, hands, face, and neck very dirty, finger-nails long, black, and ghoulish; clothes, an old threadbare frock coat, a low open waistcoat, shabby black cloth trowsers, elastic-sided boots, minus the elastic, but with a fringe of black threads where it should have been, heels well trodden over, a linen shirt almost black and quite unstarched, with glass studs, no shirt collar or neck handkerchief.   Voila tout!

Judging from the appearances of these youths there is one lesson either not taught at the college, or, if taught, not attended to.   I mean "self-respect;" and so long as this is neglected, so long will the Armenians remain the "poor creatures" they are.

I cannot believe in there being much good of any sort in men who are content to go about in *petticoats*, their heads unkempt and their faces dirty, and I am convinced there is a lot of bad in a creature that wears constantly slippers trodden down at the heel.

CHAPTER XX.

American hospitality—Missionary labours—A bishop of the English
Church—Hadji Mary—Intruders—Familiarity breeds contempt—
Rapid change of governors—A letter on Turkey.

ON waking on the morning after our arrival at Aintab, we
received a letter from Dr. Trowbridge, asking us to take
up our quarters at his house; and therefore, after a morning spent in riding about the town and chatting with
sundry Turks and others, we packed up a few necessaries
and rode out to the college, leaving the servants at the
khan.   It was specially kind of Dr. Trowbridge thus to
take pity on us, for not only was he very busy, but Mrs.
Trowbridge was ill in bed, and they already had two
guests staying with them, Dr. and Mrs. Riggs (the father
and mother of Mrs. Trowbridge).   We thoroughly appreciated his hospitality, for not only was the change from
our bare dismal dirty room to his comfortable well-
furnished house inexpressibly pleasant, but in Dr. Trowbridge and Dr. Riggs we enjoyed the society of men
thoroughly acquainted with the East and its people, and
besides, both highly educated and exceptionally clever.
Dr. Trowbridge had spent many years in Turkey working
in different parts as a missionary; but long as he had
lived in the country he was, as it were, a new comer when

compared with Dr. Riggs. As a young man Dr. Riggs had devoted his life to the work, and if not actually the first American missionary who had visited Turkey, he was nearly so. The best years of his life had been spent in out of the way towns in various parts, and during this time he had made himself perfectly acquainted with Turkish, Armenian, Greek, and other languages; a knowledge he had utilized by translating the Bible into the two first.

Like all the missionaries we saw in Asia Minor, our friends here had perfect faith in their labours producing an abundant harvest, and indeed said they had already done so; but at the same time they were not blind to the shortcomings of their flock, nor shrank from owning how often they had been disappointed. Both had great hope for the good that the college and the education it affords would do, and in this hope I share, as I believe without education the Armenian is incapable of learning or appreciating the doctrines of the religion taught them.

While we were staying at the college we had numerous visitors from the town—both Turks and Christians, and among the latter we were vastly surprised to find a man calling himself a bishop of the Established Church of England! Bishop " Migherditch Shahanyan," for I believe he *is* a bishop, was a sturdy, active, middle-aged man, by birth an Armenian, and at one time a bishop of that church. Convinced of its errors, he had seceded and become a Protestant, and his title to be considered a bishop of the Established Church had been, he said, acknowledged by Bishop Gobat of Jerusalem, who he looked up to as his spiritual chief. He told us he had gathered together a few followers in Aintab, and in this he was corroborated by Dr. Trowbridge.

A short time previous he had been to England, where, besides picking up the language fairly well, he had induced some one to give him, I think it was, £1000 with which to build a church. The money was entrusted to some Englishman who was to hand it over to the bishop in instalments as the building operations proceeded. The English consul at Aleppo had laid the foundation-stone with all proper pomp, and the walls had been run up till £400 had been expended. One instalment of £200 had been handed over, but not one penny more had the poor bishop been able to obtain; and now his life was made a burden to him by the builder incessantly dunning him for the remaining £200, and from what he told us there seemed a very good chance of his being locked up as a defaulter. He said he had written to Bishop Gobat, and he showed us letters from him expressing his sorrow, but at the same time his inability to recover the missing money. It did not appear that the loss had ever been communicated to the *donor*, who perhaps is picturing to himself a pretty little church built through his generosity. If so, he may be astonished to find some day that little beyond the foundations are finished, and that his money has gone astray no one knows where!

The bishop asked us to dine with him, but an attack of fever prevented my accepting his invitation, as I should have much liked to have done. G——, however, went, and enjoyed an excellent dinner, served after the Armenian fashion; but the bishop's wife sat down to table, and entered into the conversation like a European lady, whereas in all ordinary Armenian families the wife never appears, but in some back region prepares the dinner of her lord and master, and superintends the servants, herself being little better than one of them. This lady had performed the pilgrimage to Jerusalem and visited the holy places, and was, therefore, addressed by the bishop and his friends as " Hadji Mary " (Pilgrim Mary). As she was very handsome and agreeable, the bishop had, in seceding from his old church, been a gainer in all ways, for in it, though priests are allowed to marry, only celibates are ever made bishops, and further, he was blessed with a son, who G—— reported to be the most beautiful child he had ever seen.

One morning after breakfast we were standing on the doorstep talking to our host, when up walked two respectable middle-aged Turks who, without taking the smallest notice of any of us, quietly entered the house, and after peering about the passages below, commenced ascending the stairs. Dr. Trowbridge most politely asked if they wanted the house-master or if he could serve them in any way. They said no, they required nothing, as they had only come " to look about," and then continued to mount up. The doctor followed and accompanied them into every room, after which they took their departure, without a word of apology for their intrusion or thanks for his civility. The fact is, it never struck them they were intruding. They looked upon a Giaour and his house much as we do upon a horse and his stable, and it no more enters their head to ask permission of the man than we should of the horse. The way the horse shows its displeasure at being stared at is by using its heels, and the only way of teaching the Turk that he is offending is by the use of a toe; and I must say I longed to give them a lesson. Not so, however, Dr. Trowbridge; he took it most good-temperedly, and on our expressing wonder at this said, " Oh, use is everything. We are so accustomed to have people of all classes wandering about the house at all hours that we think nothing of it. If we wish to keep a room private, we lock the door." I have said I had an attack of fever while staying here. It was not a bad one; but while it was on me, I kept in bed for a few hours, during which time the room door was opened four times by such chance visitors as the above mentioned, who, after staring at me for a minute retired, leaving the door open and my temper anything but good!

If any exception is to be found to the admirable manner in which the American missionaries conduct their work, I venture to say it is in allowing the natives, Mussulman and Christian, to treat them with too little respect. They are so humble minded that they feel themselves on an equality with all, and allow all classes to treat them as if they had the same social standing. Even the lads of the college behave as if they were their equals, lounge in and about the house, and address their masters as they do their companions. This, I am sure, is a mistake, as cheap favours, like cheap goods, are never half appreciated, and were the missionaries to stand more upon their dignity, the people would be much more ready to listen to and follow their instructions. In one respect Dr. Trowbridge was wiser than the missionaries we had met at Kaisarieh. He never allowed the people in the streets to insult him, or the ladies connected with the mission, with impunity; when abused and called insulting names, he quietly marked the delinquent, and then called on the governor and insisted on his sending a zaptieh with him to arrest the offender, and this conduct had answered so well that it was rare that any one was troubled now.

Twice we spent the evening with Mr. and Mrs. Fuller (the former being Dr. Trowbridge's fellow-missionary), who lived about a quarter of a mile from the college, on a hill just outside the town; and as an illustration of the state of the country, I may mention that when we started to walk home at night, Mr. Fuller expressed some anxiety about us, as he said it was quite possible we might be attacked and robbed even in this short distance.

One of the greatest drawbacks to any progress in Turkey, and to the missionary work in particular, is the rapid way in which governors come and go. No one ever remains long enough to learn the requirements of the people, or to have time to improve on the administration of his predecessor. His clerks and subordinates are men whose only idea of governing well is to enrich themselves; and the pasha, be he ever so honest and anxious to do right, is removed before he can trap them and put better

men in their place. Judging others by themselves, the
pashas always begin by looking on the Americans as men
who, in some cunning manner, were swindling at the
expense of the country, and therefore ought to be opposed
and thwarted in all ways; and by the time the honesty
and uprightness of these gentlemen has penetrated the
mind of the slow-witted pasha, an order comes and he is
removed, and his successor begins all over again the old
game of obstruction and suspicion.

In the five-and-a-half years previous to our visit to
Angora, the governor-general had been changed eight
times; and though Dr. Trowbridge had not kept count of
those who had been in Aintab during the same time, he
said he believed even more had come and gone. Some
few of these men may have been honest, and might have
governed to the best of their ability without enriching
themselves, if they had had time to learn how to do so,
and if the entire system of government had not made it a
task beyond the power of any man to accomplish; but
I do not think I exaggerate when I say that for one
governor who is honest a hundred are rogues who only
accept office, or rather buy it, that they may enrich themselves in the shortest possible time, and care no more for
the well-being of their country than thieves and robbers
do for that of the unfortunates they plunder.

I have now before me a letter written by a man whose
honesty and truthfulness are beyond suspicion, and who,
from his knowledge of Turkish, and long residence in the
country, has had exceptionally favourable opportunities of

seeing behind the scenes. I have his permission to make
what use I can of his information, but am asked in doing
so to suppress names, as many of the incidents might, if
known, involve honest men in trouble. I regret this, as I
should have liked to give his letter *verbatim*, it being in
my opinion a true sketch of the state of this unfortunate
land. As it is, I will give only such extracts as can hurt
no one, good, bad, or indifferent, and I will preface them
by saying that my correspondent is not mentioned by
name anywhere in these pages, nor otherwise referred to.

"My knowledge of Turkish, and also my business, has
brought me into closer connection with Turkish officials
than is often enjoyed by Europeans, and consequently I
have had an opportunity of noting political events, and
have during the past two years often written to the
English ambassador, Sir H. Layard, thinking, perhaps,
that the giving of information to one in his position might
be of service to the country at this time of transition. It
seems to me that one of the things of primary importance
for the English public to learn is the folly of hoping for
political reformation through the Turks. I am pretty
well acquainted with officials of all grades in Asia Minor
—Abdurahman Pasha, of Diarbekir; Hassan Pasha, the
Vali of Van; Raomi Effendi, Mutirserif of Argani Madan,
and Said Pasha, recently appointed Mutirserif of Madan,
are, I think, honest men. There may be others, but I do
not know who they are; and my list goes down to the
lowest policeman. Twenty years ago the administration
of affairs was very simple. The pasha or governor had

matters pretty much his own way. He was assisted by a
megliss of half a dozen members, and business was despatched in a rude way but very briskly. Bribery was
not uncommon, but it had not grown into a *system* as at
present. Ten or twelve years ago the French system was
adopted; the machinery was much more complicated—
meglisses and scribes and attachés of various kinds were
multiplied—every wheel has its block; where formerly
one man would seek a bribe, now a dozen mouths must
receive something or the business remains unfinished.
This evil is one of enormous magnitude, as the very men
who engage in it have often declared to me. Again, with
this, is the plundering by officials of the public treasury.
For the last two or three years the tithe of the crops has
not been sold as formerly to farmers of the Moine, but
collected by agents appointed for the purpose. These
men, I have been credibly informed, pay more for their
appointment than the whole amount of their wages. Each
village has its megliss, who are supposed to assist in
measuring the crops, and who certify to the amount of the
Government tithe over their own signature. I have often
been told in the villages, even by members of these meglisses themselves, that the tithe-gatherer would give them
a small present of grain for their signatures, and then
would send to his own home from a fifth to one-half of
the grain belonging to the Government. I was told the
other day that five years ago the Government sold the
tithes of a certain district for seven thousand five hundred
measures of grain; this year, with much better crops, the

Government agent brought in two thousand six hundred
measures. A prominent member of the —— government
told me a few weeks ago that one-third of the tithes of
the last crop in his district had been stolen. This is,
perhaps, an exaggeration; but the main fact remains.
When a few weeks ago some of the chief citizens of ——
came here to complain of their kaimakam, they charged
him with taking bribes, that he allowed his agents to
steal, etc., etc., and to every charge our mutirserif replied,
'That is the way they do here.'

"—— Effendi (a vali) told me that he is utterly
powerless. His kaimakams and mudirs buy their offices
in Constantinople, and they come here to rob the treasury
and plunder the people. For example, a man, a Kurd,
presented himself with an appointment as Mudir of ——.
He also had a certificate showing that he had passed a
regular examination at Constantinople. The vali found
that the man could neither read nor write, and on pressing
him he found that he had never been to Constantinople at
all, that his brother was water-carrier for some pasha
there, and this brother had secured his certificate and
appointment. After a little the vali managed to get rid
of him; but the next one was worse still, for he smoked
essrar (hashish), and night and day lhe was under its
influence. He also told me about the kaimakam of ——.
He came there several months ago on a hired horse, poorly
clad, and in debt for his road expenses. He now has
eleven horses in his stable; he has purchased silver ornaments costing six thousand piastres; he has paid his

debts, lives luxuriously, and has surrounded himself with
every comfort. —— Effendi has summoned him to come
and give an account of his stewardship, but he has brought
with him £150, so the Kadi Mufti and the rest are bound
to get his money and set the man free if possible; and, as
—— Effendi said to me, 'The case is a plain one, but
what can I do alone?' He moreover said he could not
rely upon his own zaptiehs even. Their pay is next to
nothing; so when one is sent for a culprit, he takes a bribe
and reports that the man is not to be found. In the midst
of our conversation —— Effendi repeated several times,
' Constantinople must be reformed and purified first of all,
our troubles come from there.' —— Pasha (another vali)
has told me the same often. He said that when Hussein
Arni Pasha was Grand Vizier (he was killed by a Circassian, you may remember, about two years and a half ago
in a cabinet council), he appointed him to the vilayet of
——, and said to him, ' This is one of our richest provinces, and you will have a chance to make a good lot of
money.' —— Pasha added, 'This was our Grand Vizier,
and he was practically saying to me, ' Go and steal!'

" —— Pasha, who was governor here three years ago,
told me, ' We know our places are likely to be sold to
some one else at any time, and we make all the money
we can, so as to be prepared to go to Constantinople and
buy another place. Our system *compels* us to be dishonest.'

" —— Bey, of Constantinople, a member of the Council
of State, was appointed a few months ago Reform Com-

missioner for the —— district. His firman gave him
almost unlimited power. He has just come here, having
spent the past months among the Derzim Kurds. He
and his associates have the reputation all over the country
of taking bribes. I met a brigadier-general *en route* to
Mesopotamia from Derzim with his soldiers. He told
—— Effendi that he received orders one day from the
above-mentioned bey to arrange a court-martial, and be
prepared to execute twelve Kurdish chiefs the following
day. The preparations were made, but on the morrow,
without any reference to the case, the bey took his
departure for another place; and I think, though I am
not quite positive, that the Kurds were set at liberty. At
any rate, the general was given to understand that 'an
arrangement had been effected in the night!' This same
general told me that his troops are so poorly clad and so
seldom paid, and when paid it is in the depreciated paper
money, that when they come to a village it is almost
impossible to prevent the soldiers from sacking it. From
all quarters I hear that wherever soldiers have been sent
to protect the people from the Kurds, the people are pray-
ing to be delivered from the soldiers, preferring the tender
mercies of the Kurds to the robberies of the soldiers. The
delinquents are not all from Constantinople. Village
aghas and others, who talk most loudly about official
malpractices, as soon as they get an appointment to some
petty office, imitate their chiefs. The oppression too of
Christians by their own Turkish neighbours is great. In
every community, in every village, the catalogue is a long

one. About thirty hours from here is the district of ——,
in which live four or five beys, who, trusting to their
isolation, treat the people as they please. During the war
and afterwards, their oppressions became peculiarly severe,
even barbarous. I mentioned some of the facts to Sir H.
Layard, and he represented the case to the Porte, and an
investigation was ordered. The commission made fair
promises, and persuaded some of the people, much against
their inclination, for they were afraid of the beys, to come
and state their grievances. One hadji, a Turk, had been
particularly obnoxious to the beys, because he had helped
to defend the people against them. He had a long list of
their outrages against the people, and of their thefts from
the Government. The people looked to him to be their protector, and he seemed to be just the man to prefer charges
against the beys. The commission took special pains to
get this man to come and present complaints. He was
suspicious, and at first declined, but at last the assurances
of protection were so many and confirmed by oaths, that
he left his village and came to the chief town where the
commission was held; but without being allowed to prefer
a charge, he was seized on the charge of being a rebel
against the Government, and under an escort of cavalry
was hurried off to ——, where he was made ill by
imprisonment and bad treatment, and after a while was
brought home on a litter and died. The people who had
made charges retracted them, and made terms with the
beys, who were emboldened to undertake still greater
outrages. I again reported the case to Sir H. Layard, and

he insisted upon another investigation. Another man
was appointed, with still higher authority, and for a time
he really seemed a second Daniel come to judgment. He
unearthed a great amount of rascality, but after he had
shown the beys they were in his power, he secured his
price and made out clean papers for them, which he com-
pelled the other members of the council to sign, and then
took his departure. I forgot to say one of the beys was
kaimakam all the time! Sir H. Layard did secure his
removal at last; but on the whole the people curse the day
when an investigation was ordered.

"There is another form of oppression which is practised
in all parts of the country. An order is issued for supplies
for the army, say, in Erzeroum—for which the Government only pays one-third of the value. Great injustice
is also practised at the start in distributing this among
the villages. From one village a demand is made for
'thirty sheep, two oxen, and one hundred and twenty
okes of butter.' The man who goes to the village presents
an order for '*forty* sheep, *three* oxen, and *two hundred*
okes of butter,' but after receiving eight hundred or one
thousand piastres in caimé, he reduces the demand to the
original amount! The villagers go a couple of days'
journey and deliver the things, but they get a receipt for
only 'seven sheep, ten lambs, a cow and calf, and seventy-
five okes of butter,' the surplus being of course the per-
quisites of the receiving officer!"

The facts mentioned in the above letter have all occurred
quite recently, and are culled from spots some hundred

miles apart by a man who has spent twenty years in Turkey, and whom I have heard spoken of with great respect by Europeans, Turks, and Rayahs, all agreeing that few men, if any, know and understand the people as well as he does. Wherever we went in Asia Minor we heard similar accounts of misrule, but I often refrain from mentioning them, as the narrators were natives, for the truth of whose statements I cannot vouch as I can for those of the writer of this letter. The Turkish officials he quotes from are some of them personally known to me, and all the others are men well-known in official life there.

CHAPTER XXI.

A trout stream—A battle-field—Settled Turcomans—A blood-feud—A
German kreutze—Dovecots—Cur-Chemish of the Hittites—A ferry
on the Euphrates—Beridjik—An Armenian pastor—Buying a belt.

JUST before leaving Aintab a batch of newspapers arrived
for us, and we saw by them that Mr. Rassam had just
returned to the East, and was about to open out some ruins
on the right bank of the Euphrates, and as we had determined to extend our journey to Diarbekir, and should
have to cross the Euphrates at Beridjik, a few hours above
the spot where the ruins are situated, we settled to make
a short divergence from our direct line and visit them,
half hoping that we might find Mr. Rassam at work; but
in this we were disappointed, he having postponed his
explorations, as we afterwards learnt, till later in the
winter.

We left Aintab on the morning of November 21st,
and pushed on over a fine corn-growing country, destitute
of trees, but with a thicker population than we had yet
seen on our journey, villages of Turks or Turcomans being
met with every three or four hours. About noon we
passed by a splendid spring, which poured out at the foot
of a hill in a stream some six feet wide, and we were told
that it is the same river that passes through Aleppo. In

its beautifully clear waters we saw immense numbers of
fish that I believe were trout, from one to three pounds
in weight. My fingers itched for a fly-rod as I saw them
rising all down the stream in that quiet non-splashing,
non-jumping manner that denotes business, not play. A
small net dragged up the stream would have been full in
a few yards, but Ali Agha told us it was not the custom
of the inhabitants to eat fish, and from what he said I
fancy they look on fresh-water fish much as an ordinary
Englishman does on frogs—good enough for foreigners, but
beneath our notice.

Quitting the direct road to Beridjik just before the
evening, we rode on for half an hour to the right, and
pitched our tent at a Turcoman village called Muzerrin,
almost on the field where the Turks, thirty-four thousand
strong, got worsted by the Egyptians, under the famous
Ibrahim Pasha, in 1839, in a battle that only lasted two
hours. It may be said for the Turks that a considerable
portion of their army was composed of Kurds, gentlemen
not fond of fighting where they run any risk and quite
indifferent as to which side was victorious, knowing that
either way, directly the battle was over, they would have a
rich harvest in plundering the fugitives, be they friends
or foes. Baron von Moltke witnessed this battle from
the Turkish lines, and I believe the result of the battle
would have been very different had the advice he tendered
been followed by Seraskier Hafis Pasha. Many of the old
men of Muzerrin told us they remembered the fight, and
from the pleased expression that came over their faces

while speaking of it, I expect they, like their brethren the Kurds, picked up a thing or two after the battle.

These villagers had deserted the habits of their race, and all the year round lived in this village, growing just enough corn to keep them one degree off starvation, and keeping sufficient cattle and sheep to pay for their clothes. I looked into one or two of their rooms, but had not sufficient courage to enter one, nor did I feel tempted to do so by the luxuriousness of the interior. Just four mud walls five feet high, the natural soil for a floor, an open chimney, a window six inches wide, and a rush mat to sit upon, that was all. Bedding, I believe, there was none; and we were told that the only tool of any description in all the village, except their ploughs, was a small adze belonging to the community in general. Then the ploughs were not very much to look at, being merely one stout stake morticed through a pole, to one end of which is yoked the oxen, the other held in the hand so that the stake scratches along, making a trench in the ground about three inches deep and three wide. After this is done, the corn is liberally sown broadcast, and covered by a board being dragged sideways over the field by two oxen, a small boy driving them standing on the board.

We tried to buy milk, eggs, chickens, curds, and honey, but were told the only eatable in the whole village was the everlasting flaps of half-baked dough. Having some food with us it did not much matter, and that the villagers were really hard set was proved in the morning by an old man raking out of the dust where our tent had been pitched the dirty bottom crusts we had cut off our Aintab bread and thrown away the night before. During the evening some of the men paid us a visit, and in the course of conversation it came out that war was smouldering in the land. Some two years previously one of our guests had found it necessary or convenient to shoot a man belonging to a neighbouring village, and from that time a blood-feud had been kept up. None of the men of either village dared go far from home in the daytime, but at night the respective warriors slunk around their enemy's village in the hopes of getting a pot shot.

Other villages had been dragged into the war, and our friends had been made happy on the day of our arrival by having just concluded a defensive and offensive treaty with two fresh villages. I tried to discover what chance there was of peace, and asked if peace would be made supposing balance was struck by a villager being killed ; but no, it appeared it would then be the turn of the last murdered man's village to kill, and so I suppose it will go on till eventually there is only one man left alive. Living as these men do from year's end to year's end without the least incident, I can quite imagine that a blood-feud is a great blessing, and therefore much to be desired.

While we sat chatting, one of the men suddenly left the tent, but presently returned, saying he had a valuable "antiqua" that he had found near the village, and then commenced to undo a ball of dirty rags and with some labour finally produced a coin which he handed to us

eagerly, scanning our faces in the hopes of finding that in
it we recognized a prize. The coin proved to be a Prussian
kreutze, bearing the date 1836! Possibly it may have
belonged to the great Von Moltke, and been dropped by
him on the day of the battle! We told our visitors its
value, when at once they carefully tied it up again,
and from the nods and winks they interchanged it was
evident they still believed it to be worth a great deal, and
thought that we were crabbing it in the hopes of getting
a bargain.

A few hours' ride the next morning brought us in sight
of the grand old historic river, the Euphrates, winding its
tortuous way around low chalky hills, with here and
there rich strips of level land intervening. Nowhere
though was the scenery pretty or grand. All being spoilt
by the arid, burnt-up appearance of everything, which
extended quite down to the river's edge. We passed
several villages, in all of which I noticed great numbers
of beehives, and also of dovecots, if a row of holes placed
on the ground round the walls of the houses may be called
so. Anyhow, large flocks of pigeons inhabited these
lowly houses, and our zaptieh told us that these birds and
their eggs were the chief food of the people.

In this neighbourhood we also saw a better breed of
horses than we had yet met with, and as we were now
only some eighty miles from the home of the Arab, the
great Syrian desert, we kept on the look out for some
really fine animals, but never saw one that in England
would have been considered fitted for any work except

that of a riding pony for a young lady. Early in the afternoon we passed some earth mounds and scattered fragments of dressed stone, lying between our road and the river, which ran parallel to it, and rightly conjectured this was the spot we had come to see; but passing these we rode on to the winter settlement of a tribe of Arabs, a cluster of dirty hovels, called by its inhabitants "Yerablus," but only a few of these people could speak Turkish, and those few very imperfectly, so it was difficult to obtain any information from them.

After putting up the tent and making all snug for the night, G—— and I rode back along the riverside, over a dead flat plain, to the ruins of the ancient city of Cur-Chemish, and there we wandered about till evening, searching for inscriptions which we did not find, and taking a general survey of the place. We had heard so much of these ruins, and of the grandeur of the place in days gone by, that we were a little disappointed in finding it covered so small a space, but I dare say the remains now existing are only those of the fortified part of the town, and that formerly suburbs extended round it. All the ruins now to be seen are enclosed in a space shaped like a horse shoe, about seven hundred yards across the widest part, and of the same depth, whilst the heels of the shoe are contracted and are only four hundred feet apart. The open part of the shoe comes down to the river, along the face of which, and reaching for some distance below the ruins, are the remains of a massive high quay wall, which to this day is in fairly good repair. The edge of the shoe is formed by a huge earth mound or ramp, thirty feet high, in which are three openings, one at the toe of the shoe and one on either side, and in these are the remains of massive stone gateways. The heel of the shoe on the up-river side appeared to us to be a natural hill, and was both much higher and much wider than the rest of the wall, and it was, besides, the only part of the wall on which we saw the remains of foundations and buildings. Scattered about here were marble slabs and cornices, nearly all partially sunk in the ground. The shoe faces south-east, whilst below it extends a vast flat plain, only just above high-water level, and on the other three sides are undulating upland plains. The entire space within the walls, except a small part at the head, is thickly strewn with massive blocks of dressed stone, and foundations of buildings crop out on all sides, among which streets may still be traced. The space at the upper part of the enclosure that was not built over appears to have been the rubbish heap of the town, for it is thickly strewn with pieces of broken pottery.

Doubtless Mr. Rassam will soon be in a position to give us the history of this most interesting place, which I believe was at one time the capital of the Hittite kingdom, and has since been the stronghold of several of the different peoples who since those days have been masters of the land. Whoever the people were who carved those massive white marble columns and capitals, and dressed those grand blocks of stone, they certainly must have been a finer race than that now occupying the country, and enjoyed a higher state of civilization. I think Mr. Rassam is greatly to be envied for possessing the knowledge and talent requisite for the task that is before him, and also for having such a rich field whereon to exercise them. While the tent and baggage were being loaded up in the morning, we once more rode on to the ruins, and studied them with great interest, till they are all so clearly impressed on my memory that it will afford me double pleasure in reading any account of the forthcoming excavations that may appear.

From Yerablus (Djerablus) we rode for six hours up the right bank of the Euphrates, looking out all the time for the town of Beridjik, which we knew was on the opposite side of the river, and which was really within sight most of the time; but the houses being built of white stone, with white mud roofs, on white stone cliffs, we could not distinguish it till we were opposite to it. Here the Turkish Government has a ferry—a monopoly—and as the ferrymen get their wages by the day, and receive it whether they work much or little, they naturally work little, and look upon a traveller as a bother. At sunset the boats are moored on the Beridjik side, and any one arriving after that time must either retrace his steps some miles and sleep at a small village, or spend the night on the flat muddy bank of the river. Fortunately for us we were in good time, and the boats on our side of the river; so we rode straight into them and were at once poled across. The river here is from eighty to a hundred yards wide, and not more than eight feet deep; it runs fast, but the water is discoloured by a yellowish sediment, that

R

when the river floods its banks is left on the low-lying lands in a rich deposit. The ferry-boats each carried four horses, and in shape they were like the scoop of a coal-scuttle—one end being only a foot above the water, but the sides getting higher and higher towards the stern on which is a raised deck for a man to stand on and steer the boat, using a preposterously long and very hateful pole which works on a pivot. I consider it hateful, for I got a sound whack on the head from it as it swung round that nearly sent me into the river.

Directly we landed we were in the town, and began riding up streets as steep as the roof of a house, and so narrow that our big saddle-bags often scraped the walls on either side; but the horses, feeling sure this superior place must be the end of their journey, struggled manfully along, and soon brought us to the house of a native Armenian Protestant pastor, to whom we had brought letters of introduction from Dr. Trowbridge. On giving us these, Dr. Trowbridge warned us that the minister's house was small, and that possibly he could not give us a room; but added, "if he cannot, there is a church attached to the house, and you can make yourselves very comfortable in that; for, by piling the benches out of the way, you will have plenty of room." And on our asking if we should be allowed to smoke there, he said, " Certainly —why not ?   Oh, we have no reverence for the *building ;* it is to us a room and nothing more."

We were, however, saved this novel experience, by the pastor at once showing us up a flight of stone steps into a clean room, round which ran a soft divan, most accept-able to our weary limbs after our hot ride. Coffee and cigarettes soon appeared, and our host did his best to entertain us; but having two Circassians working for him in the garden below, he could only give us half his attention, the Circassians being such inveterate thieves that, if not carefully watched, they were sure to steal something. As long as the hoes the Circassians were using kept up a steady chop, chopping, our host was easy; but the moment this sound ceased, conversation was cut short in the middle of a sentence, and out would rush the pastor, only to return when the hoes went on again. So constantly did he run up and down the stairs to see that his men were only working and not thieving, that we felt convinced it would have been far easier for him to have done the hoeing himself, and so have saved his anxiety, his labour, and his money; not that this last would amount to much, for the men were only paid two piastres a day—that is to say, about fourpence. I had a chat with the men, and found they were a couple of merry, light-hearted rogues that had lately come from Roumelia, and were part of a gang of emigrants that the town was supporting until they could support themselves, —a feat, we were told, they were in no hurry to perform. Later on in the day, I bought, through the help of an Armenian, a leather belt mounted with oxidized silver buckles and buttons, which one of these Circassians was wearing, and paid for it a sum that I believe was much beneath its real value.

CHAPTER XXII.

Native visitors—A reign of terror—Anarchy—A Mudir—A Turkish
official—Soldiers from the war—A shot at wolves—A Caravanserai
—Oorfa—The castle—The birthplace of Abraham—A legend—
Ancient tombs—Nose-rings—Going down into the well.

AFTER supper the usual influx of visitors began to arrive,
and the usual questions were put, always including the
one, "When were the English coming?" no one believing
us when we said we did not know. All present were
Armenians, the chief men of the community, and one was
a member of the town council; but, as he said, he might
just as well have *not* been, as it would be his ruin to
oppose the kaimakam or other Mussulman members in
the smallest thing, and he therefore merely sat at their
deliberations, not venturing to offer an opinion, but always
putting his seal to whatever he was told. Thick and
fast followed stories of murders, robberies, outrages, and
wrongs; but, evidently in the minds of all, the night
when the present Sultan was proclaimed in the place of
his drunken, mad predecessor, was the climax of all
horrors. For then one of those waves of fanatical rage
and hatred, that occasionally arises amongst Asiatics,
swept over the town, and a cry went up, started no one
knew where, no one knew how or wherefore, to kill the

Christians. All night bands of fanatics rushed about the streets, hammering at the doors of the Christians, and threatening to murder all. No Christian dared open a door or light a candle, and in pitchy darkness families huddled together in remote corners and cellars, not daring to whisper, and paralyzed with fear. During that night children were born by mothers who died from fright, their fate envied and prayed for by many who momentarily expected worse than death. Children lost their senses, and to this day are babbling idiots; while to others and their children after them, the memory of that night will remain a horror only to be mentioned in suppressed voices.

Every picture has its bright side, and so has this. One Turk (and only one) was moved with pity, or saw the danger of his co-religionists' mad conduct, and ventured at his own personal risk to attempt to quiet the storm; and it is owing to him alone that the whole Christian population was not murdered. He was an old man, a descendant of the Deré Beys of the place, and fortunately retained some of the influence his father had possessed over the inhabitants. Mixing with the mob, he commanded them to be silent, and then pointed out that though in a few hours every Christian in the town might be exterminated, yet, in the West, there were powerful nations, far outnumbering the Osmanlis, who would certainly at no distant date avenge any atrocities that might be committed, and who would perhaps at once ally themselves with the Russians, and reduce the whole land to a condition of vassalage. Little by little the storm quieted down, but it was days before the Christians dare appear again in the streets and resume their usual occupations, and even then they did so in fear and trembling lest some accident —a dispute over a bargain, a trumped-up accusation or hasty word—should start the troubles all over again. A form, and only a form, of government existed in the town. There was a mutaserif, with judges, finance ministers, clerks, tax-collectors, and police; but owing to none of these having received any pay for months, all were powerless. The police refused to obey orders; the people, except the Armenians, to pay taxes, and the entire revenue of the province only sufficed to support the Circassian emigrants that lounged about the town, robbing and stealing, and who were the most worthless of all the community.

The day before our arrival at Beridjik a Turk, who was feeding five or six sheep close to the gates of the town, was attacked and murdered by the Arabs, and his sheep driven off. The deed was witnessed by others, and within fifteen minutes of its perpetration the governor was apprised of it; but on summoning his zaptiehs they refused to move unless he paid them all or a greater part of the wages due to them. But this he could not do, there being no money in the coffers. The governor first entreated and then threatened, and finally, mounting his horse, he rode unattended to the scene of the murder. There lay the victim, but, naturally, the murderers had decamped with their plunder and there was not the faintest hope of their ever being brought to justice.

During the evening a Turk, who was a sort of chancellor of the exchequer for the province, paid us a visit, and though he greeted all in the most hearty manner, it was pitiable to see the fear his presence produced in the Christians. All at once jumped up, retreated from the divans, and stood in humble attitudes near the door, salaaming at every word the Turk condescended to address to them, and agreeing to all he said; but as his conversation took the form of abuse of his own people, his padishah, and government, I dare say no great strain was put upon their consciences. Over and over again the Turk said, " All is rotten, from the Sultan downwards. Our armies are beaten in the field, or sold to the Russians by their generals, the people are starving throughout the land, justice is asleep, honesty is unknown, patriotism is dead. There is but one hope, and that is the active intervention of England." Encouraged by his line of conversation, some of the Christians repeated the stories they had been telling us, and asked him to confirm them, which he readily did, laughing at the notion of any one doubting them. Altogether he fouled his nest, but he had an excuse—he was somewhat drunk, though only sufficiently so to put him off his guard and make him dare to express his real thoughts and opinions. As we had no liquor of any description to give him, and as there was a wedding going on where he hoped to get plenty, he soon relieved us of his presence, and then we pleaded fatigue and got rid of the others.

Rolls of soft thin mattresses and thick quilted coverlids

were then brought in by the pastor's wife and daughter, and we were soon enjoying the best beds we had slept in for some weeks, the remembrance of our narrow, hard canvas camp beds making the change all the more delightful.

In the morning we were up at daybreak and off again on our journey, our direction lying east over the plains of Mesopotamia. Before starting from Constantinople we had been warned that trouble might be before us through the number of disbanded soldiers, who were returning to their villages; but in justice to these poor fellows I must mention that, though on every stage of our journey we fell in with them, they either took no notice of us or, if they did, treated us in a friendly manner. All were in rags and tatters, and none carried home with them more than a small bundle tied in an old great-coat across their backs; yet none begged of us, or seemed to think they were undergoing exceptional hardships, but seemed cheerful and light-hearted, probably rejoicing that they had escaped from the war unscathed by Russian bullets, and from the fever, sickness, exposure, hunger, and frostbites that had finished the career of so many of their comrades.

We overtook a band of fifty of these soldiers soon after quitting Beridjik, who told us they had been taken prisoners by the Russians at the fall of Kars, sent to the Crimea and other places, and kept there until the war was over, when they had been returned as prisoners to Constantinople. There they were disbanded, minus pay, and shipped off to Alexandretta, from which place they

were walking to their homes at Diarbekir and the surrounding villages. All spoke well of the Russians, who,
they said, had treated them more like friends than
enemies, giving them good food, and plenty of it, and
allowing them almost absolute freedom. They all seemed
struck with the superiority of Russia over Mesopotamia.
"Here," said one, "grass and corn are green and luxuriant
only for a month or so in the spring, all being burnt up
by the sun during three parts of the year. Here are no
trees, no rivers, and hardly any rain. In Russia the grass
is always rich and green, crops of various sorts succeed
each other month by month, while the country is well
watered, and the climate never too hot. A man may
grow rich in Russia; if he succeeds in *living* here he is
fortunate."

We soon left the poor fellows behind, but two days
afterwards we were astonished to see them late one afternoon again trudging on in front of us, they having continued their weary march a greater part of each night, and
we only succeeded in heading them into Diarbekir by a
few hours. They chaffed us merrily whenever we saw
them, saying they would tell the people of Diarbekir to
look out for us in a few days, and prophesying that if we
went no faster we should be greybeards before we got
home.

The country we rode through this day was very like
that we had passed between Aintab and the Euphrates,
except that now and again we came upon large tracts
covered thickly with huge blocks of basalt, averaging

about a ton in weight, rendering such tracts utterly profit-
less, for so thickly was the ground covered, that not only
was cultivation out of the question, but there was not
even room for any pasturage worth having.

While passing over one of these stony tracks, on reaching the summit of a hill, we saw in front of us a collection
of some fifty vultures, sitting in a ring round some dead
animal, and, on riding nearer, two big wolves trotted off
well in view. Noticing that the vultures did not even
then fall upon the carcase, I turned my pony from the
path, and picking my way among the stones, rode nearer.
I then saw there were two more wolves pegging away at
a dead donkey. One was a darkish one, the other red,
like a fox, but both looked nearly as big as the donkey
they were feeding on. When I got within a hundred
yards the dark fellow decamped, but the other, keeping
its eyes fixed on me, did his best to drag off the carcase,
and actually did tug it along some yards. Every now
and then his heart failed him, and panting and blowing
from his exertions he made a bolt, but, as I rode as if I
did not notice him and was intending to pass by, he
always thought better of it and returned for another tug.
Little by little I got within twenty-five yards of him,
when, fearing he was going to make off in earnest, I took
two shots at him with my revolver, with no further result
than giving him a scare. Off he dashed, jumping and
tumbling amongst the loose stones, while the vultures,
relieved from his presence, pounced upon the donkey, and
in a few minutes had torn it to pieces. Half a mile

further on was a low pass between the hills, and as we
rode forward vulture after vulture swooped through it
and, passing over our heads within a few yards with a
rushing sound, went to join their friends at dinner. From
the position of the hills it must have been quite impossible for these birds to have seen the donkey, but I
fancy they found it out by seeing those soaring over the
pass swoop down, and so, taking the hint one from
another, all within many miles played at "follow my
leader."

On this night we broke our journey at a veritable
caravan khan, one that in years gone by had been erected
by the Turks for the accommodation of travellers. As
we had seen these buildings extolled in books of travel
as something really fine, we thought ourselves lucky,
especially as Ali Agha and the zaptieh spoke of this as
one of the best in those parts. It was built in an oblong
form, the two long sides and bottom being a continuous
row of vaulted, cellar-like stables, with a few narrow slits
for windows, and doorways without doors to them. The
fourth side was divided into a lot of small rooms, with
arched roofs like the stables. All faced into the outer
square, which was an open space some forty yards long
and thirty yards wide, rising to a mound in the middle
that was formed of the manure cast out of the stables.
This court was entered by an arched gateway, on which
yet hung by rusty hinges part of a door. There were
no mangers to the stables, and nothing to which to
fasten a horse, and the manure and filth had been

allowed to accumulate for so long that there was hardly
room to pass between it and the roof in some places.
All was constructed of square, dressed stone, but as
breaking joint is not considered necessary by a Turkish
builder, the walls were falling down in parts, and letting
in the arched roof. Earth had been spread over the
arches, so that the top of the building formed a flat
promenade, reached by a dilapidated staircase in one
corner. We peeped into the rooms through the glassless,
shutterless windows, but found them so dirty we at once
put up the tent on the hill in the middle of the yard, and
even Ali Agha, the Armenian boy, and the zaptieh, all
preferred the open air to sleep in. There was no khanji
or any one to look after travellers ; the rule being, first
come, first served, unless the last comer is the strongest,
and then the rule is reversed. A few Arab donkey-drivers
were the only other occupants beside ourselves, and we
could have dispensed with their company, as they quar-
relled all night, the word *money* being repeated ten times
in a minute at the top of their voices. Either Ali Agha
and the zaptieh did not speak truth in saying this was a
superior specimen of the old caravanserai, or the glamour
of the East had blinded the men whose description of
these establishments we had seen.

Eight hours' ride on the next day brought us to the
town of Oorfa, which is built on a round, cone-shaped
eminence, rising out of a rich and fertile valley that runs
between two ranges of hills. The suburbs reach the main
hills on either side of the valley or rather gorge, for here

it is scarcely wide enough to be called anything else. The town is prettily situated, and from a distance looks picturesque, but, as usual in the East, on entering it one finds narrow streets, tumble-down houses, dilapidated mosques, dirt, poverty, and wretchedness. The hills on the right, as one rides up to the town, rise almost precipitously from the gorge, and are surmounted by the ruins of what must have been a very fine and strong fortress, for even now what remains standing retains considerable beauty, and the style of the massive stone walls shows plainly that they date from before the days of the Turks. The people of Oorfa believe the castle was built by Nimrod, but the town having been held by the Greeks (under the name of Edessa), I should be inclined to give them the honour of having built the castle. It is surrounded on all sides by a dry moat, some twenty feet wide and about twenty feet deep, cut out of the solid rock. In the centre of the ruins there is a beautiful white marble pillar, with a carved capital, the beauty of which we could not see, as the flat top had been taken possession of by storks, and the decaying sticks of their nests hung down in a thatch all round, hiding the carved work.

Just below this castle, and at the entrance to the town, there are two ponds of beautifully clear water, and by the side of one of these stands a rather fine mosque, built, it is said, by the Turks, over the spot where Abraham was born. Both Jews and Christians share this belief, and I believe, too, that some of our learned men in Europe give Oorfa (Ur of the Chaldees) the honour of being his birthplace. The two ponds and the small brook that leads out of them are crowded with carp, which are supposed to be most sacred, and we were assured that to kill or take one might cost us our lives. To ensure a prosperous journey, travellers on leaving the town buy a few paras worth of grain from a man who stands selling it by the side of the pond, and propitiate the fish by feeding them; but how the fish are supposed to look after him on his journey is more than I can tell. That they are well accustomed to this attention is shown by the way they all swim to the side of the water on the approach of any one, coming in such numbers that the top of the water for yards round bristles with their backs. Round the outside pond are gardens thickly planted with plum and mulberry trees, the existence of which, together with the ponds and the sacred, fish were accounted for by a Turk in this way. " *Thousands* of years ago, when Nimrod was king, some awfully wicked people tried to storm his castle on the hill, and failing to do so by the usual means, they bethought them of burning him out. To do this, they collected a mountain of wood where the ponds now are, and set fire to it. Nimrod watched the operation, but directly the wood began to burn, he stepped off the top of his castle on to the pile and stamped it out. He then slew all his enemies and went home. Where his feet first alighted in his long step (some five hundred feet !) up sprang those ponds, and the sticks that formed the fire took root around them and made the groves you now

see. As for the fishes, when Nimrod got home he found
his cook just going to dress a fish for his supper, but not
being hungry after his exertions, he took the fish by the
tail and chucked it from the castle into the ponds, and
there it is now, and all these others are its progeny." I
give this story as it was told us, but decline to vouch for
its truth!

What interested us far more than the fabled exploits
of Nimrod were the curious tombs that are cut in the
solid rocks all round the castle, and indeed all over the
neighbouring hills. Some were tunnelled out from the face
of the cliff, and others were on the flat, a narrow driftway leading down into them. They were all cut out of
the solid rock, but were of different sizes, some intended
for but one body, and others for many more. The first we
entered was down one of the sloping drifts, at the bottom
of which was a round doorway just large enough to allow
us to enter by stooping low. We then found ourselves in
an oven-shaped chamber about ten feet square, with an
arched roof only five feet from the ground. On either side
was a solid stone bench, left when the rest of the chamber
had been excavated. In front of the round doorway,
working in a crescent-shaped groove, the ends of which
were continued into the rock, was a stone exactly like a
grindstone that could be rolled aside up the groove, but
which, when again liberated, descended of its own gravity
to the lowest part of the crescent, and so effectually closed
up the entrance. We may have been mistaken, but at
the time we both felt that we must be looking on a tomb

the exact counterpart of that one made by Joseph of Arimathea.

The next tomb we saw was entered by the same sort of driftway, but the chamber was very much larger. There were the same two stone benches, but besides these the walls were pierced by ten or twelve recesses, like wine-bins, which had doubtless each contained a body. Instead of the rolling stone, the entrance had evidently been closed by a wooden door with movable bars on the outside, the holes that received the ends of these being in working order to this day. All the tombs we saw were empty, and the natives have long since abandoned this form of burial ; but near the town the tombs are made use of as residences for poor people.

In the twenty-fourth chapter of Genesis it is stated in the *original* language of the Bible that Abraham's servant presented Rebecca, when at the well, with *nose jewels*. Now it struck us as a curious fact that here in Oorfa, the reputed birthplace of Abraham, and in the country from which Rebecca was taken, all the children, young men and young women, wear nose-rings, and, further, that we only noticed this practice here and hereabouts. On asking about this custom, we were told that at an early age the rings are put in, and are continued to be worn by the boys till they reach manhood, and by the girls till they are married and have had one child. The rings are small, like an English lady's finger-ring, with generally a turquoise in them. (" Nose jewels " are also mentioned in Isaiah, chap. ii.) Another curious thing we noticed, which is also mentioned in that same chapter of Genesis (xxiv. 16). It is said that Rebecca went *down* to the well, and filled her pitcher and came *up*. Now in the immediate neighbourhood of Oorfa we saw many wells that would allow of this "going down." They were trenches faced with stone, some twenty yards long and a yard wide, with a sloping stone staircase at each end leading to the spring at the bottom. We saw girls and women descending into these wells with their pitchers on their shoulder, doubtless in the exact manner in which Rebecca did.

S

CHAPTER XXIII.

Camels at supper—An English dentist—The post Tartar—The Arab
horse—A riding mule—In the tombs—An early start—Severek—
A Turkish chaussée—Lost on the mountains—Electricity.

DURING our stay at Oorfa we put up in a wretched little
khan, but were lucky enough to get a little room on the
roof, above the dirt and smell of the yard, and it was
rather amusing to sit on the flat roof outside and observe
the life below. The yard was crowded with camels, all
wistfully watching two men kneading cakes of dough
that weighed about two pounds each, and showing their
impatience by sundry grunts and by spitefully biting at
each other. At last one of the men appeared with three
or four of these cakes, and his two camels shuffled quickly
after him to a comparatively quiet corner, where they
knelt down in a surprising hurry and remained with their
mouths wide open, like young birds when the old ones
are about to feed them. The man thrust a cake well back
in the mouth of the first camel, and then clapped a
hand on each side of its big lips to prevent it in its
munching from dropping any out sideways. This he
continued doing till the camel showed that all was
swallowed by opening its mouth for another cake. Then

the other camel was served; and so, going from one to the
other, he gave each four cakes, the poor beasts looking
as if they would have enjoyed twice that number.

We were honoured by a visit from the khanji, a Turk,
in the evening, avowedly to see if we had any brandy to
give him. On our telling him we did not drink it, and
that we thought all spirits bad, he assured us we were
quite wrong—all spirits were good, and brandy especially
so; adding, "I drink a bottle of raki every night,. and am
a new man after it." I dare say he felt so at night, but
I have no doubt he felt a very old one in the morning.
Our visitor then went on to say, "I know you English.
I have a great friend, an Englishman; he lived in this
room " (I think he said a year). " He was a tooth doctor,
quite a wonder. I dare say you won't believe me, but
not only did he pull out bad teeth, but he filled up holes
in others and made them as good as new, and when a
man had lost all or part of his own, the doctor made him
new ones far better than those nature had originally given
him. He made a whole set for the governor here, and
got £35 for doing so. I do not know why he left, for he
made a lot of money here, and soon would have been very
rich. Besides, see how comfortable he was; he had this
good room to live in!" I could quite understand why
an Englishman should have left such a place, the only
marvel being that he stopped there a week.

We were up at daybreak next morning, and leaving
Ali Agha to engage a fresh zaptieh, we went for a walk
over the town, to the fish-ponds mosque, and finally to

the castle and tombs, returning to the khan before noon
to find all in readiness for a start except the zaptieh, who
as usual had not turned up. We sent messengers to the
konak for him, and at last rode there ourselves, when the
governor, a Bosnian Effendi, swore that no one had asked
for a zaptieh, and that one should follow us in a minute—
yes, in one minute; thus telling deliberate lies, for the
zaptieh had been asked of him, and no one followed us
for half an hour.

During the afternoon G—— and I were riding on a
few hundred yards in front of our men and pack-horses,
when we heard a great shouting, and turning round saw
three brigand-looking fellows shuffling along just behind,
driving in front of them what we thought at first were
our pack-horses, but which proved to be three poor beasts
with big saddle-bags just like ours. On they came, thrash-
ing their beasts and shouting, and kicking up a fine dust,
the personification of hurry on horseback. They turned
out to be the post—a Tartar (who, by the by, is not a
Tartar but a Turk, his name being taken from the Tartars
who rode the post in days gone by) and two soradjis, whose
business it is to whack the pack-horses and do the rough
part of the work. The Tartar is supposed to ride through
the entire distance, say, from Constantinople to Bagdad,
but is in reality changed frequently. The soradjis change
with their horses at every town, and are responsible to
the postmaster for their safety. Now, if there is one thing
the Turks are proud of, it is this post, and to hear them
talk one would suppose it went quicker and better than

the Flying Dutchman or Wild Irishman. Whenever a
man wants to give an idea of rapid rides he says, " Like
the post." Europeans of all classes in Turkey have
accepted the fallacy, and writers who should have known
better have often spoken of the exploits of the post Tartar
as not to be equalled by any other mortal. From these
authorities I had in days gone by conceived a picture of
a magnificent-looking creature, riding a splendid Arab,
scouring over the trackless plains day and night, only
halting when his steed was fainting with fatigue to leap
from its back to that of another. On and on, night and
day, nibbling a crust as he galloped, and actually sleeping
in his saddle, till at last, arriving at the end of his five
or six hundred mile ride, he delivered his despatches to a
noble-looking pasha, and then fainted away ! Now for
the reality stripped from its romantic twaddle. In the
first place, the Tartar is generally a poor unhealthy,
crumpled-up looking individual, and his noble steed an
under-sized, under-bred, over-ridden, half-starved pony,
incapable of going out of a quick shuffle. Besides its
rider, it carries saddle-bags, great-coats, a gun, water-bottles,
and a few other etceteras that dangle against its poor lean
sides. It is never ridden except at a tripple, as that is
the easiest of its paces. The whole journey from end to
end occupies an hour for each four miles, so that if the
Tartar rides at the rate of eight miles an hour, he can for
every hour so ridden rest another; and this plan he invariably follows, allowing himself on every journey a
margin of from one to three days, which he accounts for

at the end by saying the roads were bad, that he was ill,
or that the horses were starved and could not get along.
At all the towns we visited, not once did the post arrive
on the proper day, and often was three days late on
such short journeys as that from Constantinople to Angora
or Kaisarieh. Travellers often take advantage of the
escort of the Tartar and his soradjis, hiring post horses
at a fixed rate from post-house to post-house, and when
this is done the post is invariably detained by them.
During the remainder of the afternoon we kept passing
and being passed by this Tartar post, and only parted from
them at sunset, when they continued their journey to the
next village, where they slept all night.

Having reduced the splendid heroic Tartar to his proper
place, perhaps I may here say a few words about the
Arab steed he is supposed to ride, but which he does not.
From what we saw of the animal all our preconceived
notions as to the Arab's excellence were dispelled, and we
came to the conclusion that he is a much over-rated
animal. It is true we only skirted his home, and were
often told that to see the horse in perfection we must go
farther; but though this may be true, we did undoubtedly
see many thorough-bred Arabs, some belonging to Arab
peasants, but the finest and best belonging to big pashas
and Turkish officials, men who are pretty sure to secure
the best horses to be had. All we saw were pretty
animals—perhaps I may say very pretty—their pure blood
showing in their clean-made heads, fine coats, and fiery
spirits; but in what good qualities they outshine a well-

bred English horse, it is difficult to say. They are under-sized (fifteen hands being an exceptionally high horse), with no action, and down on the pasterns like a brood mare. Not one in a hundred can walk well, few can trot at all, and in their boasted gallop they are as inferior to an English thorough-bred as an ordinary English pony is. Being fiery and quick in their movements they give one the impression of being very fast, but they cover little ground in their stride, and do more clambering than galloping. They are too slight for cavalry horses and for any sort of draught purpose, and even in the East no one rides them on a journey if he can get a half-bred, as their action is so bad and they get over the ground so uncomfort-ably. When one meets Turkish pashas and great men journeying they are invariably riding half-breds, while their Arabs are being led by grooms, and reserved for state occasions or to make a splash when entering a town.

It is said their best quality is being able to keep up great speed for a long distance, but their inferiority to an English thorough-bred was shown some years ago, when the late Viceroy of Egypt challenged any one English horse to race his stud of Arabs over ten miles of desert. The challenge was accepted and a third-rate old plater sent to Egypt, and the race came off, thousands going to see it. The result was that the English horse, without once being really extended to its full pace, came in at a slow, slinging canter, the Arabs actually not being in sight, though a mile of uninterrupted desert was extended to view. For £100 an English horse might be bought that would beat the quickest Arab in a short or long race as easily as a racehorse would a half-bred.

No greater mistake could be made by any man intending to make a long journey in Turkey than to buy an Arab for his own riding. The fieriness of the animal would be a continual annoyance, and his bad action and slow walk a pain and misery. The proper beast is a half-bred pony, showing that it has Arab blood in it by its well-made head, but yet with sufficient of the plebeian strain to give it strength and tissue, and make it a good walker, or, better still, a good trippler. Such horses can be bought for £10 to £15, and a ready market for them will be found at the end of the journey at a small reduction on the original price. But were I again to make a journey in the East, I would buy a really good mule, as they are more enduring, and their tripple is easier and better. I tried several of these animals, and anything more perfect than their tripple I cannot conceive. One in Angora carried me at a tripple over the rough stones of the streets, the reins lying loose on his neck, at the rate of eight miles an hour, and so even was his pace I might have read a book while sitting him with as much ease as in an armchair. Their only drawback is their price, a good mule costing as much as three ordinary horses, and a good white one as much as four horses, white being considered all over the country a most fashionable colour, and denoting that the rider is a man of substance.

On the evening of this our first day out of Oorfa, we arrived at a small settled Turcoman village, so small and miserable that there was not a stable into which we could put our horses; but as the zaptieh, who had overtaken us, assured us there was not another village within two hours, we accepted the offer of the headman to camp in the ruins of a very large tomb close by, for, though there was no roof to it, the three sides, which were of solid rock, would keep the wind a little from our poor beasts. It was a grim sort of place to sleep in, but there was no better, so we tied up the horses to pegs driven into the ground and then put up the tent. The tomb had evidently been excavated out of the side of the hill, and must have had an arched natural roof over it; but this had fallen in and been removed, leaving only the three solid faces of the rock, in which were, here and there, coffin-like recesses where formerly the bodies were placed. On the Armenian boy expressing his disgust at his lodgings, I proposed he should take possession of one of these graves, and cover all over with his great-coat, but he seemed to think it would be an uncanny sort of bed, and preferred the shelter of a big rock.

The next morning, before it was light, G—— roused me up with the always unwelcome news that it was time to turn out, or rather for me to turn out. The teapot and etna being under my charge, I always got up first to start them brewing. To do this in our small tent, my bedding had to be rolled up and the bedstead taken down. After doing this, I would light the etna and then dress, that is, put on my boots, the rest of my day garments having gone to bed with me. I had done all this, and had seated myself, cold and shivering, on the flap of the saddle-bag, when it struck

me daylight was very slow in coming; so I took a peep at
the watch, and found, to my disgust, there was still an hour
and a half before daybreak, the time we usually got up!
I could not well take off my boots again and put up my
bed, and so I sat drinking cup after cup of tea, mentally
resolving never again to turn out without first looking at
the watch myself. Fortunately we were still in a mild
climate; yet it was chill and raw in the early mornings,
and invariably the first hour out of bed was the most
disagreeable in the twenty-four.

A tent is not much of a place, and one might suppose
there would be but little shelter from the cold beneath a
piece of thin canvas, with open cracks at the bottom and
eaves; but the first peep out on a frosty morning dispels
this idea, the outer air being apparently many degrees
colder than that beneath the canvas, and one is quickly
driven in again for the sake of getting a little warm.

Being up myself, I was forcibly struck with the many
advantages to be gained by an early start, and I agitated so
successfully that I soon had all in a bustle, and we ended
by riding off while it was yet so dark we could hardly see
our way. It was well we did so, for we had a long day's
journey before us into the town of Severek, and it is
always advisable, when going to a khan, as we did there,
to get in early, so as to secure a room and get shaken
down before dark. Half an hour before reaching this
town, we overtook our friends the soldiers again, trudging
on manfully, surrounded by a lot of people who had come
out to meet them, bringing cakes, cheese, grapes, etc., which

the men were munching as they hurried forwards. We also then came upon a fairly good macadamized road that went as far as the town, and only wanted to be a little repaired to make it excellent. In fact, if it is ever finished, it will be too good for the requirements of the country, having been set out twice as wide as an ordinary high-road in England, and the traffic that passes over it is so small that only a track up the middle of the road will be used, the stones on each side remaining rough and not broken down.

Severek, which is a place of second-rate importance, proved no better than the average Turkish towns; but the khan we had to put up in was many degrees more dirty and poverty-stricken than most we had stopped at, and the town-people a shade worse mannered, so we were thankful to leave the place next morning. Again we changed zaptiehs here, and, of course, were again delayed; but when G—— called on the kaimakam to remonstrate at our being obliged to halt in the street for this tardy gentleman, he assured us it did not matter, as our journey on this day would not be a long one, and there was a perfect macadamized road all the way. The perfect road turned out to be the continuation of the one we had passed over the night before, but different to it in that it had no ballast over the rough foundation-stones. It was, in fact, an arched bank of loosely thrown-together boulders of basalt, the smallest as big as a man's head, which it was utterly impossible to ride over; and as the whole country was also covered with loose blocks of the same stone, we could only creep along, and, instead of having a quick journey as promised, it proved about the slowest and most wearying of any we had gone through.

In front of us we had a range of barren mountains, called the Caraja Dagh, and from time to time our zaptieh cheered us on our way by pointing to a low place in these hills, and telling us that the village we were to sleep at was just there. At sunset, when we had nearly reached the place, we passed a ruined khan, the appearance of which seemed greatly to astonish the zaptieh, who exclaimed, " Why, I was told there was a village here!" and it then turned out he had never passed this way before, and knew the road as little as we did. To make matters worse, the partially constructed road, along the side of which we had been riding all day, suddenly finished, and only the faintest track remained, winding and twisting at every yard round and among the huge stones that completely covered the ground. We struggled on as fast as we could, hoping to find the promised village, but the farther we went the greater our difficulties; even the horses could not follow the track, and we all had to dismount and lead them. There was a small crescent moon that gave a little light, and so long as this lasted we managed to keep going; but when it set, at about nine p.m., it was no longer safe for either man or beast, for all were tumbling about like a set of ninepins. The poor packhorses were so hungry they would keep wandering away in search of the few scanty stalks of wild oats that found root-hold among the rocks. At last, after picking our way inch by inch for another hour, we came across a tiny brook, and all agreed we could go no farther.

The horses were unloaded, and then, poor beasts! tied up supperless to big stones, whilst we rummaged out a candle, and by its light arranged the saddle-bags so that the flaps lay on the ground for beds. Then the etna was set going under the shelter of a big boulder, and each had a cup of tea and a little piece of dry bread, after which we wrapped ourselves up in our coverlets, and, with stones for pillows, settled down for the night. So thickly covered was the ground with rocks, that to erect a tent, even if we had had light enough to do so, would have been quite impossible, and we even failed to find a spot sufficiently clear to allow our stretching out at full length. As it was, I slept all night in the form of a crescent, a stone some two feet high in my lap, and when I got stiff from lying in one position I had to turn over the top of this stone and reverse my crescent. Fortunately the night was still, fine, and absolutely free from dew, and we both slept as well as we could possibly have done had we been in our own beds.

We noticed on this night what an extraordinary amount of electricity there was in the air. Almost everything we touched cracked and sparkled, and when stroking the mane of my horse my hand was followed by a continuous line of light, and touching some goat's-hair bags we carried this light was still more distinct.

On waking in the morning we found ice on the margin of the stream, and the air was so cold we were glad to get the horses loaded and walk forward to warm ourselves. We looked about in all directions, hoping to find a village where we might procure some food for our poor beasts, but on all sides of us stretched the dreary, barren, stone-covered plains, with the Caraja Dagh that we had descended in the dark rising in our rear. Not a living creature, not a sign of cultivation, was to be seen for hours, and it was not till we were within half an hour of Diarbekir that we saw a village, and then we thought it better to push forward and get to a khan in that town; but by the time we had got in our poor horses had endured a fast of thirty-three hours! In spite of this they all travelled. well, and we should not have discovered that anything was the matter with them, or that they were very tired.

CHAPTER XXIV.

The Indian telegraph—Diarbekir—Rescued by an Englishman—Inac-
cessibility of Diarbekir—Mr. Boyajian—An honest governor—A
collapse of justice—Kurdish insurrection—Insurrection a profitable
speculation—Advantage of consuls—English intervention.

FOR the last few hours into the town we followed the
telegraph, the line subsidized by the English Government
for the Indian messages, and our preconceived notions
that insulators were required were entirely upset. On an
average the wire was on one post in three, fixed by iron
spikes clenched down over it; on others it rested on the
iron shank of the smashed insulator, and in places it
trailed along the ground. For ten posts in succession it
was spiked to the posts, then, after being fixed by an
insulator, fell to the ground, where it rested for the length
of three posts; and yet we were assured by the telegraphist
in Diarbekir that it was in working order, and that he
had no difficulty in forwarding messages.

Diarbekir was in view for an hour before we reached
it, but I cannot say we fell in love with it at first sight,
for a more dismal, jail-like place is not to be found. It
stands back some mile or so from the river Tigris, on flat
ground, and is surrounded on all sides by massive black
stone walls, with old-fashioned round turrets at every

twenty or thirty yards, the walls so high that only the minarets peep over them. They are fast falling into decay, and we afterwards saw places on the river face where they had fallen down, leaving gaps fifty yards wide. As we approached not a creature was to be seen outside the gates, and we felt as if we were coming to a city of the dead, and should not have felt astonished if on passing the gate we had found a population of skeletons! There was nothing novel and nothing pleasant in the town itself; on the contrary, from being a walled-in place, the streets were even narrower and the houses smaller and more crowded than in open towns, and I think the smells were stronger. Bad times had fallen on the place, as shown by large spaces where houses had been abandoned and allowed to fall into ruin, their inhabitants having migrated to more pleasant parts, or been swept away by one of the constantly recurring outbreaks of typhus. Diarbekir contains in all about twenty-three thousand seven hundred inhabitants, rather more than one-half of which are Christians, a few Jews, and the remainder Mussulmans.

As we rode through the streets we half regretted that we had now arrived at the extreme point of our journey eastward, but at the same time it was pleasant to feel that every day's ride in future would be taking us nearer home, nearer old friends and the comforts and luxuries of civilization. As usual, we put up at a khan and engaged a room, but directly we had done so an old shrewd-looking Armenian made his appearance and offered us some empty rooms at his house, at the same time introducing himself as the English consul's interpreter. His post must have been a sinecure, as there was no English consul, nor had there been one for some years. Thinking he might be a useful man, and, as interpreter, well up in languages, we asked him what he spoke, and he at once frankly confessed he knew nothing but Turkish, a fact that must have somewhat hampered his usefulness as interpreter!

We were about to accept his offer of the rooms, when Ali Agha, who had been out searching for a Mr. Cummings, an Englishman who lived here, and to whom we had brought letters of introduction, arrived with the gentleman himself, and, as he most kindly pressed us to stay with him, we thanked the Armenian, and a few minutes later were installed in Mr. Cummings' comfortable English home-like house, having received a kindly welcome from Mrs. Cummings and her sharp, bright-eyed little boy and girl. We were now once again in the line of country where the Angora goat flourishes, and our host was acting as agent for Mr. Thompson, of Constantinople, for the purchase of the mohair; but the trade, as at Angora, was now almost at a standstill, so Mr. Cummings was having a dreary life of it, with little to do and, I fear, little to earn; but being young, strong, and light-hearted, he made the best of it, and appeared to be quite contented Besides himself and his family, there were only two people in the town who spoke English, and not half a dozen Europeans or semi-Europeans in the place; there was, therefore, little or no social intercourse. There was no shooting or sport of any kind, the surrounding country

T

was so dreary it offered no temptation for a ride, and
Weston himself would have refused to take a walk. Of
all the dreary places we had seen this was the dreariest,
and it was marvellous to find civilized human beings able
to endure it. Its position made it a prison that it was
hardly possible for ladies and children ever to get out of;
for it would be out of the question for them to ride on
horseback as far as Alexandretta, which is the nearest
seaport, and the only way to get there is by means of a
sort of sedan chair slung on poles between two horses, one
in front of the other. In this manner Mrs. Cummings
with her two children had reached Diarbekir, and the
account she gave of her journey and sufferings made our
long ride on horseback appear as nothing, and we felt she
ought to be possessed with superhuman strength to have
got through it.

There is an old saying that a Newcastle grindstone is
to be found in every spot where the Saxon has penetrated.
I cannot answer for the truth of this, but I feel convinced
the same might be said of a piano. Wherever one finds
English men and women, one is sure to find the piano.
Mountains, rivers, deserts, bad roads, and no roads cannot
exclude it. If a little feeble and out of tune in its notes,
it looks well, and I suppose is felt to be a friend by those
who are fond of music, and helps to remind them of
pleasanter and happier homes miles away across the sea.
Diarbekir, being the most ungetatable place we had seen,
yet had its piano, which stood in Mrs. Cummings' drawing-
room. It had travelled all the way from the seaport

slung between two horses, as its mistress had done, and, though it had passed some years among Turks, Greeks, Kurds, Arabs, and others, it could yet speak in the old familiar notes when called on to do so under the skilful hands of Mrs. Cummings.

We were much astonished, the first evening of our visit here, when the door opened and a gentleman entered, who appeared to be an English clergyman, for he was dressed exactly like those we had last seen months ago at home. It turned out that he was, in fact, an Armenian by birth, and his relations lived in Diarbekir and the neighbouring towns. How and where he was educated I cannot say, but we quickly discovered that he was a highly cultivated, clever, gentlemanlike man, and that amóngst his numerous accomplishments he counted a perfect knowledge of English. Our astonishment increased when he told us that he was married to an English lady, who had lived with him in that dismal spot some dozen years, without once visiting her old home. During this time he had been working among his fellow-countrymen, teaching them the doctrines of the Church of England, and persuading them to follow its precepts. While on a visit to England, where he went with the hope of interesting people in his work and getting help, he had made the acquaintance of Mrs. Boyajian, and induced her to marry and accompany him to Diarbekir; and, although she must have made great sacrifices to do so, yet I feel sure she has had no reason to repent placing her happiness in such good hands. Mr. Boyajian has never been ordained, and does not call himself a clergyman, but only a pastor, having been elected as such by the people he had taught and worked amongst. Besides holding two full services each Sunday, and teaching daily in the schools he had established, he had also been elected a member of the town megliss, and Abdurahman Pasha, the governor, consulted him in all matters, and, what is more, often took his advice.

We were indebted to Mr. Boyajian for a great deal of information concerning the people and the country—indebted to him directly and indirectly; for not only did he tell us much himself, but he introduced us to the governor, the Armenian bishops, leading Turks of the place, and several members of the megliss, all of whom had some information to impart. In one particular all were agreed. One and all declared that Abdurahman Pasha was a noble exception to the usual Turkish official, being honest, able, and poor, and more anxious for the welfare of his country than for his own. Unfortunately, his powers of doing good were extremely limited, rogues great and small being able, through the Government at Constantinople, to laugh at his attempts to bring them to justice. For instance, there are some valuable salt mines in the vilayet, worked for the Government under a Turkish director. This man in the last few years, by falsifying accounts and selling the salt for his own benefit, had been able to pocket several thousand pounds. Abdurahman Pasha collected the clearest evidence and proof, and then brought the man to account. He was

tried and convicted by the local tribunal, and nothing
remained to be done but to get his punishment awarded
at Constantinople; but part of the ill-gotten gains were
judiciously expended there in bribes, and orders came
back that all proceedings should be stopped, and the man
not only released, but reinstated in his old berth, the
ministers thinking a man who could make thousands, and
so be able to bribe highly, was a source of wealth not to
be lightly suppressed. Everybody in the vilayet knew
the particulars of this case, and it may be easily supposed how little the governor was respected by rogues,
when his efforts to bring them to book so completely
collapsed.

As at Oorfa, so was it here, and, indeed, throughout the
whole country there might be said to be no government,
or rather, what there was, was worse than nothing, being
only used in most instances to assist individual robbery
by Government officials. To add to the general anarchy
that prevailed, there were Kurdish revolutions going on
in almost every direction.

Near Bitlis, and in the neighbourhood of Lake Van, several
tribes were in open revolt, and were having a good time
of it, robbing and plundering Christians and Turks; but
as they also fought tribe against tribe, and were split up
into independent bands, they were not considered dangerous to the Government. In the Derzim Mountains,
a short distance north of Diarbekir, the Kurds had been
out for some time, murdering all who entered their district, and plundering the villages, Mussulman and Chris-

tian, for miles round; but again the danger was considered only local, and the Government did not therefore care to interfere. A more serious outbreak was, however, going on at Djeziré, a town on the Tigris, half-way between Diarbekir and Mossul, but in the vilayet of the former. Some years ago, a Kurdish chief named Beden-Khan had headed a revolution in this district. Troops were sent against him, his bands dispersed, and he himself bought over by a pension, a pashalic, and a residence at Constantinople, where apparently he lived for the remainder of his days in the peaceful bosom of his family, which, besides wives unlimited, consisted of thirty-eight children. During the late war, one of his sons returned to the old country to try and collect volunteers to fight against the Russians. Directly he appeared, the old followers of his father flocked round from all parts, and in a few days he found himself a rich man from the quantities of presents his admirers showered upon him. It does not appear that he ever induced the Kurds to follow him to the war, but he seems to have soon after returned to Constantinople, where he told his brothers of the reception he had met with. One of these brothers at once set off for the old home, hoping to fare equally well, but the Kurds seem to have had no more to give, and therefore, not to be disappointed, this young chieftain raised the standard of revolt against the Government. He collected a mob of Kurds, fell upon Djeziré, kicked out the kaimakam, took possession of the treasure, and appointed himself master of the place. Troops were collected by Abdurah-

man Pasha, and sent against him, and while we were at
Diarbekir, news arrived that a battle had been fought, the
Kurds defeated and dispersed, and the chief obliged to
hide, minus followers, and with every prospect of falling
into the hands of the Government troops.

Abdurahman at once telegraphed this good news to
Constantinople. No reply was sent back, but on the day
before we left Diarbekir, the kaimakam of Sert, not far
from Djeziré, telegraphed word to say that he had received
a telegram from the Porte, ordering him to find up the
rebel chief, and tell him that by the Sultan's orders he
would be made a pasha, and receive a good pension, if he
returned at once to Constantinople! Abdurahman Pasha
was furious. "I repress the rebellion, and have the
miscreant at my mercy, and am rewarded by having a
slight put upon me through a small kaimakam being
authorized independently of me to offer the rebel rewards
instead of punishments; and now, if the remaining
children of the old pasha do not come one after the
other, and earn a pension like their brother, they are
fools!" adding, "I am sick of it all. I do not stop
here to rob the people and enrich myself, and I shall
send in my resignation, and never take office again." As
we saw shortly after in the Constantinople papers that
another pasha had been appointed at Diarbekir, I suppose
he carried out his threat.

Scores of villages had been robbed and plundered by
the insurrectionary Kurds, and scores of others by the
unpaid, unfed soldiers who were sent out against them,

starvation during the coming winter staring in the face
all the poor peasants thus left destitute, and those villages that had not already suffered felt pretty sure their
time was coming, as the Kurds were certain to break out
again at no distant date and pay them a visit. Diarbekir
itself is not safe, and the inhabitants expect sooner or
later to be plundered and murdered by one of the
numerous tribes of the neighbourhood, who know well
that they have nothing to lose and all to gain if they do
so. We were told that near the Tigris, below Diarbekir,
there were vast plains as flat as a table that, under cultivation, would produce rich crops of all kinds, but that the
villagers dare not grow even sufficient for their own wants,
as the possession of any store was sure to tempt either
Kurds or soldiers to plunder them. Therefore with plenty
lying waste at their feet, all were verging on starvation,
in the train of which came fevers and other diseases,
which were fast carrying off the poor people, and leaving
the land a depopulated desert.

Since we left Diarbekir last December (1878), an
English consul has gone there, and his presence will be a
blessing to all, as he will be the one power in the land,
beyond corruption and beyond fear, a check on dishonest
officials and a shield to the oppressed, and if intervention
by England for the better government of the land is to be
anything more than idle talk, a better beginning cannot
be made than by sending such men to every great town.
Then when reports reach our ambassador from missionaries,
travellers, merchants, and native Christians, of outrages,

injustice, and oppression, the Porte will no longer be able
to silence him, and prevent his moving further in the
matter by declaring there is no foundation for them.
Such reports will either be confirmed or refuted by the
consuls before the Porte is spoken to on the subject, and
the good old excuses will have to be abandoned.   It will,
I know, be thought by many that to interfere in Asia
Minor is not our affair; that we should say to the inhabitants, Kurds, Turks, Christians, and others, what the
costermonger said to his quarrelsome dogs, "Fight it out,
you beggars; you find your own jackets!"   But if this is
so, let us give up all half-measures and, above all, the talk
about British interests and British intervention, that the
people may know what to expect and to hope; then,
perhaps, driven to despair, they may either right their
own wrongs, or, better still, the Christian will be forced
to emigrate to happier lands.   As it is, wherever we went,
we found all living on the hopes of English intervention
—all classes, Turks and Christians, honest men and
rogues, alike wishing for that happy event; the only people
in the country not caring to obtain it being the clique of
governing pashas at Constantinople, who know that then
their day will be over, that no longer will they be able to
swagger over a province for a few years and then retire to
pleasant houses bought by the money they have robbed
from the poor in distant parts, and lounge away their lives
at Constantinople, intriguing and scheming to secure for
their sons and other relations a field wherein to exhibit
their powers of amassing such another fortune.

CHAPTER XXV.

The Aleppo button—Ophthalmia—Mange—Environs of the town—
Facing homewards—The Taurus—Unruly horses—A child bride
—Arghana Madan—The copper mines.

SINCE crossing over the Taurus at Cilicia, we had availed
ourselves of every chance opportunity of looking at ourselves in a glass, and sometimes, when one was not to be
had, I confess I had eagerly inspected my face in the
quiet waters of a fountain or brook, dreading to see a
small red pimple, denoting the beginning of the disgusting
"Aleppo button." Why it is especially called the *Aleppo*
button I do not understand, for it is prevalent in all towns
in Cilicia and Mesopotamia ; wherever we went in those
regions, every one we saw was more or less marked by it,
and we were assured there was no hope of our escaping.
Invariably it attacks the face or hands, and beginning, as
I have said, with a small red spot, it grows and grows till
it becomes an open sore like a burn, from the size of a
sixpence to that of a five-shilling piece, eating deep into
the flesh, and driving the sufferer almost mad with the
irritation, which must never be relieved by even a rub, for
if it is the sore spreads till the whole face is more or less
covered. It often takes six months for the malady to run
its course, during which time the patient is weak and

feeble, and in general bad health. Fortunately, when once
the sores have healed, the victim is never again attacked,
but as long as he lives the great unsightly scars remain,
a sure indication that he has lived awhile in the land of
the "button." No one escapes it more than a year or
two, and often it attacks the traveller directly he enters
the country. No cure has yet been discovered for it, and
nothing seems to hasten or retard its course. Natives are
invariably more marked than visitors, from the fact of
their getting it as children, and from the impossibility of
preventing the poor little things from rubbing the itching
part. From the fact of its invariably coming on some
exposed part, and from the first appearance of it being
exactly like a gnat's bite, I am inclined to think it is
some insect, possibly the common fly, that starts it, and
my belief was strengthened by an American lady telling
me she had managed to escape it for two years, she believed
by wearing a veil almost always.

Besides this scourge there is another, as common and
yet more dangerous—ophthalmia, and few natives escape
it, weak bleary eyes being the result even in the case
of those who recover, while hundreds are permanently
blinded by it. It is fearfully catching, and is communicated from one person to another by the swarms of flies
that settle on the eyes of the sufferer, and carry away the
virus on their legs. But, unlike the "button," there is
a cure for this, namely, constantly washing the eyes with
a weak solution of alum and water, always taking care to
use a fresh piece of sponge each time. Even cold water

constantly used is a cure; but the natives, although they know this, neglect it nine times out of ten, preferring to let the disease run its course rather than take the trouble of constantly washing.

Then there is another disease that we were told half the Armenian women and girls in Diarbekir suffer from, and that is mange, exactly the same disease that dogs have, the offspring of idleness, dirt, and the everlasting "custom." Once a fortnight, or at most once a week, the women have their hair done. Then all go to the baths and spend the whole day there, carrying food and drinks with them, and besides the wash, they get their hair fresh plaited and indulge in a good gossip. I am unable to describe very exactly the method by which these ladies arrange their coiffures, except that the hair is twisted and plaited into scores of thin tails which are wound round and about a thick saddle-like pad that sits on the head, and on this, covering the ears and temples, is a great silver or brass oval-shaped plate, weighing several ounces, that gives the wearer the appearance of a lop-eared rabbit. Except on the weekly or fortnightly bath days, the hair is never touched by brush or comb, and naturally becomes a den of all that is unpleasant, generating this terrible disease, which often covers the head with sores, and frequently produces total baldness.

We were told that when a young man wishes to marry, his mother proposes to the parents of the desired one, and that whilst doing so she is supposed to find out if the lady has the mange; but on my saying, " I suppose if she has,

the negotiations come to an end?" our informant replied,
"Not often, for in that case not half the men would get
wives, as most girls have it."

Twice during our stay at Diarbekir we passed a pleasant
hour chatting over five-o'clock tea with Mrs. Boyajian,
and the sight of her nice clean house and rooms furnished,
as far as circumstances would allow, in English fashion,
was most refreshing after the dirt and squalor and
wretchedness of all around. She had two pretty children,
a boy and a girl, about ten and twelve years old, who
chatted freely in several languages besides English, and
whose education occupied the chief part of their mother's
time. Mrs. Boyajian did not complain of her life, but
said she longed, chiefly on account of her children, to get
once more into civilization, and I yet hope to see her in
England, and her husband an ordained clergyman, with a
flock around him better able to appreciate him than the
natives of Diarbekir. Later on we heard a great deal of
him and his work from some American missionaries, and
though they sighed heavily over him because he was not
of their way of thinking in some doctrinal matters, yet
they all declared that he was a thoroughly good hard-
working man, a brilliant exception to Armenians in
general.

The town of Diarbekir stands, as I have before said,
about a mile from the river, on a cliff some fifty feet high,
from the foot of which to the river extends a flat piece of
ground, cultivated as gardens and planted thickly with
fruit trees, the whole being irrigated by the water of the

town, which is carried all over it, after having enriched itself by passing through filthy streets and open drains. The crops grown are very great, water-melons and sweet melons in particular attaining great size, two of the former often being, we were told, as much as a donkey could carry. Immediately opposite the town the Tigris is fordable at low water, and about two miles below there is an old-fashioned stone bridge, with the usual numerous high-pointed arches. As far as the eye could reach on the other side of the river extended vast bare upland plains, while to the north appeared snow-clad mountains, apparently not more than twenty miles distant. Communication with the towns lower down the river is carried on by means of rafts, which are made by inflating a number of goat-skins, over which is placed a platform, with sometimes a small hut upon it. Two men pole this raft along during the day, but at night, for fear of concealed rocks and whirlpools, it has to be anchored. It travels at the rate of three miles an hour, and from thirty to forty miles are got over in the day. To the Turk this style of travelling is very delightful, as he has nothing to do but smoke, eat, and sleep, but I should think it must be weary in the extreme to a more active-minded people.

Before crossing Mesopotamia we had planned to retrace our steps from Diarbekir as far as Beridjik, and then, after passing through Aleppo, to hit off the sea and terminate our ride at Alexandretta; but so dreary and uninteresting had we found this almost depopulated land, and so wearisome had we found it to ride day after day amidst the loose masses of basalt with which more than two-thirds of the surface of the country is covered, that on reaching Diarbekir we made up our minds to risk being shut up in the Taurus by the snow and storms which now might be expected to begin any day, rather than face those dismal plains again. Keipert's map was deeply studied, and various old travellers consulted, all of whom, I am bound to say, assured us we should never get through. On pointing out to old Ali Agha by the map that the distance to the sea at Trebizond was shorter than to Alexandretta, we scoffed at his saying measurement was nothing and the only thing to be trusted was *hours,* and we silenced him by pointing out that *viâ* Trebizond to Constantinople was shorter even in hours than by the Mediterranean. We had, in fact, quite made up our minds about it, and so on the morning of the 6th of December we said good-bye to our good friends, and turned our horses' heads to the north, feeling we had at last commenced the homeward route. We had started somewhat late, so only made six hours' ride, but this brought us to the first slopes of the mountains, where we slept at a village, occupying the strangers' room, as it was a little too cold for our tent; and for this same reason we did not pitch it on any of the succeeding nights, so had to endure the tortures of the million, in dirty stuffy rooms.

We were off early on the 7th, and at once entered among the hills, which rose higher and higher every mile we went. We passed just below the town of Arghana, which is perched, as is so often the case in Asia, house above house on the face of a cliff; but not stopping there, we pushed on and soon turned off from the partially made chaussée that we had followed from Diarbekir, and which was a continuation of the one we had seen near Severek. The scenery here began to be somewhat grand and imposing, the mountains rising almost perpendicularly from narrow gorges only a few feet wide. These gorges run in all directions, cutting the mountains up into one huge jumble and making them look as if quite impassable. The mountains are nowhere wooded, and hardly a blade of grass or vegetation of any description grows on them, but the colours of the rocks and different soils of which they are composed struck us as being most remarkable. Standing on the summit of a hill and looking away to the north, every colour and every shade of colour presented itself for miles upon miles, making the hills look as if they were the coloured morsels of a giant kaleidoscope that had been broken and spilt. Conspicuous on all sides were greens of every shade, now in the bottom of the gorges, now on the hill-tops, and it required no deep knowledge of mineralogy to tell us we were in a land of copper and probably of other rich minerals.

The path on which we were riding became so narrow, and in places so steep and covered with rocks, that we could only cast momentary glances at the scenery, all our attention being required by the pack-horses, that, as usual, whenever the road became specially bad, went as ungainly as possible. They kicked, they fought, they scraped the saddle-bags against projecting rocks, they bolted up gullies or along precipitous ridges, and, in fact, did everything they could to bring destruction on themselves and their loads, and it seemed as if the prospect of the mountains before them made them think their lives not worth having.

At one village, perched up on some high crags, we found great excitement, as a wedding was about to take place, and the whole male population were out on the road, beating a drum and snapping off pistols as a welcome to the bride, who was shortly expected to arrive. A mile farther on we met the damsel herself, a poor little creature with a baby face, who could not have been more than thirteen years old. She came ambling along on a well-bred Arab, sitting on a man's saddle *a la garçon*, with an attendant on each side guiding her and her horse. All, bride, attendants, and horse, were decked out in the most gorgeous colours and seemed very much pleased with themselves. The bride's veil was loose and low on her face, and she showed, by turning her head towards us, that she had no wish to hide her beauty, but from the peep I got I do not think she had much to be proud of.

Not long after meeting the bride, we came down upon the Tigris, which is here a rapid mountain stream only about ten yards wide, running very fast over and among rough boulders. Two hours later on, when we had passed over a considerable hill, we came upon it again, and following its course for an hour arrived at Arghana Madan, where the richest copper mines known in Turkey are worked, and have been worked since the days of the

U

Romans. A few minutes sufficed to settle men, horses, and baggage in a khan, and then, with a young Greek as guide, we went all over the place and examined the mines. The ore is extracted from a steep hillside, where it crops out some three hundred feet above the Tigris, which runs at its foot, and, after being calcined in open kilns at the surface, is carried away on mules' backs to a rude furnace, where it is smelted and run into ingots, two such ingots being a load for a horse. Most of the miners are Greeks, but there are a few Turks. Any one is allowed to sink a shaft where he pleases so long as he does not interfere with his neighbours' workings, and to enable him to carry it on, the Government advance him money as the mine deepens. All the copper ore, after being calcined at the miner's cost, is sold to the Government for seventeen piastres the six okes (a batman), but as the payment is made in caimés, it does not amount to much, and, further, it varies so much from day to day that the miner cannot make any sure calculation as to his profits. Probably he gets about tenpence for seventeen pounds. All the wood in the neighbourhood has long ago disappeared, and none can now be obtained nearer than thirty-five miles distant, and then it is only in sticks some two feet long and not as thick as a man's wrist. This has to be transported to the mines on donkeys, and costs 10s. 4d. per ton. The rough stone yields from twenty-five to sixty per cent. of copper, but about this it was difficult to get dependable information, and I fancy what we heard was chiefly guesswork. The transport of the smelted copper to the sea at Samsoon costs about a shilling for seventeen pounds, camels being chiefly used for this purpose.

The governor told us that there was in stock at the furnace over two million okes of ore ready smelted and awaiting transport, a statement that astonished us when we considered how hard pressed the Government is for cash; but it was afterwards told us that, owing to the camel-drivers having been paid in caïmés and abominably cheated, they had refused to come near the mines—in fact, were out on strike. Owing to the same cause, nearly all the mines had been abandoned, and there was only enough ore raised to keep one of six furnaces employed. It was the old story; the goose that laid the golden egg had been all but killed, and Turkey was fast losing this source of wealth. We first visited the furnaces, and found them to consist of a large shed with a row of eight huge chimneys, very wide at the bottom and narrowing towards the top. In the rear of this are eight pairs of bellows worked by a small stream led out of the Tigris, which force air in at the base of the chimney. Some ten feet from the ground in the front part of the chimney is an open hole four feet wide; into this is pitched the ore and fuel, whilst the molten metal is tapped below. The shed, the bellows, the chimneys, and all connected with the place was in ruins, and unless quickly repaired the work must stop.

We afterwards climbed up to the mines on the hill, passing over on our way a perfect mountain of old slag. We only descended one mine, but were assured all the others were just like it. They consist of a slanting shaft some eighty or a hundred feet deep, supported by timber, down which one descends by very bad steps, up which the ore has to be brought to the surface on men's backs. The mine we selected belonged to a Turk who had within an hour of our arrival found ore. The old fellow was most anxious for us to inspect his mine, as he said our doing so was sure to bring him luck, and as he proved a pleasant, civil man, willing and anxious to give us all the information in his power, I am sure I hope it may. He told us that the fate of all the mines on the hill was to be flooded with water, and we saw several with the water up to their mouths.

In the whole district there are no other mechanical contrivances than the pick and hammer, no roads, no carts, no pumps; all is done by animal and human labour, unassisted. At different times search has been made in the neighbouring hills for coal, but as yet without result. All the wood within reach has been used up, no provision having been made for the future by planting or protecting young forests. Unless coal can be found within reasonable distance, these valuable mines must be abandoned as unprofitable. The miners told us that though these mines had been worked ever since the days of the Romans, there yet remained large tracts having ore that had never been touched. One hill especially was pointed out to us close by, where copper ore, we were told, cropped out in all directions.

On returning to the khan we sent our compliments and also our firman to the governor, and were in return invited by him to pay him a visit after we had supped, and, I suppose to make this possible, he sent us our supper, which consisted of five or six dishes. When these were disposed of, G—— went down to call on the old fellow, and sat with him for an hour, while I remained at the khan, chatting with a number of the miners and others, who begged me on my return to England to persuade a company to work the mines; but as the reason they assigned for desiring this was that they could not work them themselves at a profit, I fear Englishmen will not be induced to run the risk. Many attempts have been made at different times to procure these mines for European companies, and offers made to the Turks that would, if accepted, have far exceeded in value anything ever made out of the mines under the present system. These offers have been invariably refused, the Turks believing that some day enormous sums will be made out of the mines. The thought of outsiders making money is always so hateful to the Turk, that he would rather forego any advantage he might derive than give the foreigner a chance. The only concession he will ever give is one that he knows won't pay, or where payment depends on the faith of the Government, as, for instance, the guarantee for a railroad. Then by breaking faith with him, the foreigner is sure to be brought to grief, and the Turk rejoices thereat.

CHAPTER XXVI.

A good chaussée—A pasha's railroad—A freak of nature—Soldiers on
the march — Kharpout plain — Kharpout — Turkish honesty—
Americans in Kharpout—A Philo-Turk.

FROM Arghana Madan we continued along the side of the
Tigris for about five hours, on what is *very nearly* a good
road, and which might be made quite so with a very little
labour.   It has been carefully and well laid out with
regular gradients along the face of the hill, and throughout
it has been thinly ballasted, and when first finished must
have been one of the only good roads in Turkey.   From
the time it was finished, four or five years ago, till the day
we rode over it, not an hour's labour had been expended
on it.   The crumbling earth from the hills had been
allowed to roll down and bury one-half of it, thus reduc-
ing the original width of twelve feet to six.   The numerous
bridges over water-gullies that come down between the
hills consisted of two stone abutments with thin poplar
poles laid across and covered with earth.   These poles
have rotted, and about one-half have given way.   All that
is required to make this road ready for wheeled traffic is
to have the earth removed from the side and a drain cut
to receive the water that drops from the face of the high
bank, the timber poles over the bridges replaced by stone

arches, and a little more ballast put on over all. Nowhere
is the road straight for fifty yards, and the points of the
hills are often turned at acute angles, and yet, will it be
believed, this was intended for a railroad, and to this day
is called our "vapore yol." It was made by Kurd Ismail
Pasha, when Governor of Diarbekir, by forced labour, and
was intended to join the Black and the Mediterranean
Seas, starting from Trebizond and ending at Alexandretta.
Scratchings were made at it, extending from Severek to
Kharpout, but nowhere had a mile of it been finished,
except up this valley from the Arghana mines.

When the road had been thus far finished, a Polish
engineer passed over it on his way to Diarbekir. Ismail
asked him what he thought of the road, and on the Pole
saying it would eventually, when finished, make a fairly
good road for carriages, Ismail flew in a rage, called him a
fool, and informed him that what he in his ignorance had
thought a partially made carriage-road was in reality a
railroad, only requiring rails to make it equal to the best
in Europe. In vain the poor engineer tried to explain
that engines would not work up a hill as steep as the side
of a house, or go round acute angles; he was told he knew
nothing, and, further, was insolent for daring to contradict
the pasha. Ismail then reported to Constantinople that
the earthworks were all finished for his line, and begged
that rails and rolling stock might be sent at once. It is
needless to say this request was not attended to, and
Ismail, after having visited Constantinople and taken a
trip up the line from there to Adrianople, confessed that

his road was not quite perfect, and might require a little more work before the rails were laid.

In the afternoon we emerged from the valley and arrived on an open stretch of high land, with a good many villages scattered about, and most of the level ground showing signs of cultivation; and here, up in the clouds, we came upon a big lake, called Gulchuck. From what I can remember of it, I should say it is at least twelve miles long by eight broad, and evidently very deep. Five years ago, Nature played a queer trick with this piece of water. The surrounding country was visited by a violent earthquake that upheaved some metres the valley through which the lake emptied itself by a stream running into the Tigris. At once the stream ceased to flow, and the lake began to rise steadily. Roads and tracks that ran along its shores were submerged, and villages on its margin were swamped and had to be abandoned, till about two years ago the water had almost reached the level of the heaved-up valley. Then came a further upheavement, and since then the lake has risen four metres, and is now threatening to overflow down the old valley. We were told all this by a Prussian engineer from Cologne, who has been some twenty years in the Turkish service, and who is now manager of the Arghana mines. He thinks there is great danger of the lake, when once it begins to find its way out, rapidly cutting through the new obstruction, which is only formed of shingle and loam, and the enormous mass of pent-up water rushing down to the Tigris, carrying destruction to the mining town and many

other villages. The Governor of Arghana Madan shares
this fear, and further believes that the town of Diarbekir
is doomed and will be swept away. Both the engineer
and the governor have stated their fears to the authorities
at Constantinople, and asked for sufficient money to cut
a small canal along the side of the valley, so as to relieve
the lake, but the only answer they can get is, " Please
God, nothing will happen." We did not share these grave
fears, believing from what we saw that the water would
simply restore the old watercourse as it was before, but
on a higher level, and that the lake would retain its new
level, only discharging the same amount of surplus water
as formerly. I hope we may be right, for if not, Arghana
Madan and many other villages have a *mauvaise quart
d'heure* before them at no distant date.

We stayed the night at a khan near this lake, and,
thanks to the weather being very cold, and our room
having a door at one end that was about as airtight as a
hurdle, and a huge chimney at the other, we were kept
actively employed most of the night stoking the wood fire,
and were obliged to lie down with all our usual clothes
on plus fur coats. In the yard of the khan we saw a
curiosity. It.was the first, last, and only wheeled conveyance that had ever passed over Ismail Pasha's new road.
It had been built at Diarbekir, and a man paid to drag it
with two ponies thus far, but he found the task so difficult
that he would not attempt the return journey, so left
the cart and rode his horses back, and I have no doubt
that during the past winter the cart has been broken up,

and has helped to warm some chance traveller like ourselves.

The next morning, while descending from the high lands to the Kharpout Valley by a track so narrow, so bad, and often so near the edge of a precipice that we dare not and could not sit on our horse, we met a Turkish regiment on the march from Kharpout to Diarbekir, and, on the principle of the weakest going to the wall, we had to stand aside for half an hour whilst they passed. The miserable state of dirt and squalor of these men is more than we can describe; nothing short of a collection of the poorest beggars could equal them. So threadbare, so ragged, and so scanty were their old uniforms, that they could only have been retained as souvenirs of better days, and the men might be said to be clothed by their muskets and side-arms. They had no tents, no spare baggage, and no food with them; some half-dozen half-starved pack-horses carried a few pots and pans and officers' luggage. Snow was on the road they were passing; it was bitterly cold, and the only shelter for the poor fellows for that night was the small khan we had just quitted, which was not large enough to hold a third of them, and where there was not sufficient fuel to be had to make a camp-fire. Many of them stopped and asked us questions, and they seemed vastly astonished to hear that Diarbekir was three days' march farther on, as they said they had been told they should arrive there that evening. As raw material, nothing could be finer than these men, though it struck us they were somewhat old for soldiers, the beards of many

being streaked with grey. We felt sorry for them, but we
felt still more sorry for the villagers on their line of march,
for it was self-evident that to exist the soldiers must
plunder and rob wherever they went, and as winter had
now begun, no fresh stores could be obtained to replace
those taken. Even supposing all were paid for in cash,
the roads to and from the villages to the towns would
be impassable, and the transport of stores quite impracticable before the spring.

By noon we had left the hills, and had reached a spot
that might be called the gem of this country—the great
plain of Kharpout. Nowhere in Asiatic Turkey had we
seen any part half so fertile, or a quarter so well cultivated.
It is a dead level plain of deep rich alluvial soil, and is, I
should say, twenty miles long by twelve wide, surrounded
on all sides by high rugged mountains, from which descend
numberless little streams and rills. Villages are to be
seen in all directions, chiefly inhabited by Armenians, who
have here taken to agriculture, and prove, by the clean
state of the land and by the use they make of the streams
for irrigation, that they are much better husbandmen than
the Turks. Every yard of the plain is cultivated, cotton
forming the chief crops, but great quantities of wheat and
barley are grown and sold to the villagers in the mountains
in exchange for goat-skins, horses, sheep, and such things
as the almost barren rocks can be made to produce. Here
and there, on moist, swampy spots, and by the side of
streams, groves of poplars are cultivated, which are cut
and sold when as thick as a man's leg, to be used as rafters

to cover in the flat-roofed houses. These poplars, with a little stunted oak scrub, are the only representatives of the forest within miles.

On our ride across the plain we passed through several Armenian villages that were wretched in the extreme. From being built on the flat in deep rich soil, the surroundings are poached up into a lake of black mud, some eighteen inches deep, and often the only dry spot in the village is the large manure heap, whereon squat the elders of the community, surrounded by children, dogs, cows, sheep, and ponies, all looking more than half starved. Rinderpest or some other disease had been rife among the cattle, and in every village we saw numerous skeletons sticking out of the mud around the houses. Nowhere did we see any haystacks or any provision, except half-rotten straw, for the cattle in the winter, and as the poor beasts at this early part of the season could hardly drag one leg after the other from weakness, many must have died before the grass began to grow in spring.

All domestic animals in Turkey are undersized. Cows, sheep, horses, and even chickens are little more than half the size of those in Europe, and I think this may be accounted for by no one thinking it necessary to select the finest or healthiest of his stock to breed from. Nowhere are bullocks fattened for the butcher, and the animals are often killed just "to save their lives." The consequence is the beef is stringy, hard, and rank, and I do not think the very poorest in England would eat it. As for the mutton, it is always what is called *woolly;* that is, has a strong goaty taste about it that you can't get out of your mouth for days. The chickens, which are not much bigger than partridges, are invariably tough, stringy, and thin, and when boiled are very like what I should imagine a wet woollen comforter would be to eat. Eggs, when they can be had fresh, are the one clean and wholesome food to be got, but even these are very small.

After crossing this fertile, level plain, an hour's ride up a very steep ascent brought us to the town of Kharpout, which is placed on the summit of a high hill. At the entrance to the town are the ruined walls of an old fortress, perched on the edge of a cliff, but the space thus enclosed is all built over and forms part of the town. In summer the governor and his officials live and conduct their business in Kharpout, but in winter they descend to a miserable sort of place in the plains, called Mezireh. On entering the town we spent half an hour before we could get quarters anywhere, and when at last a room was given us at a khan, it was full to the ceiling with cotton, and we had to wait till it was emptied, and when that was done it proved to be without glass in the windows and with an open fireplace, the hearth being some three feet from the floor, thus leaving one's lower extremities out in the frost, while the upper parts were roasting. We had, however, scarcely settled down when a young Constantinople Greek called upon us and invited us to come and stay with him at Mezireh, an offer we gladly accepted, as in our present room we stood a good chance of being frozen. But as it was already dark, and our things all unpacked, we put off our migration till the morning, when we rode down the hill and took up our abode with our new friend.

During the evening we spent at the khan we called in one of the zaptiehs who had escorted us from Diarbekir, and gave him a bakshish, telling him to divide it with his companion. He salaamed and retired, but shortly afterwards the other zaptieh appeared with Ali Agha, and inquired of us how much we had given, and on our telling him he turned to Ali Agha, and said, " There, you see, it is as we expected ; he has given me one quarter, and kept three quarters for himself." We then told Ali Agha what it had always been our custom to give the zaptiehs, and it turned out that almost invariably the man who received the money had robbed the other. Yet I fancy I have heard it stated that the lower orders in Turkey are honest, and those only are dishonest that have been corrupted by intercourse with the West. Among any other people than Turks, the way this zaptieh had cheated his friend would have caused a row between them, and we expected to hear high words in the yard below ; but no, the two men apparently continued the best of friends, and both escorted us next morning to Mezireh, chatting amicably as they rode along. I did not, however, envy the culprit his ride back to Diarbekir, and should not be the least surprised if his horse made a false step and blundered over a precipice in some lonely spot.

Scarcely had our Greek visitor left us when a Mr. Allen, an American missionary living in Kharpout, arrived and invited us to stay at his house ; and when we explained that we had already accepted another invitation, he begged us to spend the evening with him and his friends, and also to visit him whenever we could from the lower town. To this we agreed, and we spent several pleasant hours in the comfortable missionary house. Like all the other missionaries we had met with, these good people had devoted their lives to their work, and spoke quite cheerfully of ending their days here. Most of them had been half a lifetime in Turkey, only visiting America about once in fifteen or twenty years.

Here, as at Aintab, missionary work had taken the practical form of educating the young Armenians, both boys and girls; large schoolrooms were attached to the mission house, and we were told that as soon as sufficient money could be obtained for the purpose a college such as the one at Aintab would be built. Besides the three missionaries, with their wives and families, there was an American lady, a Miss Seymour, who worked in what the mission call "the field," her chief task being to teach in the girls' school, and read to those of the Armenian women who would attend to her. Now and then, she told us, she made tours to distant towns with the missionaries, and tried to sow "the seed" amongst the women, the gentlemen, from the way all the Armenian women are excluded from man's society, being unable to get at them. When we thought of the fatigues and hardships, the filth and wretchedness that we *men* had gone through in our journey, we realized indeed how devoted and earnest these ladies must be, and what marvellous pluck they must possess. At the same time, I cannot think any lady should submit to it, or be encouraged by any one to undergo such hardships. We do not dig our gardens with a silver spoon, and I am sure a fitter implement might be found wherewith to cultivate " the field " than refined, delicate American ladies.

In one of these missionaries we found what we had not before met with since we left Constantinople, a real genuine Philo-Turk, who assured us that the Osmanlis were little short of perfect; but as he failed to bring forward any evidence to prove this, and as his two brother missionaries in no wise agreed with him, I shall content myself with stating the fact that at Kharpout a believer in the Turks exists! I am sorry to say that this gentleman, though a believer in the Turks, did not, apparently, think much of Europeans, as he declared what little evil there was in the noble Osmanlis was derived from their intercourse with the West. In this I partially agree with him, for I do think the Turks have been apt pupils in learning all the *bad* we had to teach them, drunkenness being the last lesson they have learnt, while they have neglected to adopt any of our virtues. But to show that the Turks were not altogether such sweet gentle-minded creatures before they were demoralized by contact with outsiders, I may give the following copy of a *permis* to bury. It was given me by H.B.M. Consul at Angora, who stated that t was a literal translation of an old document held by the Armenian Bishop of Sivas. We heard of many other such elegant effusions, but this was the only one we could obtain.

Translation of an " Izinnamey " or Turkish *permis* to bury
a Gregorian priest, issued by the local government of
Mossul, Asia Minor, A.D. 1848.

> "On earth who wore the pitchy gown
> Now wears elsewhere the devil's crown;
> An outcast from Heaven, in Hell doth drown.

"Let it be known to all that this unholy big Priest
called ——, an infidel man, a sectary of the most odious
religion, and the offspring of an adulterous woman, having
died in wickedness and filth, let the detestable carcase be
carried forth; and though the very ground may well reject
it, lest the fœtid odour should cause a pestilence and so
torment true believers, let a ditch be dug, let the above-
mentioned carrion be put therein, the earth thrown upon
it and firmly stamped down, and thereafter return to your
affairs."

Signed and sealed by Mevlevu Sheykh
(leading Mussulman
ecclesiastic)

 and the kaimakam
or civil governor's
seal.

CHAPTER XXVII.

Visitors—Insurgent Kurds—Incorrect information—The view from
Kharpout—A military road—Keban Madan silver mines—Cheap
hospitality—Crossing the Euphrates—A misunderstanding.

WE arrived at the Greek's house at Mezireh the next
morning in time for breakfast, and immediately a flood of
visitors set in and continued to flow without intermission
till dark.   Not one in ten had anything to ask us or a
scrap of information to give.   All sat a dreary long time,
staring at us as if we were wild beasts, and we could not
give a hint that their visits were wearying, as we otherwise
should have done, because they were all friends or business
acquaintances of our host.   The governor called, the megliss in detachments called, binbashis called, merchants
called, and priests called.   From the governor we learnt
the unwelcome news that we could not continue on our
direct road to Trebizond, but must turn to the west and
prolong our ride two days, as the country on the direct
line was the Derzim Daghlar, inhabited solely by Kurds,
who cut the throats and robbed all who entered their
mountains.   They had been very brisk lately, and troops
had been sent against them, that is, moved up to such
towns as Kharpout and Erzingan; but we failed to learn
that they had ever entered the disaffected district, and we

afterwards met numbers of troops on the march from
Erzingan to Kharpout, going round the long way so as
not to get into danger. Why should they? The Kurds,
with their predilection for robbery and murder, are an old-
established institution. They had never been subjugated;
and though they did plunder the villages for miles round,
refuse to pay taxes, and send no men to the regular army,
yet custom had made them sacred, and it was absurd to
risk fighting with them! As long as the present government lasts, uninterfered with by Westerns, so long will
these gentlemen be perfectly safe; but I suppose if the
gendarmerie of Turkey is placed under European officers,
wholesale robbery will hardly be allowed, even in the
Derzim Daghlar, and steps will be taken to bring the
Kurds to order. As they live in high mountainous regions,
on almost barren rocks where corn will not grow—and
even if it would the people do not know how to cultivate
it—and as their only idea of earning a living is to take
one from some one else, nothing short of extermination
will stop their lawlessness. The only way to prevent the
wolf killing the sheep is to kill the wolf, and the Kurd
will have to be treated the same, or else allowed to
plunder as he does now. I do not envy any commander
who may have to undertake the task of catching the
Kurds, for the Derzim Daghlar, as the crow flies, measure
from east to west some hundred miles, and are about fifty
miles wide, and are also surrounded on all sides by hundreds
of miles of mountainous region. There are no roads anywhere into the Derzim, and hardly a track. Mountain

rises from the foot of mountain in one dense mass, twisted and split up in all directions, with deep chasms and inaccessible peaks. There are no villages, no stores of any sort, and no guides to be found. The Kurds can move about from hill to hill and district to district, doing ten miles to one that any troops could accomplish, and when driven into a corner they can always, as a last resort, split up and squander themselves among other tribes who are not in rebellion until the troops are removed. It will be fighting a shadow, which will over and over again become a substance directly the troops are withdrawn.

M. Fischbach, the Prussian engineer, whom I have before mentioned as the director of the copper mines, was staying at the Greek's house with us, and was to proceed to Egin in a few days, hoping to discover coal in that neighbourhood. For twenty years he had been in the Turkish service, and, being a clever, intelligent man, he had picked up a mass of useful information which he freely placed at our service. To meet such a man is a Godsend to a traveller, for from him one may learn more in half an hour than in a month from the natives, whose ignorance regarding their own country and immediate neighbourhood is so dense that one often thinks they make false statements intentionally, and that they do so under certain circumstances there is no doubt. When the Turk can see what are the wishes of his questioner, he cannot resist making statements that will be in accordance with them, letting truth take care of itself. For instance, we never wish the journey before us to be long, fatiguing, or dangerous, or the

roads bad; therefore, invariably, on starting the distance
is shortened about a third, the roads are made good,
mountains removed, robbers banished. We inquire how
many hours it is from here to such and such a town, and
are told *ten*. The ten hours are ridden, and then the
same question put to some villager, and the answer will
be, "Three more," but it generally proves to be four.
When we left Oorfa we asked the khanji whether he had
ever been to Diarbekir, and whether the road was stony.
Yes, he had often been there, and we should not see a
stone as big as a nut on the entire journey; but before we
had gone half an hour out of the town we entered upon
a perfect sea of big loose stones, that were never lost sight
of for four days. Unless information can be derived from
some such man as M. Fischbach, the only hope of arriving
at the truth is to collect some half-dozen people together
and pit them against each other. Make them quarrel,
if possible, and then, by carefully attending, a few genuine
grains may be sorted from the chaff. Then all are such
inevitable liars they will swear black is white to obtain
any small advantage to themselves. About the stopping
at small towns Ali Agha and we always clashed. We
loathed them because of the dirt and dust and the numberless annoyances we were sure to encounter, and preferred
resting in our tent in some quiet village; but Ali Agha
liked the towns. He was saved the trouble of pitching
the tent and packing it again, he met congenial spirits,
and got what he considered good food. It therefore
happened that whenever one of these small places was on

our road, Ali Agha would declare the distance to it was just our usual day's ride, namely, nine hours; that the nearest village on the other side was six hours further on, and that we could not possibly stop at any this side, as either there was a bad sickness in them, or the inhabitants were very bad. Not only would he tell us these stories himself, but he made others come forward and back his statements; and when, after having passed a miserable night in some dirty town, we reached a village next morning but an hour farther on, Ali Agha would pretend to be furious, and bemoan the sins of the wicked people who had deceived us. If we paid no heed to him, but pushed on through a town, his horse knocked up, the loads came unfastened, and the zaptieh did not know the way; and if we still persisted, the old fellow made life a burden by sulking and pretending he was ill. The Armenian always sided with him, and nine times out of ten we had to give way. Every day's ride proved to be some hours longer than we had been led to suppose, and each stage from one large town to another was a day's ride farther than we had been told at starting. Governors and officials, being generally new-comers, could give us but little local information, and, besides, they usually wished to get rid of us, so would tell any lies to induce us to move on quickly. Such men, therefore, as M. Fischbach were our only real helps, they and Keipert's map; and Ali Agha hated both, for they often made us refuse to listen to him.

Besides being liars, the people of the land are steeped

in ignorance. A mudir asked M. Fischbach lately if England was near Vau or Batoum. Another man, the son of a pasha, informed him that the new Sultan had shut up all the theatres in Paris, as they were forbidden by the Koran. Nearly all the lower orders firmly believe England and France are under the dominion of the Sultan and pay tribute to him, or rather that we ought to do so, for that we sometimes escape this tribute is admitted, but our doing so is rebellious, and our conduct the same as the Kurds, who refuse to pay taxes, and we are sure sooner or later to be justly punished. We are worse than the Kurds, for they are poor, whereas we are rich, and could therefore afford to pay up.

On the day after our arrival, our host, accompanied by M. Fischbach, started for Egin, leaving us in possession of his house, and our first proceeding was to lock the door and station the Armenian inside with orders to open it to no one but the Americans, so secured for ourselves a day of complete rest and quiet, in which we could write journals and letters for England. In the evening we rode up to Kharpout to dine with the American missionaries, and we wished to dispense with any one's attendance, but this Ali Agha would not hear of, assuring us we were pretty sure to be robbed if we ventured alone. We therefore took the Armenian, carrying Ali Agha's old gun, and further took the precaution of strapping on our own pistols.

The view from the top of the Kharpout hill was, without exception, the finest we had seen since leaving Brusa.

For some days rain had been falling in the low hills, but snow had fallen on the mountains, and we could from our elevated position look over miles of distant summits thus covered, looking like a series of surf-capped monster waves hastening forward to dash into the plains below. Light fleecy clouds floated on the foot-hills or nestled down into snug ravines, whilst a soft mist partially veiled the foreground, through the hazy light of which might be seen, dotted about in all directions, tiny villages that looked (the reverse of what they were) clean and pretty. On the high mountains the cold had cleared the air of all vapour, and as far as the eye could reach crags and peaks stood boldly out as if cut out of burnished steel. They were very grand, some rising to eight or nine thousand feet above the sea; but we should have preferred to see a level plain in their place, for our onward route was through those hills, and they looked terrible in their savage beauty, and absolutely impassable for anything that had not wings.

We left Kharpout on December 12th, and rode due west for five hours over hilly but cultivated ground, and then entered a gorge between high hills, down which poured a rapid torrent. From here, for three hours into the small town of Keban Madan, we had the good fortune to find a road partially made, but even on this the ingenious Turk had in places succeeded in making riding on horses an impossibility. Wherever a spur of a hill had to be passed, instead of going round it on the level at its base, the road was carried straight over the top, and to get up and down

the steep slopes the road had to be made in steps like
a big staircase, each step being about two feet high,
making it necessary for the horses to travel in a series of
bounds. Now and then a gap was left on the face of the
hill where the old narrow track was the only road, and
yet we were assured by the Governor of Kharpout before
we left that this road was, as far as it went, quite perfect
and intended for artillery.

On speaking of it to M. Fischbach afterwards, he
shrugged his shoulders and said, " Ah, yes, it is, like everything the Turks attempt, a failure and a total waste of
labour. Since I have been in their service I have commenced numberless undertakings, roads, bridges, canals,
etc., but I have never been allowed to finish anything ; and
generally, as on this road, by leaving a break in the work
such as the gaps you mention, the whole of the labour
and expense has been rendered useless, when a very little
more would have finished it."

Year after year the villagers are forced to give their
labour on this road, but what they do will be equalled
by what falls into ruin, so the road will never be finished.
Edhem Pasha, the late Grand Vizier, began this road
years ago, when he was quite a young man, and since
then thousands of days' labour have been expended on
it, but it never advances a step. While riding down
the gorge we passed an almost perpendicular cliff some
two thousand feet high, composed of the most beautiful
marble, white, blue, red, and green ; and one could
but feel regret that what might be such a source of

wealth should have to lie buried in these mountain fastnesses.

Keban Madan is celebrated for its mines of argentiferous lead ore, which were a few years ago worked at a profit by the Government, but which are now almost wholly given up, owing to all the wood within (profitable) reach having been burnt. The town, which must have been one of some importance, is now almost in ruins; only some five hundred houses remain, and these become fewer year by year. Edhem Pasha built a large shed with six blast furnaces in it, some thirty years ago; but now there remains but one furnace in working order, the shed and the other furnaces being in ruins—ruins that are past repair, and all will have to be reconstructed if the work is ever to be commenced again. M. Fischbach hoped to discover coal within ten or fifteen miles, on a hillside higher up the Euphrates, down which river it might be floated at small cost. If he succeeds in this, he will indeed prove a profitable servant; for the ore is very rich in both lead and silver, and with a good seam of coal to take the place of the destroyed forests it would yield each year, let us say, an ironclad, a mosque, or a sultan's kiosk, to say nothing of the houses, horses, and wives that the mine managers and others would be able to buy with the pickings they would get out of the undertaking.

Just as we entered the town we were met by our late host, the Greek, and M. Fischbach, and with them inspected the old furnaces, but there was little to be learnt and less to be seen in the ruins. While doing this, a zaptieh

arrived with a message from the governor to say he hoped
we would become his guests, and that a house was prepared for us. We rejoiced to think we should escape
spending the night in a khan, and thoroughly appreciated
his kindness. Later on, we discovered that his generosity
cost him little—in fact, was a decided gain to him; for he
had forced an Armenian to take us in and provide us
with supper, the governor himself sharing it and playing
the pleasant part of host. The owner of the house
explained this to us, saying at the same time he was
delighted to receive us, but that it would have been
pleasanter to his feelings if the governor had not utterly
ignored him and behaved as if he were our entertainer.
The room prepared for us was a long one, with a row of
windows at the far end, under which ran the principal
and most comfortable divan. G—— was shown to one
snug corner of this and I to the other, and soon after we
had settled down the governor arrived, and he occupied
the place of honour on the divan between us and facing
down the room. The owner of the house, his grown-up
son, and a relation stood for some time at the lower end
of the room with their shoes off. At last, in the most
condescending manner, the Turk waved them permission
to be seated, upon which they crouched just on the
extreme edge of the extreme end of the side divan, not
venturing to speak till spoken to, allowing the Turk to
give all the necessary orders to the servants, and often
themselves hastening to supply his demands. We tried
our best to give the poor fellows a lift by offering them

cigarettes, and inviting them to come higher up the
divan and to get farther on to it, but this evidently made
them uncomfortable, and the Turk looked very sour when
we did so. Supper was eaten à la Turk, the dishes being
ordered in one after the other by the governor, but at
our request the real host, his son, and friend shared them
with us. When the supper was over and a friendly
cigarette had been smoked, we adopted a masterful silence,
which we kept up for an hour, only answering the Turk
in monosyllables, after which he retired—the Armenian
said to get drunk, as was his nightly custom.

The town of Keban Madan stands on the steep banks
of a little brook, a few hundred yards from its junction
with the Euphrates, which, by-the-by, is here called the
Kara - Su (Black Water). On the morrow, when we
again continued our journey, we found just below the
town a ferry-boat awaiting us (like those we had seen at
Beridjik), and, squeezing all our horses into it, we were
taken across the river, a back current on both shores
being taken advantage of in such a manner that only one
or two long sweeps of the oars were required in the
middle of the river to carry us from current to current.
The river here was sixty or seventy feet wide and ran
like a mill-race, the water clear and deep, and we were
told large-sized boats could proceed up it for some
miles. Should coal, as is hoped, be found up the river
beyond the mines, a flat-bottomed steam-tug will have
to be used to tug the barges up the stream, there being
no path along the craggy shores from which to tow them,

and the current is much too fast to allow of their being rowed.

From Keban Madan our road lay north-east, parallel to the river, but some distance from it, over hills, many of which it took us an hour to ascend, and through a country treeless and barren. At night we reached the Armenian village of Enchicle, and had the pleasure of sitting half an hour in the street while the zaptieh tried to find us a room, and finally we had to sleep on a raised platform at the end of a stable. For not having a better lodging I believe *I* was to blame. Whilst waiting in the street, a young Armenian, dressed in à la Franca clothes and his feet in slippers (slippers always make me hate the wearer), stood staring at us, with the sort of air that said, "I am a thoroughly civilized creature, and as good as you are." Just after the loads had been taken off and the horses and our baggage arranged, I heard a lot of talking at the door, and, on going out, found this civilized gentleman and some dozen uncivilized friends, apparently quarrelling with the zaptieh. All flew at me in a moment, and talked all at once in shrill, high tones, using shoulders, arms, and bodies to assist their tongues. Not one word could I distinguish in all this din, and seeing I did not understand, the young swell grasped my shoulder with a filthy, claw-like hand, which hand I immediately struck with my stick, sending the owner off howling with rage. M. Fischbach, who arrived shortly afterwards, said that the man had been to him to ask for an explanation, saying, "I offered this Englishman a house, I pressed him

to accept one, and in return he struck me, hurting my
hand a little, and my feelings very much." Poor fellow!
I am very sorry I did not understand his civilized ways,
and therefore struck him; but I was not sorry we did
not go to his house. If the horses smelt a little and
fidgeted a good bit, yet they could not talk platitudes,
and it was not necessary for us to pay attention to them,
as we should have been obliged to do to the Armenian
and his friends.

CHAPTER XXVIII.

Adepsis—Kurdish raiders—A mule track—Egin—Bad fare—A novel
bridge—On the mountains—Starving villagers—Turks at prayer.

WHEN we were about to start next morning G——'s horse,
which by kicking and fighting all the other horses whenever a chance offered had gained the name of "Adepsis"
(unmannerly), came out with a bad sore back. The poor
little beast had done its work well, and had carried its
master all the way from Brusa at an easy tripple, keeping
its condition and spirits to the last; so, thinking it had
earned a little rest, G—— mounted a pack-horse, and
Adepsis was allowed to run loose. After an hour's
bargaining we hired a mule to take the place of the pack-
horse, with its owner, who engaged to run on foot and
keep up with us all day, a task he performed apparently
without the least fatigue. His mule, the only one we
could get, was only a year and a half old, and could carry
little more than the pack-saddle, and its difficulties were
increased by having its tail hauled tight round to the
right and there tied to the pack, while its head was
pulled to the left and tied rigidly on the other side, giving
the poor beast the shape of the letter S. We did our
utmost to induce its owner to liberate its two ends, but

this he utterly refused to do, saying that if we made
him he would not go a yard with us.

"Do you not see," he said, "that the mule is only a
baby, and must be tied together to support it?"

"How does it support it?"

"I don't know; but I know it is our custom, and that
if I did not do it the beast would be ruined, so I must
stick to it."

Our old fool Ali Agha backed him, saying, "Tchellaby,
you do not know, but it is necessary to tie it like that,
for our custom says so."

Perhaps the mule from custom liked its unnatural
position; anyhow I hope it did, for not once during the
day was it allowed to straighten itself.

Just before our visit, the people of Enchicle had received
a visit from a gang of Kurds from the Derzim Daghlar
on the other side of the village, who, after spending a
night there eating and drinking of the best they could find,
retired in the morning, not only forgetting to pay for
what they had had, but taking with them fifty sheep and
all the chickens belonging to the place. These were
taken down to the Euphrates and hauled across in a noose
working on a rope suspended between two high crags.
Only five Kurds came out on this raid, and as there must
have been two hundred men in the village, we naturally
asked why they submitted to be robbed; but we were
assured that resistance was madness, as, if any were used,
the Kurds were certain to come down in force, carrying
off all the cattle, the young girls, and household goods,

and firing the village before they left. I suppose the villagers were right ; but if so, it does seem strange that in a land where there are thousands and tens of thousands of uncultivated acres, rich and good, these people should not move away out of the reach of their troublesome neighbours.

About two hours after leaving the village we came down a steep descent, and then followed a road that runs along the banks of the river, and, thanks to the bad state of the road, we had to do half the journey on foot; but use is everything, and fatigue cures one of being particular, so on the latter part, though it was just as bad, we stuck to our horses. Nowhere was the path more than six feet wide, often less than two. It was strewn with big stones, and in places where an intervening point obliged it to mount perhaps a thousand feet, it was made in steps from a foot to three feet high, and even these in places had been washed away. The path zigzagged up and down the hills, there often being but ten or twelve feet between the turns, and when near the river it often ran along the edge of the precipices, and was so narrow that there was nothing under one's right stirrup but the rocks and water from ten to two hundred feet below. The scenery would have been glorious had the mountains been clothed with forests, and as it was it had a wild and savage grandeur that was very striking. In places the mountains rose line over line from the water's edge, till lost in snowy peaks high up in the clouds. In others the river came rushing and leaping through clefts, the rocky sides of which rise

Y

in sheer precipices two or three thousand feet high, while yet in other parts the river turned so abruptly that it appeared as if emerging from under the foot of the wall of stone that faced us. On neither bank was there a level spot, and the few huts we passed were perched high up amid what looked like inaccessible crags. We rode north, south, east, and west; up this gully, down that, now on a mountain summit, now on the river's edge, the track everywhere bad, in places horrible, and necessitating the pace to be a slow crawl.

In the afternoon we reached the top of one of these high mountains, and from it saw the town of Egin lying at the foot, on a piece of sloping ground on the bank of the river, which here emerges from a deep gorge just above the town, and enters another just below it. On all sides rise lofty mountains; from no direction can it be approached except down zigzag staircase-like roads, and from where we first saw it, it looked as if in the bottom of a monster pit; yet on entering the town we found it superior and more civilized looking than most of the places we had visited. To a certain extent its poverty makes it rich. The surrounding country is so mountainous and so barren that nothing will grow, and the inhabitants are driven to seek money in other parts wherewith to import food. Therefore it has become the custom of Egin to send forth its young men, generation after generation, to Constantinople, Smyrna, the Islands of the Archipelago, and even to Egypt, as bankers and money-changers. They remain away ten years, then

return, marry, and build a house. After a son is born
to them, they go away for another ten years, leaving their
families behind. At the end of this time they return for
good, often bringing with them considerable riches.

There are good houses built all round the town, standing
in pretty, nicely kept gardens, which gives the place an
attractive, well-to-do appearance. As we rode along we
often got a peep in at the open doors that made us long
to turn in and enjoy the comfortable, warm, snug divan-
encircled rooms; but having no acquaintances nor letters
to any one here, no such luck was in store for us. On the
contrary, we had to put up at about the most miserable
lodging we had yet had. It was a small, dingy, earth-floored
room, through a café so wretched that we made an effort
to escape by presenting our firman to the head of the
zaptiehs and asking him to procure us better quarters,
offering to pay anything he liked to ask. But no, it was
not to be; the zaptieh reverently kissed the Sultan's
signature, but stated that he was powerless to help us, a
custom having arisen in this town, unlike that in any
other towns, which debarred the governor from quartering
strangers on the inhabitants. The only result of this
application was to make our condition worse instead of
better, for by the time we got back to our dismal den it
was dark, and the shops were all shut, and nothing to be
bought but some "saddle-flap" bread and a little very
dirty honey. Not only did we fare badly, but our poor
horses nearly shared our fate, for some barley was obtained
with great difficulty, and was only to be had at a

ridiculously high price. As we were so uncomfortably lodged, and as we and our horses ran the risk of (to say the least) losing condition, we only remained at Egin one night.

The next morning, while riding down the zigzag street that led to the bridge over the Euphrates, one of our horses tried to shirk the journey, and therefore at a sharp turn trotted along the roof of a house, the back part of which ran into the bank on a level with the road. From this house he stepped on to another, and so on and on till he had gone the length of a street, and was finally caught on the roof of a mosque, and fetched back to his work.

The architecture of the bridge over which we passed was novel, if not good. On each side of the river, a stack of long squared baulks of timber was placed, each layer projecting three or four feet beyond the one beneath it, in the direction of the stream—the whole forming an erection like a flight of steps turned upside down. When the steps had extended well over the river from each side, long baulks spanned the intervening space, and the bridge of rough planks was placed over all.

If possible our road on this day was worse than ever, and to add to our troubles we constantly passed donkeys and pack-horses, and in one part, where we had a precipice on our left hand, a regiment of soldiers straggled over the road for a mile. The donkeys and horses had all to be turned aside into niches in the hillside for us to pass, but it was different with the beasts carrying the soldiers' baggage; they were driven straight at us, and to avoid shoving them off the narrow track, or being shoved over ourselves, we had to drive our horses into some place off the path.

For four hours we were continually ascending, sometimes up hills so steep that our horses could scarcely carry us, but at the end of this time we reached a summit, and, passing over a sharp saddle-backed ridge, a sight presented itself before us that reduced our spirits to zero. We had always expected sooner or later to emerge from the mountains, or reach a part of them less rugged and more open, and even ventured to hope we might get into a pretty wooded district. The first forward glance dispelled all these hopes. In all directions, for mile after mile, till lost in space, there stretched before us one vast region of mountains, their sides often precipitous and jagged, and everywhere excessively steep ; no valleys were to be seen, one mountain springing from the foot of the other, and the entire mass one great jumble. If one could look down upon a field that had just been scarified, through spectacles that would magnify some thousand times, it would form the sort of picture we saw. Not a tree, not a house, not a moving creature ; desolate, barren, rock-encumbered mountains ; and as we gazed we reviled ourselves for being such fools as to have come to such a place, and looked back to the plains of Mesopotamia with loving regret.

Heavy clouds came drifting over from the north, and every hour we expected snow, and felt that if caught by it within the next week, we must be prisoners in some dirty village for weeks, perhaps months, or, failing to reach one

of these, our fate might be still worse. To go back was
out of the question, so, remembering that every minute
saved was of consequence, away we went sliding and
blundering down the hillside; but at last we reached a
tortuous gorge between the hills, and followed it up till
dark.

We passed one khan, but the one room as well as the
stables were crowded, so we pushed on, finally reaching a
Turkish village up a narrow valley, where we were made
happy by getting a fairly good warm room, a few eggs,
honey, and youatt (curds). It was very good of the villagers
to sell us these things, for they said, and I believe truly,
that they were only one remove from starvation. During
the past two years troops had continually passed to and from
the Russian frontier, and had over and over again cleared
the village out. Bullocks, cows, sheep, and fowls had all
disappeared. New had been bought, which went the way
of the first. So steep and sterile are the mountains that
no corn can be grown, or at all events very little, therefore the winter store has to be fetched from the neighbourhood of Sivas. Twice this year the requisite quantity
had been brought in, but the first had been devoured by
soldiers, and the second by Kurds, and as one man said
with grim humour, " Now our teeth will have hard work,
for the only thing left us is stones; " adding, " We have
no more money to buy a third supply, and if we had it is
too late, for the roads in a few days will be impassable
from snow."

The Kurds, we were told, had harassed the country

more than they had done for years, as during the war all
had been away hovering round the battle-fields—a flock
of vultures, plundering friends and foes alike. During
this time the little plots of ground they usually cultivated
had been left untilled, and there was not a grain of corn
in the whole of their region, except what they had robbed
from the neighbouring villages.

Even in the best of times, the mountains will not support these villages. The men, therefore, spend the best
years of their lives in Constantinople and other distant
towns, the Armenians as hammals and pashas' servants,
and the Turks as butchers, bakers, sailors, etc., returning
to the home of their childhood only when well on in years,
and not even then unless they have been fortunate enough
to save a little money. So frugal and careful are these
poor fellows during the years of their voluntary exile, that
all amass money ; but this is unfortunately well known to
a lot of swindling Greeks and others, who, by offering to
pay cent. per cent. interest for the loan of it, often transfer
it to their own pockets, and then either decamp and are
no more seen, or more frequently still bring forward
numerous witnesses to prove they have never had it.

Our road all the next day was a repetition of that we
had just passed over, and no incident occurred on the ride
that is worth recording. We stayed that night at another
small village, and on the morrow, December 17th, we
once more descended to the level of the river, and following this up passed through the town of Komer, where we
changed zaptiehs. While this was being done, we were

asked to pay a visit to the governor, a kaimakan, at his official room. On going in, we were somewhat astonished to find that gentleman with four more respectable Turks all on their knees in a line across the room, hard at work saying their prayers. No one rose, but the kaimakam motioned to us to be seated, and said, "Make yourself comfortable and smoke a cigarette, and in a few minutes I shall be at liberty." I have thousands of times seen Turks at prayer, but never before saw it so carefully gone through as by these men. Short snatches were repeated out loud in high pitched tones, first by one, then by another. All fell on their knees, touched the ground with their heads, sat back on their heels, placed their hands behind their ears, rose again, and bowed in the most perfect line and with the precision of clockwork. But the reverence of the performance was somewhat spoilt by the way one and another looked us over out of the corners of their eyes, making one doubt whether they paid any real attention to what was being repeated.

Once, and once only, have I ever seen a Turkish woman at her devotions. It was in a quiet spot in the Taurus that, on rounding a sharp turn, we came upon an old lady so engaged, whilst her husband stood by holding the donkey upon which she had been journeying. She took no notice of us, but went steadily on, kneeling and bowing just in the same manner that men do.

CHAPTER XXIX.

Erzingan—An inactive army—Foreign news—Garrison towns—Military
character—Over the watershed—The life of a soldier—Village
elders—A forest—Signs of civilization.

FROM Komer we followed a road parallel with and near
the river, upon which we continued all that afternoon,
and after sleeping one more night in a Greek village and
proceeding again the next morning, we emerged from a
gorge on the afternoon of the 18th, and found ourselves
upon a plain some ten or twelve miles square, on the
middle of which stands the town of Erzingan. This and
the one at Kharpout were the only plains we saw on the
entire ride from Diarbekir to Trebizond, but this, unlike
the fertile, well-cultivated one at Kharpout, was little
better than a vast moraine. From all directions mountain torrents pour down over it, bringing with them, when
swollen by the melting snow, thousands and tens of thousands of tons of stones, which are deposited everywhere,
making the plain almost utterly fruitless. A very little
engineering skill and labour would direct and keep these
stone torrents within proper bounds, and the plain might
then little by little be made into one large garden, irrigated
and enriched by the streams that now are its destruction.

Erzingan is little more than a big military station,

standing on flat ground which is a dust heap in summer and a mud lake in winter, most of the streets being left unpaved. In the town and its environs there are large ugly white-washed barracks, and the whole place swarmed with ragged soldiers, and every café was crowded with officers—generals, colonels, captains, etc.—all huddled up on raised wooden benches, spending their entire day in drinking coffee and smoking. These men were busily engaged putting down the Kurds, whose mountains were only a mile or two distant on the other side of the river that separated them from the plain.

All day and most of the night bugles were kept too-tooing, and as this was the only military duty ever performed, we wondered whether the generals expected the Kurdish mountains to fall at the sound as did the walls of Jericho. Mind, I am not blaming the troops for their inactivity, and can see no reason to do so, for in keeping with their colours they were behaving as no other soldiers in the world would have done under like circumstances. Unpaid, unclothed, and poorly fed, what might they expect if they went gadding about in the mountains after the Will-o'-the-wisp Kurds ? They had no guides, no transport waggons or beasts, and there were no villages to plunder and live on. Ten days in the hills and all would be starved; besides, by stopping where they were, they were doing all Government required of them. They enabled those in authority at Constantinople to say that so many thousand troops were at Erzingan towzling the rebellious Kurds.

So crowded was the town with soldiers we had some difficulty in getting a room, and if it had not been for the assistance of an officer, a captain, who kindly came to our aid and showed us one through a café shop, we should have run the risk of passing the night in the open air, and as the rain was falling in the low lands and the snow on the hills we should have fared badly. Besides thus helping us, our friend gave us the news of the day; amongst other things, that "the troubles of Turkey were over, England had declared war against Russia, the fleet was in the Bosphorus, and already thirty thousand of our troops occupied Gallipoli." We did not quite believe his news, but I think we were the only people in the town that were at all sceptical in the matter.

As soon as we had shaken down, we sent our firman with many salaams to the general in command, and besides asking for the usual zaptieh, we begged him to send us any European papers he might have. A civil message was returned that the zaptieh should be in readiness, but as there was not a newspaper of any sort in the town, he was sorry he was unable to oblige us.

Besides Adepsis' bad back, nearly all the other horses had come to grief on the wretched roads we had travelled over, and were getting very thin and stale, so we determined to rest one clear day in Erzingan for their benefit; but as we saw the snow-line descending lower on the mountains hour by hour, we dared not give the poor beasts a longer time. Having only one more stage before us, we cleared out our baggage and drafted everything we could dispense with, and as everything in the shape of provisions had long ago disappeared, the horses' loads were a mere nothing.

In any other country, Erzingan, from always being occupied by troops, would have enjoyed considerable commercial prosperity. Houses would be required for officers, and these, together with hotels, cafés, shops, and stores, would spring up in all directions; merchandise of all sorts would find a ready market, and the road to the sea would always have a heavy traffic. But here one simple fact puts a stop to all this. The soldiers have nothing to spend, and the officers little more. If the common soldier can scrape together enough to buy tobacco, get shaved, pay for a bath, and as a great treat get a few onions or garlic, he is fortunate, and readily pays away all he has. If he has no money, he will, if he can, procure these luxuries and delicacies without paying. He *takes* from the shop tobacco, never hoping to be able to pay. The first barber he meets is made to shave him, and when he has done so is accused of having cut him, and thinks himself fortunate if he is not paid with kicks. Gardens and shops where onions and other vegetables grow, or are stored, are constantly visited, and one by one a few of the tempting bulbs obtained; and if the owner says anything, the soldier displays the single onion he has taken, and calls the man a mean brute for expecting to be paid for *just one*.

No one dares to build a house better than a pigsty, for if he does it will be requisitioned by an officer and no

rent paid for it. Hardly any goods are brought to the
town, for if they are they are sure to disappear. The
officers and soldiers know that if they can get things on
credit, a day will come, sooner or later, when they will
receive orders to march, and then no debts are remembered
and they are never heard of again. For these reasons no
one ever thinks of carrying on any sort of commerce
where soldiers are stationed in any numbers, and a
military place is always the poorest and most miserable
of all.

In the course of our journey we visited many towns
where soldiers were quartered, but not once did we see
any sort of drill going on. The men lolled about in
sunny corners, or waddled up and down the streets by
twos and threes, generally hand in hand. Nowhere did
we see them playing at any games, or taking any real
exercise. They just vegetated, their only duty being to
fetch their food from the kitchens in big tins or go to
the fountain for water. The lives of the officers were no
better. They, like the men, lolled through life, generally
sitting all day cross-legged on the divan in some café,
their only occupation being counting and playing with a
string of beads that never leaves their hands. Not one
in a thousand ever, in the course of his life, opens a book,
not one in five hundred a newspaper, and their entire
knowledge is obtained by conversation with men as
ignorant as themselves.

As it is among civilians, so it is in the army, the higher
the social rank the lower the character. The common

soldiers are rough, dirty savages, but they have some good points. They are obedient, uncomplaining, patient, and brave. Sergeants may share some of these good traits, and yuzbashis may be found who are not all corrupt, but as one gets higher all are despicable in the extreme. They are as ignorant as the soldiers, have no honesty and no bravery, and are effeminate and lazy ; most are drunkards, and many are opium-eaters. Sins and crimes the names of which are unknown, or if known are not mentioned in civilized countries, are committed by them, and are the common subject of café-house jokes. Like the soldier's, the officer's pay is often in arrear, and is always small ; but, unlike the soldiers, they can make shift without it by robbing the inhabitants and purloining the military stores that pass through their hands. Their men have always despised and hated them, and the almost universal incompetency displayed by officers of all ranks during the late war has intensified this feeling. We talked with many soldiers in various places, and one and all exhausted the rich vocabulary of Turkish abuse when speaking of their superiors, most of them finishing by saying they would never fight again if led, or rather driven, by these men. This word "driven" is the right one to use, for hardly ever does an officer above the rank of captain precede his men into battle. He remains in the rear and orders his men to advance, and the only time he is found in the front is in a retreat, when he displays great alacrity.

On the 20th of December we left Erzingan, and with our horses' heads turned due north for Trebizond, we were

for four hours passing over high mountains by a mule
track, with snow and sleet falling, and we were most
thankful when, on getting to the foot of the northern
slope, we found our road led down a long sheltered valley
by the side of a small brook, and here we also came in for
finer weather and dry roads.   All day in looking back we
could see snow-clouds passing over the hills in our rear,
and felt we had escaped so far without an hour to spare.
As it was, the track on the high part of the pass was
difficult to follow, and yet there was only a few inches of
snow upon it.   Had a really heavy storm come on I do not
think we could possibly have found our way, and as there
were no villages, and no wood of any sort with which we
could have made a fire, it would have been no joke to be
lost there.

We had another reason for congratulating ourselves.
The water in the brook beside us ran northwards, so we
were over the great watershed, and on the slope leading
to the Black Sea and home.

On riding into a large village at sunset, we were met
by a soldier, who at once took us under his care and
quickly found us a room in a stable; but on a fire being
lighted it smoked so badly we were driven out again.
However, our soldier friend soon procured us another,
which we shared with five of our horses, and found them
to be anything but pleasant companions.   Not one of
them laid down all night, or appeared to sleep, but kept
munching the corn and straw, fidgeting, kicking, and
biting, and yet the stupid beasts had had a long journey

and must have been tired. True, they had had nothing to
eat all day, and had to eat at night for the whole twenty-
four hours, but one would have thought they might have
finished their supper and got a snooze in the course of
the twelve hours the night lasted.

In the evening our soldier patron paid us a long visit,
and we learnt from him that his activity in procuring
a lodging for us was part of his duty, as he was stationed
here by his superior to see that the villagers provided for
the requirements of travellers of all sorts, rich and poor,
soldiers and civilians. He had no money himself, therefore the village had to feed him; and as he looked fat
and sleek, I feel sure he did not put up with the worst of
fare. After he had left us in the evening, I jotted down
notes of his conversation with us. He told us he had been
eleven years in the army, during which time he had only
had one month's leave of absence, to visit his village near
Sivas. For thirty-one months he had now been without
a paras of pay, and he said, "If I do get it, which is most
improbable, it will be paid in paper, so will only be worth
a quarter of what is due to me." He had fought before
Kars under Muchtar Pasha, and, after escaping from that
town when taken by the Russians, had helped to defend
Erzeroom till peace was proclaimed. As usual with all
the soldiers we had met, he heaped abuse on his officers,
adding, " I have done a lot of fighting, and am quite willing to do more, but, by Allah, I will never fire another
shot unless I am led by Europeans; and all my fellow-
soldiers say the same. When we were nearly starved at

Erzeroom the padishah sent us food, clothes, and tobacco, all of which our officers stole. They lived in luxury, so did their civilian servants, while we, who were doing the fighting, wonld have given, oh! so much for one whiff of tobacco, but could not get it." Here the man sucked down a cloud of smoke with such evident relish, it went a long way to confirm his statement. He had no idea how much longer he would have to serve, and would give anything to be able to go home, marry, settle down, and "make rest." We asked did many men desert. "Thousands," he said; "they had deserted before the enemy, after their defeats, and since peace was proclaimed; all the wicked men ran away home, and wicked men were on the increase." We asked if they were never caught and punished. "No. How could they be caught? They were scattered all over Turkey in their various homes, and, besides, there is no Government now, and if a meddlesome zaptieh ever did hunt them up, why, a few piastres would settle him."

If he could get permission he could walk home to his village in five days, and would gladly do so, and come back again, if he might remain with his friends and relations only one week; but there was no hope of getting leave. "Why, Tchellaby, are we not disbanded? The Russians beat us and we can't fight again; besides, there is peace now, and our officers said we should all go home when the war was over. We think we are kept so that the officers may be able to stop on full pay and live by robbing our provisions." This man was a sergeant, about

z

thirty-five years old, tall, strong, active, and remarkably pleasant looking; in fact, a man to rejoice the heart of the most fastidious recruiting sergeant or colonel.

Besides this soldier, a discharged sailor paid us a visit. He had lately served his time in an ironclad, and had been to England to fetch the vessel out, but the only impression England had made on his mind was that there were lots of people there, and the bread was white. No one speaking to him for five minutes could have doubted his being a sailor, one of the regular noisy, rollicking, careless, happy-go-lucky sort to be found among all nationalities, but in physique he was inferior to his companion the soldier, and not to be compared with him for sharpness and intelligence. The mudir of the village and four of the elders also came in. They squatted all in a row, salaamed, asked after our health, and then after our spirits—I mean those generally carried in a bottle; but on hearing we had none, they arose, and giving a hasty salaam, scuttled off in a great hurry, and we felt convinced they did so because some one else in the place was having a debauch, and they only visited us to see if our spirits were not better than what they could get elsewhere; or perhaps the other liquor was on sale, whereas ours, if we had any, might have been got for nothing. The sailor followed them with alacrity, but the soldier, giving an expressive shrug of his shoulders, kept his seat.

During the first half of our ride on the next day, the 21st, our road lay through a less rugged country. Villages were more frequent, and a considerable tract of land had been cultivated, but the soil, except in a few valleys, looked of a poor cold, clayey description, and, judging from the thin, weedy straws of the long stubbles we saw, I should say the crops of serials grown on it were not at all good. We saw very few cattle, and our zaptieh accounted for their scarceness by saying they had all been swallowed up by the armies and the Kurds, and that the latter often came from the Derzim Daghlar, now forty miles distant, on marauding expeditions.

About noon we entered a narrow valley that ran up among high snow-clad mountains, and here our eyes were once more gladdened by the sight of trees—the first we had seen, except a few in gardens, since we had left the Cilician Gates, close down by the Mediterranean. With the exception of a few nut-bushes and dogwood, the trees were all pine, but nowhere did we see any fine timber, and ninety-nine out of every hundred were partially decayed. All had been tapped near the ground to procure resin, and this at once stops the growth, and ultimately kills the trees. Many, apparently for no purpose, had been felled, and were rotting on the ground, branches and all. Never mind, poor as they were, they were *trees*, a refreshing sight after the endless expanse of bare lifeless mountains we had been passing over, and denoting that we had opened out another stage on our journey.

It took us some four hours to pass through these mountains, the road all the way being very bad and impassable for anything but pack-horses. Just before sunset the little ravine down which we had been riding

opened into a wide valley, and on reaching this we saw
directly in front of us a handsome, well-constructed stone
bridge, leading over a river that flowed down the valley,
and a few minutes later we were on a really good chaussée,
and found we had, in fact, hit off the road that runs from
Trebizond to Erzeroom, and over which the chief part of
the Persian trade passes to Turkey. Where we first came
upon it, it was in all respects as good as one of the old
turnpike roads in England, and had at one time been equally
good throughout its length, but we afterwards found that,
new as the road was (it had only been made five years),
it had become almost impassable in some places, and
dangerous in others. At every mile or so there stood
a roadside khan, but we had to pass three or four of them,
all the rooms being occupied by travellers, and the stables
by their horses. At last we came to one with a village
perched up amongst some crags just above it, and we
made a halt, calling for the khanji. No one came, but on
mounting to a couple of small rooms on the flat roof of
the stable we found them fairly clean, so determined to
take possession.

The zaptieh rode up to the village, and soon returned
with a man carrying a lot of firewood, and straw and corn
were procured at a khan close by. Ali Agha went forag-
ing in the village, but all he could procure for supper was
eight eggs by no means fresh, so we once more put off
satisfying our hunger and supped chiefly on cigarettes
and tea.

CHAPTER XXX.

The Trebizond-Erzeroom road—Pitched roofs—Soghanli Dagh—A beautiful gorge—Last night on the road—Trebizond—Trade with Persia—Quitting Asia Minor.

WE were off at daybreak next morning, and jogged merrily along on the chaussée, admiring as we went the remains of its former excellence. We afterwards heard that enormous sums had been expended on it, sufficient indeed to have carried it on beyond Erzeroom (where it now ends) to Van, or even farther, but sundry pashas had made fortunes out of it, and many others had well feathered their nests. No expense had been spared in the construction. Excellent bridges and culverts had been made of finely dressed granite or hard limestone, huge embankments thrown across valleys to maintain a uniform gradient, and points of rocky mountain had been cut through, sometimes hundreds of yards long. All had been deeply metalled, and, in fact, made quite perfect, down to the milestones with the distance in both kilometres and hours cut upon them. So complete must it have been, that it might have been kept in perfect order at a mere trifling expense—a toll of a penny on every beast that passed over it would have left a margin; but, like every-

thing in Turkey, no provision was made for repairs, and
the road was left to fall into utter decay. Already the abutments of bridges had been undermined and fallen in; the
river, for want of a retaining wall, had here and there swept
the road away, and in places the mules and other animals
had worn deep trenches, winding over its face in all
directions. In some low parts near the sea the road had
altogether disappeared in quagmires, and had I not seen
arabas actually on the road, and afterwards the same ones
in Trebizond, I should have said the road was impassable
for wheeled carriages. Much of the excellent work, such
as the rock cuttings, must remain for ever, but the greater
part of the road, if not quickly repaired, will have to be
reconstructed.

An hour or so after we had come upon the chaussée,
we passed the town of Gumish-Khanné, and here, for the
first time since leaving Eski-Shehr (four days from
Brusa), we saw once more pitched roofs in the place of the
wretched flat mud-covered affairs that are never waterproof. With this improvement in roofs came other
improvements. Gardens and orchards surrounded every
house where a piece of land sufficiently flat existed, shops
appeared all along the road, and as we went farther khans
and cafés multiplied. Then we noticed another welcome
change. We were no longer stared at and jeered as if we
were some curious foreign wild beasts. Hardly any one
looked at us, and only a very few made any remarks, and
when they did it was only "There, goes the post," or, quite
in a friendly tone, "There go two Muscovs."

Three hours below Gumish-Khanné the road left the
valley, and, bearing to the right, began to wind up the
slopes of the mountains, and before we had followed it far
we came across forests of fine spruce-fir, intermingled with
beech and pine, and the country became prettier and
prettier every mile we rode. For four hours we were continually ascending, and at nightfall had not nearly reached
the summit of the mountain, which, by-the-by, is named
the Soghanli Dagh after the small village of Soghan, which
stands just where our road left the valley.

Such as it was, there was no want of accommodation
now for man and beast. Khans, often three or four
together, were constantly passed, and so, picking out the
one that looked the cleanest, we turned in for the night.
Two hours' ride in the morning and we stood on the
summit, probably close to the spot where the Greeks,
under Zenophon, rejoiced over the sight of the Black Sea.
Our eyes were not so gladdened, for the day was misty
towards the sea, and no extensive view was to be had.
Besides, where we crossed, the summit of the road passed
through a narrow gap, the hills on both sides closing
round in front only a few miles below, which must, I
think, completely shut out the view of the sea. The "Ten
Thousand" probably were scattered over these side hills,
from the summits of which I have no doubt the sea is in
sight. We halted for a few minutes to smoke a cigarette,
and then, after taking one last look at the great sea of
mountains behind us, we started down the last hill of our
journey. Yes, the last, but by no means the least, for

here we were eight thousand feet above the sea, which was only thirty-six miles distant. There was not a quarter of a mile's rise in all the way, and in some parts the road was so steep it must be slow work, even for a light well-horsed carriage, to get up.

For the first half-hour after passing the summit, bare, down-like hills surrounded us, and then beautiful spruce-fir forests filled the gorge we entered, while the ground beneath them was a tangle of rhododendrons. Although it was mid-winter, the scenery through which we passed on this day's ride was very lovely, and must be in spring, when the rhododendrons are in flower, and the spruce, beech, and other trees in full leaf, simply perfect. Greek villages soon came in sight, and detached houses began to dot the hillside; green grass, the first we had seen since entering Turkey, stretched in glades by the river-side, while every available spot on the hills was under cultivation. Here and there, near a village, where fir trees did not hide the view, the sides of the ravine might be seen rising often in sheer precipices for hundreds of feet, terminating high up in the clouds in rugged peaks and crags, on some of which might be seen the ruins of old stone castles. Wherever on the cliff a tree could find root, there stood a tall tapering spruce or a dense patch of rhododendrons. In some parts wear and tear, a shock of earthquake, or a flash of lightning had rent a rocky summit and toppled the greater part of it down the face of the hill, where masses as big as cathedrals remained, looking as if the push of a hand might send them rolling on.

Some of these rocks had fallen into the brook, completely blocking its course, and the water had risen behind them till it reached the top and came rushing over in a pretty cascade.

Had our horses been fresh we might easily have pushed on and reached Trebizond this day, but to spare the poor beasts, and also to avoid arriving in a strange town at night, we made one more halt on the road, sleeping this time at the café of a villainous-looking Persian, who, before we dismounted, assured us every khan farther on was full of soldiers, and that his room was just about the most perfect on all the road. Naturally he lied, or he would not have been a Persian. There were, as we afterwards found out, no soldiers on the road, and his room was a pigsty, miserably filthy, and with a smashed door that would not shut. But we did not mind; it was our last night on the road, and on the morrow we should, Inshallah (please God), be in Trebizond. We were only six hours from it, and, come snow come storm, nothing should prevent our reaching it next day, if possible.

The storm *did* come. When we turned out at daybreak we found a bitter wind blowing in our faces and a deluge of rain coming down, but we hurried on, and in four hours came to the end of the gorge, and straight before us was the Black Sea, pitching and jumping, rolling and tumbling, surf-capped and streaked, as no other sea ever is. Turning sharp to the left, we soon reached the suburbs, and constantly passing good detached houses standing on the slope overlooking the sea, we reached the town itself, and pulled up in an open square called Giaour Meydan (Infidels' Field).

Espying a European-like looking individual, we asked which was the best hotel, and he pointed out one close by, which on entering surpassed our fondest expectations. When, chatting with the Greek miners at Arghana Madan, we asked about Trebizond—were there good streets, good houses, good shops, and, above all, a good hotel? all was answered by "Trebizond? Trebizond? Trebizond Europa!" (Trebizond *Europe*). The man was scarcely justified in his exclamation, but at the same time the town was sufficiently civilized to make it excusable. Had we entered Asia Minor by Trebizond instead of Mondanieh, I should probably have stated that the hotel was beastly dirty, the rooms draughty and comfortless, and the food greasy and coarse. Coming as we did from the interior, from cafés, khans, and hovels, the hotel was just all that could be desired; the rooms clean, warm, dry, and snug, the *table d'hôte* a thing to be lived for, and the company *crème de la crème*. But of all the luxuries, the one we appreciated most was privacy—the fact of having a room one could call one's own, from which an impertinent intruder might be kicked and a bore excluded, and our luggage might be tumbled about and left in handy confusion, and where a quiet reasonable stare might be taken in the looking-glass without the doing so inviting criticism from friends and strangers.

I can fancy that in bright weather Trebizond is as pretty and pleasant a spot as any in Turkey. The town stands

on sloping ground, its front close on the sea beach, the
waves, when high, actually washing against the walls,
while clustering close behind it are steep, flat-topped hills,
except on the western side, where the hills recede for
some miles, leaving a rich tract of several thousand acres
between them and the shore, cultivated near the town
as gardens and vineyards. Our hotel stood on a small
promontory, and from its windows we had a splendid
view of the rugged mountain range of Lazistan, covered
apparently to the level of the sea with deep snow. On
the sloping hill to the east of the town are a few really
good houses, one of which was pointed out to us as
formerly the residence of Mr. Palgrave, the English
consul. I believe I am right in saying that the population
of Trebizond is about thirty-seven thousand, of which
two-thirds are Mussulmans. The chief industry of the
town, and that for which it is celebrated, is the construction of silver ornaments, but though I searched through
the shops, I could find nothing quaint or pretty, or that
could not have been bought in the Burlington Arcade, of
better workmanship and at half the cost.

The comparative prosperity of the town is chiefly due
to its being the port where most of the merchandise for
Persia and the greater part of Central Asia is landed.
Nearly two-thirds of the entire imports find their way
there. The return caravans bring to the town, for ship-
ment, silk, carpets, haricot beans, saffron, and a few other
things. During the war almost all export and import
was stopped, and we heard that Russia was trying hard

to prevent its ever again flowing through its old channel —a channel that was made by the Romans and Genoese, but which has been used less and less each year since the Turks drove the latter out of the country. Russia hopes to secure the Persian trade for her newly acquired town of Batoum, and rumour said she was about to open both railroads and roads for this purpose. That Trebizond may thus be robbed no one can doubt, but it is uncertain if Russia will reap any very rich advantage, as there is another road by which the traffic is likely to pass, namely, by Alexandretta and Aleppo ; and now that England has possession of Cyprus, perhaps steps may be taken to remove the only real obstruction that has closed the road, the Arabs and Kurds, who plunder and rob all caravans that pass. In Batoum Russia has a convenient port, and therefore it is in a better position than Trebizond, which has not even a good open roadstead ; but an obstruction far greater than open seas is fondly maintained by the Russians, viz. prohibition duties, that will, unless done away with, shut out Europe, and especially England, from their old market.

During most of the time we were at Trebizond, it rained in torrents, but we succeeded in paying several visits. We dined with our kind and hospitable consul, Mr. Biliotti, and, besides, we spent several pleasant hours in the house of an American missionary, who had been driven from Erzeroom by the late war. We also took a walk to the beach to look at the remains of the old boat harbour made in the days of the Genoese, but which is now utterly destroyed. Probably it was from this spot that a part of the great Ten Thousand took ship, and so finished their memorable march, while the more robust of their companions marched westward along the coast.

It was a pleasant sight for us, on the morning of the 30th of December, to see the French steamer, the *Miranda*, at anchor in front of our windows, and pleasanter still was it, later in the day, when we found ourselves on board her. The long ride had been undertaken chiefly for the pleasure of it, and in all ways it had been a success; nevertheless it was delightful to think it was over, that the scorching plain, dreary wastes, and desolate mountains were behind us, and that we had been brought through all in safety, and were actually in better health than when we had started. No accidents worth thinking of had happened to man or beast. We had had no difficulties or rows with any one, and had parted friendlily with all, Turks and Christians, Kurds and Arabs, etc. The entire journey from Constantinople had occupied ninety-six days, out of which fifty-three had been spent in the saddle; and of these fifty-three days, two only were really wet, and two were showery.

We had ridden fourteen hundred miles, the average distance done each day being about twenty-two and a half miles; and if the miserable mountain roads are taken into consideration, I think this was very fair work for a lot of ponies.

Ever since leaving Diarbekir we had been racing against the winter, and though it had now and then come up with us, yet we just beat it into Trebizond, but it was a very near thing. The rain that had been falling as we rode into the town turned to sleet and snow in the afternoon, and though it melted as it fell near the sea, yet we could see far away inland the mountain ranges deeply covered. Had we been two or three days later we should have been trapped, and must have spent days, perhaps weeks, in some small village or khan. As it was, during the night after our arrival, travellers were caught in the snow ; several perished, and a great many horses were lost.

A few days' run in the comfortable but sadly slow steamer—days in which we revelled in rest and quiet, and thoroughly appreciated the successful efforts of a super-latively good cook—and we once more found ourselves in Meseri's hotel. But, as I have now completed my circle in the home of the Turk, I will lay down my pen, fearing lest it may run away with me, and launch me again on the journey that lingers still so pleasantly in my memory.

THE END.

LONDON: PRINTED BY WILLIAM CLOWES AND SONS, LIMITED,
STAMFORD STREET AND CHARING CROSS.

Printed in Great Britain
by Amazon

45852340R00209